M000282695

# THE WORSHIP OF THE ENGLISH PURITANS

# The Worship of the English Puritans

by

Horton Davies
Professor of Religious History
Princeton University,
Princeton, NJ

Soli Deo Gloria Publications
*. . . for instruction in righteousness . . .*

**Soli Deo Gloria Publications**
P.O. Box 451, Morgan, PA 15064
(412) 221-1901/FAX 221-1902

*

*The Worship of the English Puritans* was first published in 1948 by Dacre Press. This Soli Deo Gloria reprint is
© 1997. Printed in the USA. All rights reserved.

*

ISBN 1-57358-043-0

The cover illustration is reproduced courtesy of:
Historical Reproductions
12324 Big Pool Road
Clear Spring, MD 21722

# Preface to the 1997 Edition

*The Worship of the English Puritans* was written within three years. The first two were completely dedicated to it since I was engaged in doctoral studies at Mansfield College, Oxford University. The third year I wrote only in the spare time allowed by my first calling as minister of the Wallington and Carshalton Congregational Church in South London, England, in between sermon preparation and visitations. It was a good diversion from the blasts of the fire bombs of the German blitz, which kept us awake night and day since we were adjacent to the Croydon airport.

This thesis gave me great pleasure to write because it was a recapitulation of the lives and achievements of the earlier Congregationalists, variously known as Independents, and of their colleagues, the Presbyterians and the Baptists, who agreed on most topics except that of infant baptism.

The only delay I faced in getting this doctoral dissertation published was that the Dacre Press, my first publisher, had used up all the paper he could buy in these hard economic times on a successful account of High Anglican Worship. This delayed the publication of my book from 1944 to 1948. Yet I could hardly feel slighted since my tutor, the Rev. Edward C. Ratcliff, Lecturer in Liturgiology at the University of Oxford, a High Anglican Churchman, had recommended it for publication. It came out during my second year as the inaugural professor of Divinity at Rhodes University in Grahamstown in the Union of South Africa. And here it is now to be reissued some 41 years after I was appointed a professor of Religion at Princeton University!

This book could easily have have been entitled *Worship in the English Free Church Tradition* but for the fact that it did not include the origin of the Methodists in the mid-to-late 18th century, who are part of the English Free Churches. Although descended from the Anglicans, the Methodists were not critical of them, as the other three

Independent Churches had been. What gives Puritanism its strength is its bedrock foundation of committed Biblicism, its public and private worship in the church and in the home which reinforce each other, and its ethical committment of service. Despite the defections of some sections of the present churches, it will endure.

I am delighted that the new paperback version will appear under the imprint of Soli Deo Gloria Publications, because the Puritans themselves attempted to live to the sole glory of God.

Horton Davies
Department of Religion
Princeton University

# PREFACE

*The Worship of the English Puritans* might equally well have been named 'The Free Church Tradition of Christian Worship in England', but for the fact that it does not include a consideration of the worship of the Methodists, and for the further reason that it was produced as a historical thesis for the degree of Doctor of Philosophy in the University of Oxford. Its purpose is not, however, strictly historical or academic, but practical. It is an attempt to shew the relevance of the Reformed tradition in Christian worship to-day, and to re-awaken the interest of members of the Reformed Churches in Great Britain in their own rich liturgical inheritance. I would also wish it to promote amongst the members of other Communions a recognition of what Presbyterians, Baptists and Congregationalists hold dear and increasingly value as part of their Christian heirloom. My hope is that it may, in a necessarily limited way, assist the Ecumenical Movement whose momentum, happily, increases year by year. The re-union of the Christian Churches cannot, the author feels sure, come to fruition on the sand of expediency, nor on the clay of sentimentalism; it is the fruit of the Holy Spirit, whose seed is sown on the soil of souls that is both receptive in its understanding of our deep spiritual unity in Christ, and also firm enough to refuse to give up what is most precious in our own traditions. Unity cannot come, as Karl Barth has recently reminded us, in a crepuscular setting, which blurs distinctions, 'where all cats are grey'. My sincere desire is that this study of the Puritan and Reformed tradition of Divine worship in England, from the days of Cranmer to Watts, may assist the fulfilment of our Lord's High-Priestly Prayer for his disciples 'that all may be one', thus mirroring the Divine unity within the Godhead.

The debt of gratitude which I have incurred in the preparation of this volume is not exhausted by the Bibliography. It is a debt that is inexhaustible as Divine grace, and as wide as the One Holy Catholic and Apostolic Church, spanning the Christian centuries and traversing the continents. It leaves me amazed as ever at the 'givenness' of all that is worth-while, though it is humbling for a research worker to learn that he is no discoverer! The scale of the indebtedness also forbids adequate recognition of it in a brief preface.

It is a delight to be able to put on record the assistance of my kith and kin, of my wife, and of my father, the Reverend Dr. D. Marlais Davies, Minister of the Avenue Congregational Church, Southampton, in particular. Their encouragement was beyond praise. This debit side of the account (of which the book is the poor attempt to balance on the credit side) must include, as its chief items, the names of my teachers in Theology, Church History and Liturgics, respectively, Professor H. Cunliffe-Jones and Principal the Rev. E. J. Price (both of the Yorkshire United College, Bradford), the Rev. Dr. Nathaniel Micklem (Principal of Mansfield College) and the Rev. E. C. Ratcliff (Fellow of Queen's College and Lecturer in Liturgiology in the University of Oxford) who was my tutor during the preparation of the thesis. I acknowledge with gratitude the assistance of the Rev. Alan Beesley, my contemporary, in the preparation of Chapter X and of Appendix A; the help of Mr. H. V. Molesworth Roberts (Assistant Librarian of the Royal Institute of British Architects) in the preparation of the Index, and drudgery of friendship undertaken by the Rev. George Cleaves, C.F., in the proof-reading. My many benefactors, in different ways, are too numerous to mention, but this brief acknowledgment is due to the Viscount Leverhulme, Sir Angus Watson, Mr. H. L. Reynolds, and to the members of the congregation of Christ to whom I minister, the Congregational Church of Wallington and Carshalton, especially to the following office-bearers: Mr. Walter Holman, Mr. F. H. Ireland, and Mr. Leonard Watson.

It is also a pleasure to thank the Librarians of the Bodleian and Queen's College Libraries (in Oxford) and of the Dr. Williams' Library (in London), for their courtesy. My gratitude is also due to the publishers for accepting the responsibility of publishing my manuscript and to the printers for risking their admirable reputation in reproducing the inconsistencies of sixteenth and seventeenth century English spelling! The reader is warned to look out for these wayward spellings and not to attribute them to the printer. If any blame is to be apportioned, the culprits are the original authors who are cited, and they were in the good company of Shakespeare! For all other errors the author accepts entire responsibility, though he does not for the deliberate errors!

H. D.

Y.M.C.A. with B.A.O.R.,
H.Q./G.H.Q. Troops, Germany

*Lent*, 1946

# CONTENTS

# CHAPTER I

## THE NATURE OF ENGLISH PURITANISM

Puritanism is most accurately defined as the outlook that characterised the radical Protestant party in Queen Elizabeth's day, who regarded the Reformation as incomplete and wished to model English church worship and government according to the Word of God. The first official reference to the nickname by which the reforming party was known occurs about the year 1580. This we gather from the following protest made by members of the party concerned to the Privy Council about this time. They write:[1]

> 'We pray your good lordships to give us leave to advertise you how the adversary very cunningly hath new-christened us with an odious name, to the end, no doubt, that we being occupied in defence of our innocency, they might have greater freedom to go about their hateful treacheries. It is the name of *puritanism;* we detest both the name and heresy.'

The detested name was a most subtle choice. It suggested, as the above citation shows, that the reforming party was a revival of the mediæval heretical *Cathari.* It also implied that its members were over-scrupulous and over-precise. Indeed for some time the nicknames 'Puritans' and 'Precisians' were interchangeable.

Whilst in time the name 'Puritan' was proudly accepted by the radical reformers, as a veteran might display a scar received in honourable combat, it never lost its suspicious and sinister connotations. It was a stick used to beat any bad dog. Even in 1692 an anonymous author protests against the indiscriminate manner in which it was employed in theological debates. He refers[2] to

> 'the new nick-named Puritan in our times, wherein the Papists calleth it Puritanisme to oppose the Roman hierarchy. The Arminian . . . to defend God's free grace against man's free will. The Formalist thinketh it Puritanisme to stand out against Conformity. The Civilian not to serve the time, and the Prophane thinketh it essential to the Puritan, to walk precisely and not be prophane . . .'

[1] *A Parte of a Register* p. 129

[2] *The Pastor and the Prelate* (Edinburgh 1692) p. 23

The most objective account of the origin of the nickname given by a member of the opposing party appears in Heylyn in his *Ecclesia Restaurata, or History of the Reformation*. Under the caption 'Anno Reg. 7' he writes:[1]

'This year the *Zuinglian*, or *Calvinian* Faction began to be first known by the name of *Puritans*, which name hath ever since been appropriated to them, because of their pretending to a greater Purity in the Service of God, than was *held forth* unto them (as they gave it out) in the *Common-Prayer Book;* and to a greater opposition to the Rites and Usages of the Church of Rome, than was agreeable to the Constitution of the Church of *England*.'

The name 'Puritan' was justified only as a description of the concern of the radical party that the Church in England should be reformed according to the 'pure' Word of God. The authors of the Waldegrave Prayer Book are at pains to shew in their introduction that the Scriptures are the pattern of their worship.[2]

'We, therefore, not as the greatest Clerks of all, but as the least able of many, do present unto you, which desire the increase of God's glory, and the pure simplicity of his word, a form and order of a Reformed Church limited within the compass of God's word, which our Saviour hath left unto us only sufficient to govern all our actions by; so that whatsoever is added to this word by man's device, seem it never so good, holy, or beautiful, yet before our God, which is jealous, and cannot admit any companion or counsellor, it is evil, wicked, and abominable.'

The Word of God was the foundation of this, the Waldegrave Prayer Book, and the same criterion guided the Puritans in every department of church life. The closing appeal of the introduction might have been said by any Puritan, so typical is it of the Puritan genius.

'We . . . desire you, in his name, with judgment to read our doings, trying them only by the touchstone of his word: that either if they be found faulty, they may be rejected, or else if they be profitable, God may be glorified, his Church edified, and the malicious confounded. Farewell, dear brethren, and let us pray to our loving God, that he would be merciful unto us, restore his holy word, comfort and strengthen his children, and, finally, confound Satan, Antichrist, and all his enemies.'[3]

[1] (ed. 1661) p. 172 [2] Hall *Reliquiæ Liturgicæ* i 115 [3] *id.* i 123*f*

This citation reveals the Puritan's undeviating obedience to the Word of God, his tender solicitude for his brethren facing persecution, and his implacable enmity towards all enemies of the Gospel.

Puritanism, as the original definition given shewed, began inside the Church of England in Elizabeth's day. The impetus to further reformation according to the Word of God came from Geneva, whence a number of influential English exiles returned including William Whittingham, who became Dean of Durham on his return, and Bishop Coverdale. The party came to England with high hopes of accomplishing their project.[1] But opposition became quickly so virulent that disappointment succeeded.[2]

We are now concerned to demonstrate that the division in the Anglican Church represented by Cartwright and Hooker respectively, was due to a different conception of the authority of the Bible. Both parties subscribed to the Sixth of the Thirty-Nine Articles which declared:

> 'Holy Scripture conteyneth all things necessarie to saluation; so that whatsoever is not read therein, nor may be proved thereby, is not to be required of any man, that it should be believed as an article of faith, or be thought requisite as necessary to saluation.'

Wherein lay the watershed of opinion between the Established clergy and the Puritan clergy?

The next chapter will shew that Luther's conception of the Bible was that it contained the articles of belief necessary for salvation, but that in matters of worship and church government the Bible is not to be treated as a new Leviticus. Calvin, it will be shown, regarded the Bible as authoritative in doctrine, government and worship. Roughly the Established clergy accepted Luther's doctrine of the authority of the Bible, while the Puritans accepted Calvin's conception of the authority of the Scriptures. The Puritan said that if the Bible is binding on one issue, it is binding on all issues. He could see only inconsistency in the attempt of the Established clergy to regard the Bible as authoritative in matters of belief, but not binding in matters of government and worship.

Richard Hooker is the clearest expositor of the Anglican or Established conception of the authority of the Bible. For

[1] *Zurich Letters* (ed. Parker Soc.) ii 1 [2] *id.* i 11, 17, 63

him the Bible is God's revealed Word on the broad, general principles of the Christian religion. God has not meant to prescribe in his Word the ordering of his worship or the method of church government, or details of conduct. These He has left to the discretion of men. Such matters are to be decided by the use of reason guided by considerations of propriety, decency, and proportion, according to the circumstances and nature of the case. The Bible provides man with such information only as cannot be achieved by the exercise of his reason. Otherwise, if the Bible were to be the only and absolute criterion, the law of reason and the law of nature would be finally abrogated by the Scriptures. He speaks directly to the Puritans in the following words:[1]

> 'Let them with whom we have hitherto disputed consider well, how it can stand with reason to make the bare mandate of sacred Scripture the only rule of all good and evil in the actions of mortal men. The testimonies of God are true, the testimonies of God are perfect, the testimonies of God are all sufficient unto that end for which they were given. Therefore accordingly we do receive them, we do not think that in them God hath omitted anything needful unto his purpose, and left his intent to be accomplished by our devisings.'

Thus, for Hooker, the Bible is authoritative in doctrine and in the outstanding ordinances of worship such as prayer, praise, the proclamation of the Word, and the two Sacraments of Baptism and Holy Communion. But in the details of the arrangement of worship it was never intended to be authoritative. Times, circumstances, ceremonies are rightly to be decided by the church rulers in accordance with the proved wisdom of antiquity and the use of right reason.

The reply of the Puritan was, in effect, that the Anglican accepted the authority of the Bible in theory but not in practice. To his mind the Anglican was inconsistent in accepting the authority of the Bible as his touchstone in doctrine, but not in government or worship. He appeared to set aside such parts of the Bible as told against any contemporary institution in the Established Church by declaring that they were peculiar to the historical times of their origins and not part of the eternal law of the Christian religion. In short, the Puritan

[1] *Eccl. Pol.* II viii 5

maintained that the Anglican did not really believe in the authority of the Bible at all.

By contrast, the Puritan held that the Bible was the revealed Word of God from beginning to end, authoritative not only for doctrine but for every aspect of ecclesiastical and human life, an absolute code in everything that it dealt with. It was the expression of the will of God in matters theological, moral, sartorial, military, economic and judicial. Hence it was necessary not only to look for general laws but for detailed guidance in its pages. The Puritan would not concede the Anglican contention that some ordinances in the Bible were for an age and not for all time. William Ames, one of the leading Puritan theologians, writes in *The Marrow of Sacred Divinity*:[1]

'But although divers parts of the Scriptures were written, upon some speciall occasion, and were directed to some certaine men, or assemblies: yet in Gods intention, they doe as well pertaine to the instructing of all the faithfull thorough all ages, as if they had been specially directed to them.'

Not only is all Scripture authoritative, but it is as binding in church government as it is in doctrine.

'The Scripture is not a partiall, but a perfect rule of faith and manners: neither is here anything that is constantly and everywhere to be observed in the Church of God, which depends either upon any tradition, or upon any authority whatsoever, and is not contained in the Scriptures.'[2]

From the Puritan elevation of the Scripture over the use of human reason, it would be wrong to conclude that the Puritans were anti-humanists. They shared with their opponents the rich cultural legacy of the Renaissance. Their leaders were all men of learning and many of them had held high positions in the Universities of Oxford and Cambridge. Cartwright was Professor of Divinity in Cambridge and gained his followers mainly from that University. In Commonwealth days the Puritan centre had transferred to the sister University where John Owen was Vice-Chancellor and Thomas Goodwin the President of Magdalen. Even when the Universities were forbidden to the Nonconformists after 1662, they maintained

[1] p. 169; Ames was Professor of Divinity in the University of Francken in Friesland.

[2] Ames *op. cit.* p. 170

the scholastic tradition of a liberal education in their Academies.[1] The Puritans of New England were apostles of education as well as of religion. A recent tribute to this feature of their work declares:[2]

'The greatness of the Puritans is not so much that they conquered a wilderness, or that they carried a religion into it, but that they carried a religion which, narrow and starved though it may have been in some respects, deficient in sensuous richness or brilliant color, was nevertheless indissolubly bound up with an ideal of culture and learning. In contrast to all other pioneers, they made no concessions to the forest, but in the midst of frontier conditions, in the very throes of clearing the land and erecting shelters, they maintained schools and a college, a standard of scholarship and competent writing, a class of men devoted entirely to the life of the mind and of the soul.'

The supreme example of the fusion of humanism and Puritanism is the man John Milton. Every Puritan would have subscribed to John Cotton's dictum that we learn by experience and education 'yet there is also an essentiall wisdome in us, namely, our Reason which is natural.'[3] It is erroneous to suppose that the Puritans despised the achievements of human reason because they subordinated them to the Divine Revelation.

We have already seen that Puritan and Anglican were divided over their conceptions of the authority of the Word of God. They were also at variance in their anthropology. The Anglican apologists believed that everything that God reveals to men must be comprehended by the human reason, because both reason and revelation come from the same author, God. Jeremy Taylor expresses the Anglican viewpoint that what is contrary to reason is therefore contrary to the will of God:[4]

'when both sides agree that these are the words of God, and the question of faith is concerning the meaning of the words, nothing is an article of faith, or a part of religion, but what can be proved by reason to be the sense and intentions of God. Reason is never to be pretended against the

[1] cf. I. Parker *Dissenting Academies in England* (Cambridge 1914)

[2] Miller & Johnson *The Puritans* (New York 1938) p. 11*f*

[3] Cotton *A Practical Commentary upon the First Epistle Generall of John* (London 1656) p. 8

[4] Miller & Johnson *op. cit.* p. 49, quoting Taylor's *Ductor Dubitantium* (ed Alex. Taylor, London 1851) ix 74

clear sense of Scripture, because by reason it is that we came to perceive that to be the clear sense of Scripture.'

The Puritans were of the opinion that this was to make reason a judge over revelation. Taylor would have replied that there could be no discrepancy between what is reasonable and what is revealed. But the Puritan would have urged that the human reason is not fitted for this task, since it is a corrupt instrument. He would have pointed to the perverseness of human nature. History, he would have claimed, and daily events confirm that men are not, as Taylor supposes, naturally reasonable or naturally noble. You may allow them an education in the wisdom of antiquity and let them examine their hearts for an innate and instinctive knowledge of right and wrong, but men will still continue to be mean and cruel, stupid and carnal. The galleon of human nature, richly laden with the treasures of antiquity, and steered by the natural reason of man, is bound to shipwreck on the rock of human perversity. The Puritan, however much he might appreciate the legacy of the Renaissance, was a believer in the doctrine of original sin. This, with his doctrine of the all-sufficiency of the Scriptures, was the theological legacy of John Calvin. His mental journey had taken him to Athens but his destination was Geneva.

There was the sting of truth in the broadsheet issued against the Presbyterians with the title *The Presbyterian Pater-Noster*.[1] The taunt applied equally to other Puritans who looked to John Calvin as their spiritual leader. It is claimed that their creed was:

'I believe in *John Calvin*, the Father of our Religion, disposer of Heaven, and Earth, and in *Owen*, *Baxter* and *Jenkins* his deare Sons our Lords who were conceived by the Spirit of Fanaticism, born of Schism and Faction, suffered under the *Act of Uniformity*.'

From Calvin the Puritans inherited two important tenets: the all-sufficiency of Scripture and a thorough-going restatement of the doctrine of original sin. And it was precisely on these grounds that the Puritans differed from the Anglicans.

The characteristic differentia of the Puritans coloured their whole theological outlook. It was impossible for them to con-

[1] *Transactions of the Congregational Historical Society* vi 419; the broadsheet is dated 1681

ceive of God as an impersonation of the rational principle. God was the Omnipotent King as he was to the Psalmist who cried 'The Lord reigneth, let the people tremble'. He demanded inflexible, unquestioning obedience. It was absurd for puny man to pit his corrupt reason against the inscrutable decrees of the Most High. It was not only absurd, it was presumptuous. For was not God a 'jealous God' brooking no rivals? Hence the Puritan's exact adherence to the guidance of Scripture was a confession of his loyalty to God. Thus the Anglican's claim to institute ceremonies and customs that were not contradicted by Scripture, was an affront to the Divine Majesty in the Puritan's eyes. It was, moreover, a denial of the doctrine of original sin.

The Puritan insisted that the primary principle of the Reformation was adherence to the Word of God. It had been thoroughly applied in doctrinal matters by the Fathers of the Church of England. Naturally and inevitably the second stage of the Reformation in England was the application of the same criterion to the unreformed worship of the Church. Puritanism in England was, therefore, of necessity a liturgical movement. On its positive side it wished to restore English worship to the simplicity, purity and spirituality of the primitive Church. On its negative side it wished to reject those symbols in which Romanism expressed its character.

The Puritan's fear of Rome is not difficult to understand, even if it led to unnecessary iconoclasticism. Rome was a corrupt Church, which had set aside in many ways the authority of the Scriptures to make way for her own innovations. The Puritan feared that the adoption of Roman symbols might make way for the adoption of the substance. Had any ceremony not explicitly commanded by the Scriptures and by nature indifferent not been used by the Roman Church, he would probably not have objected to it. But in order to safeguard against a reintroduction of the Roman errors he had to insist that only what was explicitly commanded by the Word of God was to be accepted. The use of the ring in marriage, the practice of crossing in Baptism, the custom of kneeling at the reception of Holy Communion, and the use of the surplice, were of themselves things indifferent, neither commanded nor forbidden by the Word of God. But because they had been used by the Roman Catholics and were hence 'badges of Antichrist' to his mind, they ceased to be things indifferent. Hence he would only tolerate what was explicitly commanded by the Scriptures. It is to be remembered that the Marian persecutions, with their Smithfield fires, had not burnt out in his memory. The drama of the Reformation had not yet reached its finale and Jesuitism was still in the ascendant.

The Puritans naturally turned to Calvin because in his theology he opposed the Word of God to the infallibility of the Pope. As Bayne declares:[1]

> 'In considering that urgency of appeal to Scripture, and Scripture alone, which throughout its whole history was made by English Puritanism, an appeal which, with our modern prepossessions, may seem to us to be a wilful searing of the eye-balls of reason and conscience, it is essential to recollect that it was against the authority of Rome that Calvin and his followers asserted the supremacy of God's written Word.'

Calvin had no alternative but to appeal from the authority of the Church, to the only authority higher than the Church, namely, the revealed will of God enshrined in the Holy Scriptures. For this reason it will be found that the Puritans to a man are in the main Genevan tradition in public worship, whilst the Anglicans are in the Wittenberg tradition of Luther. As will be seen in the next chapter, the Anglicans followed Luther in his conception of the authority of the Bible and with him were prepared to accept any traditions which were not directly forbidden by the Scriptures, whilst the Puritans pleaded for a type of worship which was in its entirety modelled upon the Word of God.

It would be a mistake to assume that because the Puritans joined combat with the Anglicans on a liturgical issue that their concern was only liturgical, although this will be our concern in succeeding chapters. Puritanism began as a liturgical reform, but it developed into a distinct attitude towards life. Its peculiar ethos in the interpretation of the Christian life is admirably stated in the following definition given by the wife of a famous Puritan soldier:[2]

> 'By Christianity I intend that universal habit of grace which is wrought in a soul by the regenerating Spirit of God, whereby the whole creature

[1] Bayne *Puritan Documents relating to the Settlement of the Church of England by the Act of Uniformity of 1662* (London 1862) p. 10

[2] cited Bayne *op. cit.* p. 64*f*

is resigned up into the Divine will and love, and all its actions designed to the obedience and glory of its Maker.'

Their theory of life was that man's chief end is not to amuse or be amused, but, in the words of the *Westminster Catechism*, 'to glorifie God, and fully to enjoy him for ever.'

In its earlier days it seemed as if Puritanism might eventually triumph within the Church of England. The great divines who flourished in the reign of King Edward VI, and died at the stake in Mary's reign, were all strong supporters of further reformation. Whilst Hooper, Latimer and Ridley can only be called 'Puritans' by perpetrating an anachronism, they were Puritan in outlook. Moreover during Edward's reign John Knox, Calvin's second-in-command, was a royal chaplain. The Marian exiles on the Continent (as will be seen in the third chapter) were predominantly Calvinistic. They returned to England in high hopes that Queen Elizabeth was supporting their plea for a further reformation in worship. And during that Queen's reign, Archbishop Grindal was known to be a fervent supporter of the Puritans.

In these days the Puritans hoped to be able to establish a reformed worship and government within the Church of England. Cartwright and his fellow 'Disciplinarians' believed that even if the Queen were unsympathetic, Parliament would lend a willing ear. Hence the first and second *Admonitions* were addressed to Parliament. But official opposition from the hierarchy proved too severe for open combat and the Puritans were driven underground. Some of them, not always the most learned, left the Established Church and established a more Biblical way of worship in their secret conventicles. These were the Separatists. Others, and they were the majority, remained within the Anglican Communion in the hope that the theological climate would brighten. Others, again, the semi-Separatists, went voluntarily into exile on the Continent where they set up Churches after the Puritan ideal. On the accession of James I, the Puritans came out into the open again, hoping that the monarch of Presbyterian Scotland who now occupied the English throne would prove more sympathetic to their aims. When the Stuarts proved as adamant in the defence of the Establishment as Elizabeth had been, other Puritans set out for the shores of North America, and in New England set up Churches such as they had wished to constitute in old England. The more patient, however, remained even then in the Establishment. Puritan forces within and without the Establishment were to present a united front only in the Civil War. The long-awaited Puritan official recognition came only in the Commonwealth period. Then the Westminster Assembly of Divines, by their *Directory of Public Worship* and their *Confession* and *Catechism*, effected the further reformation of which their Puritan forefathers had dreamed. While Presbyterians predominated, Independents were also represented. The latter came to receive special recognition when Cromwell declared his Protectorate of England.

It will be seen that the term 'Puritan' is used to cover all those who longed for further reformation in England according to the Word of God. Whilst the term is strictly applicable only to the ecclesiastical party who urged this concern in Elizabeth's day and renewed it in the days of James I, it may be extended, in a wider sense, to the semi-Separatists such as John Robinson, who would never allow himself to deny that the Church of England was a true Church. Its main subdivision was into two parties, the Independents and the Presbyterians. Whilst each party had a different method of church government, they were both united in accepting the same doctrine of the all-sufficiency of the Word of God in doctrinal and liturgical matters. Despite small differences in detail, they are substantially the same and their spiritual father is John Calvin. When the Act of Uniformity forced them into Nonconformity and their denominational differences were thereby accentuated and sharpened, they worshipped God in the same fashion, according to his revelation in the Scriptures. George Herbert's disapproval of the bareness of Puritan worship was aimed at both Presbyterian and Independent worship.

> 'She in the valley is so shie
> Of dressing that her hair doth lie
>    About her eares;
> While she avoids her neighbour's pride,
> She wholly goes on th'other side,
>    And nothing wears.'[1]

Compared with the beautiful ritual and ornamentation of the

[1] *Poems:* The British Church

Anglican worship, Puritan meeting-houses and services were bare. The truth was that the Puritan was never aware of any æsthetic impoverishment in his services. The very intensity of his realization of the presence of the Holy God rendered all adventitious, sensuous aids to worship otiose.

'In the eloquent silence of God's presence, he required not the melting strains of music; in the piercing blaze of God's truth, he desired not the imagery of symbolic forms.'[1]

Ceremonial was not simply displeasing to him because of its apparent congruity with the Old Dispensation rather than with the New; it was unnecessary for him. In the words of the late Bernard Lord Manning,

'to call on the name of God, to claim the presence of the Son of God . . . is in itself an act so tremendous and so full of comfort that any sensuous or artistic heightening of the effect is not so much a painting of the lily as a varnishing of sunlight.'[2]

The roots of Anglican worship in Luther and the roots of Puritan worship in Calvin are at the heart of their differing expressions of public worship. They remain to be considered in the ensuing chapter. There it will be seen that the differences are not æsthetic in essence. They are fundamentally theological in character.

[1] Bayne *op. cit.* p. 24
[2] *Christian Worship* (ed. N. Micklem, 1936) p. 162

## CHAPTER II

## THE THEOLOGY OF REFORMED WORSHIP

It is often supposed that the liturgical reforms of Luther and Calvin agree only in their condemnation of the abuses of the later mediæval Church. It has also been urged that the differences in their respective conceptions of worship and in the essential genius of their Orders of service, reflect their contrasting temperaments. This, it is hoped to shew, is a grave misunderstanding of both Luther and Calvin in two respects. An attempt will be made to demonstrate that the twin pillars of the Reformation were agreed not only on what constituted the abuses of the later mediæval Church, but also in their desire to return to a primitive simplicity in Christian worship. It is hoped to shew that their agreement as to what were the abuses to be righted, far from being the expression of their subjective preferences, was due to the theological doctrines they held in common. In the second place, it will be shewn that it is a spurious simplification of the issue to declare that the disagreements between Luther and Calvin are to be explained as a result, respectively, of Luther's conservatism and of Calvin's ruthlessly logical nature. Even if this statement is altered so as to produce the impression that Calvin was entirely true to his principles, whereas Luther was conservative, it still remains an unjust estimate of Luther. His apparent conservatism can be explained by theological principles.

The Reformers were agreed on the abuses of the mediæval Church, which had to be righted. In particular, they inveighed against four false conceptions. Their common *bête noire* was the late mediæval teaching on the Mass. They agreed that the teaching was to be condemned in proclaiming that in the Mass there was once more offered up the sacrifice which had been made once for all upon Calvary. It seemed nothing less than blasphemous to them that men should dare to assert that the sacrifice made upon the Cross should require to be repeated. They were equally confident, in the second place, that the Mass as celebrated in their time was no Communion. The people did not communicate in both kinds; they were merely spectators of a drama in which the priest was the main actor and in which the choir sang incidental music of an intricate kind. Nor was this all; the service of the Mass was not even intelligible to the great majority of the people, for where it was audible, it was spoken or chanted in an academic tongue. The Reformers also objected to the propitiatory character of the Mass, whereby Masses could be offered up to placate God for the individual's offences or to obtain special favours from God, as for example, before setting out on a journey. In fact the Reformers contended that the mediæval Mass was regarded as an *officium* rather than as a *beneficium*.[1]

Allied to their disapproval of the Mass was their objection to the current views of the priesthood. For if the priest was to be regarded as the indispensable instrument for procuring God's good favour, he became not a vehicle of grace but an impediment and an obstacle to communion between God and man. Further, the priests were, as Luther scornfully insisted, tyrannical, greedy, worldly and mercenary.[2]

A third conception which both the Reformers condemned was a false view of the authority of the saints, which regarded them as potent mediators between God and men, who could be influenced by the individual to remit his purgatorial pains and penalties, and who constituted a pantheon.

It is not surprising that both Luther and Calvin emphasized the primacy of preaching the Word of God both to offset the abuses which had encrusted the Sacrament of Holy Communion and to declare what was the true will of God in the matter.

The Reformers were not only agreed in their negations, they were of one mind in many positive affirmations. They both wished to restore the pure worship of the primitive Church. In the *Formula Missae* Luther avers that it is not his intention 'omnem cultum dei prorsus abolere' but only 'eum qui in usu est, pessimis additamentis viciatum, repurgare et usum pium monstrare.'[3] He does not thereby jettison the whole tradition of the undivided Church, since he agrees that 'primorum patrum additiones . . . laudabiles fuere, quales Athanasius et Cyprianus fuisse putantur.'[4] In fact his aim is to restore the uncorrupted Communion Service of the primi-

[1] James Moffatt, 'Luther', ch. viii of *Christian Worship* (ed. cit.) p. 127

[2] Luther's *Formula Missae*, in Carl Clemen *Quellenbuch zur praktischen Theologie*, I[er] Teil (Giessen 1910) p. 27*f* [3] Clemen *op. cit.* p. 27 [4] *ibid.*

tive Church. Calvin's intention was similar. This was made explicit in the full title of the Genevan Service Book of 1542. This title ran: ' La forme des prieres et chantz ecclesiastiques auec la maniere d'administrer les sacrements, et consacrer le mariage: *selon la coutume de l'eglise ancienne.*'[1] It was, therefore, the declared aim of both Reformers to restore the worship of the ancient Church. The common ground of agreement both on the abuses of contemporary worship and on the positive conception of a restoration of primitive Christian worship, far from being coincidental, is based upon common theological presuppositions. The basic doctrines held in common by the Reformers were three: the Bible as God's Revelation, Justification by Faith, and Christ as the sole Mediator between God and men. The last two doctrines, of course, were derived from the first all-inclusive doctrine of the Scriptures. Once the Bible was reinstated in all its authority, then it followed that any traditions that conflicted with the Word of God, regardless of the sanction of the Church, had to be abolished. Furthermore, the primacy of the Scriptures determined the desire for a return to the principles and practice of the primitive community of Christians, as envisaged in the Acts of the Apostles. These two conclusions went hand in hand. For the errors of the contemporary Church were seen to be deviations alike from the Bible and from the primitive Church. Further, there were two controlling principles in the Bible which contemporary practice flouted. If men were justified by their faith in the righteousness of Christ, accepting his sacrifice as the all-sufficient guarantee for the pardon of their sins, then all practices motivated by a belief in justification by works had to disappear. Such practices included attending the Mass as a good work and going on religious pilgrimages. Further, the notion that the saints had a thesaurus of merits which was available as credit to offset the debts of the sinner, also had to be abolished. The very conception of the efficacy of the intercession of the saints and of the necessary mediation of the priesthood, nullified the Biblical doctrine of Christ as the sole Mediator. If saints and priests were indispensable, it would be untrue to say of Christ 'there is none other name under heaven whereby we must be saved'. Thus these three doctrines, integral to the thought of both

[1] Maxwell *The Liturgical Portions of the Genevan Service Book* (1931) p. 70; the italics are mine.

Luther and Calvin, made necessary a liturgical reformation.

The results of the Lutheran and Calvinist liturgical reforms are admittedly different. How then are the differences to be accounted for? It is insufficient to explain the differences on the assumption that Luther was a conservative and wary of reform, while Calvin was logical and radical. The real difference between the Lutheran and Calvinist reforms in worship may be summed up as follows: Luther will have what is not specifically condemned by the Scriptures; whilst Calvin will have only what is ordained by God in the Scriptures. That is their fundamental disagreement. It is of vital importance in the history of Puritan worship, since the Puritans accepted the Calvinist criterion, whilst their opponents, the Anglicans, accepted the Lutheran criterion.

Luther's view, it will be shewn, was in the main directed by theological considerations, but some account of his temperament and of practical exigencies which he had to face, must be taken in estimating the reasons for his so-called conservatism. He made it perfectly plain that he did not wish to introduce a 'nova lex' in liturgical matters. He was quite averse to the instatement of a Christian Leviticus. This, he held, was contrary to the believer's Christian freedom.[1] Moreover, he held that the Word of God, if faithfully preached, would of itself create new and adequate forms of Christian worship. It was not for him, he declared, to produce a binding liturgy which should act as a fetter on the consciences of Christian men. Even in promulgating the *Formula Missae* he disclaims any wish to coerce Christians into accepting it.[2] It is merely introduced as a suggested alternative to the Mass of the Roman Church, not as an authoritative declaration that must be submitted to. The variety of rites and ceremonies practised in present-day Lutheran churches on the Continent is a legacy of Luther's doctrine of Christian Freedom. Furthermore it should be remembered that he favoured fluidity on the ground that a uniform liturgy by its very uniformity might blind men to the inwardness of worship.[3] All he required was that the rites of the Church should not conflict with the guidance of Holy Scripture.

Allied to this concern for Christian freedom was his advocacy of the principle of 'Festina lente' in liturgical matters.

[1] Moffatt *op. cit.* p. 125 [2] Clemen *op. cit.* p. 26 [3] Moffatt *loc. cit.*

This was based upon St. Paul's advice to consider the weaker brethren. Lest they should be bewildered by any iconoclasticism, he proposed to abolish only what was contrary to the plain teaching of the Scriptures. For the rest, he would prove all things and hold to that which was good.

This tendency to regard the tradition of the Church as valuable, when and where it was not contradicted by the Scriptures, was confirmed in Luther by his doctrine of the 'Orders'. The implications of this doctrine were that God has so ordered the world that man must not live as a mere individual isolated from society, but as a being sharing certain communal relationships. Such communities ordained by God are the Church and the State. Since they depend for their continuance on the divine sanction, men ought to respect them. Therefore, except when they definitely contradict the revealed will of God, they are to be obeyed. Such a doctrine puts a heavy premium upon tradition and as such it may be regarded as the religious basis of Luther's conservatism. It also helps to explain why the bishops have such an important part to play in deciding what particular liturgical reforms are desirable. Theoretically Luther left the choice of accepting or rejecting his liturgical reforms to the Christians of the local churches, but in practice the decision was left to the discretion of the bishop.

One point has yet to be treated. That is Luther's attitude to ceremonial. In contrast to the bare Calvinist *cultus*, the Lutheran liturgy is rich in the use of symbolical action and vestments. On this matter, we have Luther's round assertion that God had given man five senses with which to worship him and that it would be sheer ingratitude to use less.[1] Doubtless he would have regarded Calvin's order of service as an example of worshipping God with only two of the senses: hearing and speaking or singing. By contrast the Lutheran service appeals to the sense of smell in the censings and to the eye in its use of vestments and ceremonies. To this criticism Calvin might legitimately have replied that worship was primarily for the glory of God, secondly for the edification of men, and not in the least for their pleasure. One doubts whether Luther would have been satisfied with such an answer, since with his sense of the amazing condescension of God in Christ, he held that God had given men aids in their devotions. Such aids were

[1] Moffatt *op. cit.* p. 129

ritual and ceremonial. As Christ, by his Incarnation, had sanctified humanity, so earthly things might be sacramental of the divine. Luther was therefore not prepared to dispense with the 'eye-gate' to the soul, as Bunyan was later to term it. As will be seen later, this view was unacceptable to Calvin, since he maintained that man was essentially corrupt and that his worship was only acceptable in so far as it conformed to the law of God in the Scriptures. He held that the Decalogue in declaiming against 'graven images', had sufficiently dispensed with the need for ceremonial and vestments.

Luther's attitude, it will have been seen, was capable of being defended on theological grounds. But his attitude was not strictly theological, nor was it always based upon principles. Sometimes he was inconsistent with his principles. Luther did not always carry his theological convictions to their logical conclusions. For instance, his appeal to the secular arm to punish the peasants who had revolted against their masters was contrary to his doctrine of the freedom of a Christian. Similarly, in liturgical matters, it may fairly be claimed that his doctrine of the Word of God was not logically developed. In extenuation it should be remembered, however, that he was the first of the Reformers and that by the time of Calvin the situation was more stable and men had more time for reflection on the issues. Nevertheless, it cannot be denied that in Luther's later years the Reformer displayed a growing conservatism. He desired more uniformity both in the use of ecclesiastical vestments and of liturgical forms. What had previously been optional, became obligatory.

Finally, it cannot be doubted that Luther's opinion was to a certain extent moulded not upon principle, but by events. The method was *solvitur ambulando*. This is definitely the case in the order in which his reforms were accomplished. His preaching of Justification by Faith made it necessary for him to reform the Canon of the Mass. This in turn produced the abolition of separate priests for each guild and also of the custom whereby each priest was allowed to say only one Mass each day. This led to more clergy being out of livings and therefore meant that less money came into the coffers of the Church. The attack upon monastic life caused many monks and nuns to leave their solitary lives and they too were unemployed. The complete collapse of finances led to Luther's seeking the aid of the Prince. A further effect of Luther's reforms was that the Roman Church refused to ordain candidates who were Lutherans or who would not take vows of celibacy. All these circumstances forced Luther to make his one provision for ordaining and training future ministers of the Word. To a considerable extent, therefore, Luther was guided not by principles but by events. At the same time it is also true that it was the faithful proclamation of theological principles that led to these happenings. Luther's attitude to liturgical reform was therefore mainly grounded upon theological bases, but it also was partially determined by considerations of expediency.

The doctrines that are logically applied by Calvin are not distinctively his. He and Luther were united in their agreement upon most of them, but it was Calvin who gave them their distinctive emphasis and applied them logically to the theory and practice of worship. For both Luther and Calvin the Bible was the Word of God. But their conceptions of the authority of the Word of God were different. Luther described the Bible as the 'Trostbuch', the cradle of Christ; whereas Calvin defined it as 'la sainte loy et parole evangelique de Dieu'.[1] Luther accepted the guidance of the Bible in doctrinal matters but refused to regard it as a directory of worship. Luther would admit in his worship any liturgical elements that were not inconsistent with the teaching of the Bible. Calvin would only accept what the Bible specifically warranted. If the Bible was the revealed will of God, he contended, then only Biblical ordinances could be acceptable to God. Human additions were therefore to be utterly abhorred, for God had made known his will in the Scriptures.

Calvin's rooted objection to human additions to the legitimate worship of God had another basis. Man was essentially corrupt; he bore the *damnosa haereditas* of original sin and therefore he could not worship God aright however he might wish to.[2] He was utterly sinful and therefore his own ideas of what constituted correct worship were vitiated by his sinfulness. Being in this quandary, he could yet take heart from the fact that God had declared what true worship was in his holy Word. Man must therefore learn there how to glorify God aright.

[1] J. S. Whale, 'Calvin', ch. x of *Christian Worship* p. 156 [2] *Inst.* I iv

Further, since we are able to pray to God aright only as the Holy Spirit intercedes for us, we must submit ourselves to the guidance of the Spirit. These three doctrines: the Word of God, original sin and the fall, and the intercession of the Holy Spirit, are logically applied in the Calvinist *cultus*. Hence the Biblical character and the Biblical precedents for the service; hence, too, the centrality of the Word, invisibly in preaching and visibly in the Sacraments. This also explains the opening invocation of God's aid in the Genevan liturgy, stressing human helplessness apart from God. Hence also the following confession of sins and the invocation of the aid of the Holy Spirit before the reading of the Scriptures, so that they may be rightly understood.[1] All three doctrines which were so carefully worked out in the Genevan order might be comprehended under the single, all-controlling Calvinist doctrine of the sole causality of God.

The doctrine that Calvin made even more distinctively his own was that of Election. It may be said that he rediscovered the sense of the Church as the New Israel, the people of God. This doctrine is unmistakably reflected in his theory of worship. It produced both the deep sense of homage and reverence before God emphasised in his service by the reading of the Decalogue and by the confession of faith that was made by the believers as a solidarity in Christ. It is seen no less in the deep and spontaneous gratitude that bursts forth in the psalms sung by the congregation. And it is this doctrine, as well as that of the Communion as a 'sigillum Verbi' that makes Calvin emphasise the unity of the ante-Communion with the Communion. The Communion is therefore no mere appendage to a preaching service; it is the service for the faithful where God seals his promises to the Elect. The doctrine of Election with its reflection in the corporate nature of the Calvinist *cultus* contrasts with the individualism that characterises the Lutheran service.

To leave the matter there would be an injustice to the memory of Luther. It must also be recognized that Calvin had to accommodate his views on three matters. He made a distinction between fundamental and unimportant matters in the ordering of the worship. He did not for a moment waver in his conviction that all worship must proceed from the

[1] Calvin *La forme des prières ecclésiastiques*, in Clemen *op. cit.* pp. 51–58

divine inspiration, and human traditions therefore carried no weight with him. On the other hand, he maintained that in the matter of worship there were both fundamental doctrines and also superficial aids conducive to peace and concord which might be left to the judgment of individual Christians. He made three concessions only, every one of them a matter of order, not of doctrine.[1] He gave in to the Genevan populace when they decried his formula of absolution as a novelty. He also allowed the Lord's Supper to be celebrated with unleavened bread. He did not disapprove of the use of unleavened bread in the Sacrament, but he disliked the method by which the change was introduced to Geneva; that is, he disapproved of the high-handed way in which the neighbouring Canton of Berne insisted that Geneva should follow its practice. His third and greatest concession, however, was to yield to the request of the Genevan magistrates in allowing the Lord's Supper to be celebrated only four times yearly. The point was not easily conceded and Calvin left it on record for posterity that his conviction in this matter had been overruled by the Genevan magistrates.[2] These three concessions are not to be compared in seriousness or extent with Luther's concessions. Furthermore, Calvin cannot be accused of inconsistency or conservatism in the matter of accommodation, for he knew both the logic of his position and that he must yield because he was in the minority and the points at issue were only of minor importance.

It is, however, in the comparison of Calvin's doctrine of the Sacraments (and particularly of the Lord's Supper) with Luther's, that the former's consistently theological basis becomes clear. This is not to assert that Calvin was a mere logician in his treatment of the Sacraments, for he recognized that there is an impenetrable mystery in the gracious dealings of God with men, which reason can rarely probe. His was an adoring as well as an acute mind. However, his doctrine of the Sacraments was more consistently theological than Luther's. As Barclay shows,[3] the two Reformers were agreed on four main contentions. They both condemned any doctrine that

[1] F. O. Reed *Public Worship in XVIth century Calvinism* (an unpublished thesis for the degree of B. Litt. in the University of Oxford) ch. ii

[2] Maxwell *op. cit.* p. 203

[3] *The Protestant Doctrine of the Lord's Supper* (1928) ch. ii

denied the necessity of a living faith in the recipient and taught that the Sacraments conferred grace *ex opere operato*. They both repudiated the doctrine which held that the Sacraments were to be understood in a merely etymological sense as badges or testimonies of the Christian profession. Thirdly, they rejected as inadequate the view that represented them as mere allegories or significant exhibitions of truth. Finally, they were both opposed to the doctrine that regarded the Lord's Supper as a commemorative rite only. For both the Sacraments were, positively, 'sigilla Verbi,' that is, they were signs by which God confirmed or sealed his promises to his people. The radical difference between the Lutheran view of later years and Calvin's doctrine consisted in the fact that Luther maintained that the Sacraments had inherent efficacy, whereas Calvin referred their sanctifying power to the accompanying aid of God.[1] Luther thought that the objectivity of the Sacraments could only be maintained if their inherent efficacy was postulated. To assert faith as a pre-condition of their effectiveness seemed to him to make the Sacraments depend upon the faith of the recipient. Calvin was well aware of the imputation, but his doctrine of the Lord's Supper cannot be accused of subjectivity, since he declares that faith itself is a gift of God mediated by the Holy Spirit. Luther also found it difficult to maintain a belief in the mystical union of Christ with the believer in the Lord's Supper, if one held that the Lord's risen body was circumscribed.

In order to obviate that difficulty, he held the doctrine of the ubiquity of Christ's body. Calvin, on the other hand, did not resort to a dubious metaphysical theory to substantiate conclusions reached on theological grounds. He claimed that Christ's risen body was in heaven, but that this did not prevent him operating by the power of his Holy Spirit.

'Christ with all his riches is there presented to us no less than if he were set before our eyes and were touched by our hands.'[2]

It may thus be seen that Luther's later doctrine of the inherent efficacy of the Sacraments departs from his earlier doctrine of them as 'sigilla Verbi', presented to and responded to by faith. On the other hand, Calvin is consistently theological without conceding any of the objectivity of Luther's later view. At the

[1] *Inst.* IV xix 2 [2] *Le Catechisme français de Calvin,* cited F. O. Reed *op. cit.*

same time his teaching, equally with Luther's, preserves a sense of adoring gratitude at the condescension of God as well as a deep sense of mystery.

The first main difference between the Lutheran and Calvinistic worship, considered as a whole, is that the former is more subjective, the latter more objective. For Luther the Bible is the Word of God in which he finds the corroboration of a spiritual experience. For Calvin the Bible is the declaration of God's will and has authority in its entirety. The Lutheran service tends to become the expression of the experience that the Word engenders. Its atmosphere is one of glad thankfulness for God's gracious forgiveness. In the Calvinist service more prominence is given to the Bible as the declaration of God's will for doctrine, conduct and church government. The characteristic atmosphere is that of reverential awe before the Sovereign Will. The Sermon in the Calvinist *cultus* is an objective element in worship, for it is the announcement and exposition of a Will declared in every part of the sacred Writ. Furthermore, while the Lutheran service appeals to the individual and expresses its confession in the first person singular, the Calvinist service is corporate and congregational. God is conceived as declaring his will to the Elect and their prayers were the corporate response to the Word, as were their praises sung in the metrical psalms.

A second difference is that the Calvinist service was more Biblical in nature than the Lutheran. Whereas Luther's service contained hymns which were paraphrases of the Christian's experience and of Christian teaching, Calvin's praises were entirely Scriptural. He would allow only the Psalms. Furthermore, while Luther was not opposed to the use of sequences and proses, provided their doctrine was sound, Calvin insisted upon reading the Word of God without embellishment. Again, while Luther's prayers might proclaim Christian experience, such as penitence or adoration, Calvin's original orders of service contained a prayer of confession that was exclusively Scriptural. Furthermore, Calvin included the Decalogue as an integral part of the Strassburg liturgy.

A third difference between the Lutheran and Calvinist rites is one of accent. Whereas Luther's service is composed of two elements, the descending movement of God to man and the ascending movement of man to God (these being roughly equal in proportion), Calvin's service is mainly a descending movement. If the thought uppermost in Luther's mind is that of gratefulness, the dominant thought for Calvin is that man must obey the *ius liturgicum*—the Bible—since apart from such obedience he cannot offer an acceptable tribute of worship to God. The keynote of Luther's service is gratitude; of Calvin's, obedience. Although there are elements both in the prayers and the praises of the Calvinist *cultus* that represent the ascending movement, the prevailing sense is one of reverential abasement before the living God. This is instanced by the lack of a specific prayer of adoration in the Calvinist service. If Lutheran worshippers are 'laeti triumphantes', Calvinists are 'miseri et abiecti'. The distinction is not absolute, but it points to a real difference of emphasis.

Fourthly, the Lutheran service is richer in the use of ceremonial than the Calvinist service. Earlier it has been shewn that there are theological not æsthetic reasons for the difference. Suffice it here to state that the Lutheran *cultus* is rich, the Calvinist bare.

The theological differences between Luther and Calvin, issuing in differences of liturgical emphasis, are all-important because this liturgical watershed prepares the way for the differences between the Anglicans and the Puritans in England. It will be seen that the position of the Established clergy in England is that of Luther, whilst the views of the Puritans are those of Calvin. The analogy is not exact in detail, but in the main it holds good. It can certainly be maintained, however, that the different conceptions of the authority of the Scriptures in the mind of Luther and in the mind of Calvin, reappear in the liturgical controversy between the Puritans and the clergy of the Establishment. They were the inheritors of the Reformers.

# CHAPTER III

## THE TRANSMISSION OF THE REFORMED HERITAGE

The origins of English Puritan worship are to be sought in the liturgies of the Churches of Geneva and of Strassburg. The transmission of this liturgical heritage, with which we are now concerned, is the work of eminent exiles. In the reign of King Edward VI the Puritan influence was spread by Continental refugees who found a welcome asylum in England under the protection of Archbishop Cranmer, and also by Ridley and Hooper, who had been exiles on the Continent in the time of Henry VIII, but became bishops under his successor. On the other hand, during the reign of Queen Mary the guardians of the Puritan tradition were English exiles who found a refuge in the Low Countries and in Switzerland.

### *A. The Edwardian Puritans*

The influence of the Puritans of King Edward VI's time can clearly be seen in the Prayer Book of 1552. Pre-eminent among the distinguished foreigners in England during this reign was Martin Bucer. His influence, however, preceded his arrival. For in 1547 there was printed in London a translation of the system of doctrine and worship which he and Melanchthon had drawn up for the Protestant Archbishop of Cologne, entitled, *Nostra Hermanni Archepiscopi Coloniensis simplex et pia Deliberatio et Christiana in Verbo Dei fundata Reformatio*. This was certainly in the hands of the English Reformers when they were engaged on the revision of the Book of Common Prayer.[1] From it the Baptismal Offices of the Prayer Book were substantially taken. Furthermore, in the Communion Office the Confession of sins, the Absolution and succeeding Sentences and the Thanksgiving in the Post-Communion, are of similar origin. It should also be noted that the Second Exhortation is extracted from a work of Bucer's friend and fellow-exile Peter

[1] Baird *Eutaxia, or A Chapter on Liturgies* (1856) p. 192

Martyr.[1] Further evidence of Bucer's influence is supplied by C. H. Smyth's consideration of Bucer's Criticisms of the 1549 Communion Office in Chapter VII of *Cranmer and the Reformation*. There it is shewn that the rubrics which Bucer objected to were omitted including the 'Certayn Notes'. Further, the petition for departed souls in the prayer for the Church was omitted at his suggestion; similarly the petition for the mediation of angels in the prayer of Oblation was expunged, as were the words of administration. Also, at Bucer's request, the title was altered from the 'Mass' to 'Order for Administration'.[2] It should also be remembered that Bucer was Calvin's predecessor at Strassburg, and that Bucer's order of worship was substantially the basis of Calvin's Strassburg Liturgy. Furthermore, Bucer holding the Regius Chair of Divinity in Cambridge, was able to exert a profound influence over the clergy, as to a lesser extent did his opposite number, Peter Martyr, in Oxford. Baird asserts:[3] 'We may fairly claim the Liturgy of Cologne as a fruit of the Calvinistic Reformation, for Bucer, who had the chief hand in it, was a disciple of Calvin.'

John Knox, Calvin's most fervent disciple, was also able to introduce an important rubric into the Second Prayer Book. On visiting England in 1551 he was invited to assist in the revision of the Prayer Book then in progress. The 'Black Rubric', which completely excluded the notion of 'anye reall and essencial presence there beeyng of Christ's naturall fleshe and bloude' in the Sacrament, was inserted at his suggestion.

An even more direct instance of Calvin's influence is the introductory portions of the Daily Service in the 1552 book. Bucer and Martyr recommended the Sentences, the Exhortation, the Confession and Absolution, which were borrowed from Calvin's Strassburg Liturgy. It is also probable that the introduction of the Decalogue into the Communion Service was due to Calvin's influence.[4] Furthermore, the Responses to the recitation of the Ten Commandments are taken from

[1] *Liturgical Services* (ed. Parker Society) p. 186, n. 4

[2] Again, practically the whole of the Solemnization of Matrimony will be found in the Cologne Ritual, as well as a large portion of the Order for the Burial of the Dead

[3] *op. cit.* p. 194

[4] There is the further possibility that Miles Coverdale paved the way for the introduction of the Decalogue in his *Ghostly Psalms* (1539); *v.* his *Remains* (ed. Parker Soc.) pp. 543*ff*

Pullain who was Calvin's successor in Strassburg and who translated the Strassburg Liturgy which he used in Glastonbury in 1551 under the title, *Liturgia Sacra.*[1] Pullain, as we shall see, is also an important influence upon later English Puritanism since he shared the Church of the White Ladies in Frankfort with the English Marian exiles. Further, the very words accompanying the distribution of the elements in the Lord's Supper are taken from the Calvinistic liturgy of John a Lasco who derived them from the Calvinistic liturgy of Strassburg.

Calvin's influence was also mediated by John Hooper the Bishop of Gloucester who inaugurated the Vestments controversy, basing his objection to the use of vestments upon the sufficiency of the Word of God as a directory of ceremonies. Further, both he and Ridley were insistent upon a more thorough reformation of the worship of England.

All these, then, were media for the transmission of Puritanism in the reign of King Edward VI. Their influence was considerable, as we have shewn, upon the Book of Common Prayer. But more, they were not satisfied even with the radical reforms introduced into the 1552 Prayer Book, but hoped for a more thorough reformation, until the English liturgy should completely conform to the Word of God and the practice of the Apostolic Church. For this reason they were the parents of the radical Puritans among the Marian exiles and later of the Separatists in the reign of Elizabeth. Two of them, Pullain and John a Lasco, Superintendents of the Churches of the Strangers, respectively, in Glastonbury and London, were enabled by royal protection to employ Calvinistic liturgies in their diets of worship, thus exemplifying in practice the goal at which the radical Puritans aimed.

## *B. The Marian Exiles*

For our liturgical information in this period the chief sources are two: the first is entitled, *A Brief Discourse of the Troubles begun at Frankfort in the year* 1554 *about the Book of Common Prayer and Ceremonies.* It is written by a contemporary and from the radical Puritan standpoint of a member of Knox's party. It is conjectured with considerable probability by Pro-

[1] Maxwell *op. cit.* p. 21

fessor McCrie[1] that the author is Whittingham. This document is of first-rate importance, since it describes the origins of the struggle between the Knoxians and the Coxians who represented respectively the left wing and the right wing of the Puritans among the English exiles. This important watershed of opinion or rather of conviction (since it was no less) produced the two divergent streams of Puritanism which coursed through the reign of Queen Elizabeth. The second document of equal importance is *The Forme of Prayers and Ministrations of the Sacraments, etc., used in the English Congregation at Geneva: and approved by the famous and godly learned man, Iohn Caluyn. Imprinted at Geneva by Iohn Crespin. MDLVI.* This, commonly known as John Knox's Genevan Service Book, was the work of Knox and his party at Frankfort and became the service-book of the English Puritans, as we shall prove later.

We shall re-tell very briefly the narrative of the *Brief Discourse*, emphasising the salient points. On the 27th June 1554, Edmund Sutton, William Williams, William Whittingham, and Thomas Wood came with their companies to Frankfort.

'The same night came one Maister Valaren Pullan Minister unto their lodging and declared how he had obtained a church there in the name of all such as should come out off England for the gospel, but especially from Glastonbury which were all Frenchmen.'[2]

He invited the English exiles to share in the worship of the French Church, but they being in the majority ignorant of French, had to decline. They were, however, granted permission by the Magistrates

'to preach and minister the Sacraments in that Church . . . the French one day and the English on the other day, and upon the Sunday . . . but it was with this commandment that the English should not dissent from the Frenchmen in doctrine or ceremonies . . .'[3]

The English then drew up an order of service providing that

'the answering allowde after the minister should not be used, the litany the surplice and many other things omitted, for that in those reformed churches, such things would seem more than strange.'

[1] *cf.* his letter on the question of authorship given in the Introduction to the reprint of 1875 [2] *A Brief Discourse* (ed. Arber, 1908) p. v [3] *id.* p. vi

It was also agreed that in place of the Confession of the Book of Common Prayer another should be used 'both of more effect and also framed according to the state and time'. Further, this concluded, the people were 'to sing a Psalm in metre in a plain tune' according to the practice of the other reformed churches. Then the minister was to pray for the assistance of the Holy Spirit before proceeding to the sermon.

'After the sermon a general prayer for all estates and our country of England was also devised at the end of which prayer was joined the Lord's Prayer and a rehearsal of the articles of our belief, which ended the people to sing an other psalme as afore.'

Finally, the minister pronounces the blessing, 'The Peace of God, or some other like effect, the people to depart'.[1] Similarly, an order for the celebration of the Lord's Supper was agreed upon. One point calls for comment, namely the Blessing which was taken from the Anglican Communion Service and not explicitly based upon the words of Scripture.[2] The order of service we have detailed belongs to the Strassburg family of liturgies upon which Pullain's order is based. It was not, however, a complete break with the Book of Common Prayer as the Blessing shows.

When these arrangements had been made, the Frankfort exiles sent invitations to their fellow countrymen in various towns including Zurich, Emden and Strassburg to come and join them. The Zurich brethren asked whether they would be allowed to use the 1552 Book. Chambers, their emissary, returned with the reply that the Frankfort exiles were willing to use it, 'so far as God's word did commend it', while they utterly rejected all 'unprofitable ceremonies'. The reply of the Strassburg exiles carried by Chambers and Grindal as liaison-officers, declared that they were certain that the Frankfort Church was eager to reduce the Church of England to its former perfection and therefore to conform to its usage. This was reinforced by the plea,

'least by much altering of the same we should seem to condemn the chief authors thereof, who, as they now suffer, so are they ready to confirm that fact with the price of their bloods and should also both give occasion to our adversaries to accuse our doctrine of imperfection and us of muta-

[1] *id.* p. vii
[2] McMillan *The Worship of the Scottish Reformed Church* (1931) p. 49

bility and the godly to doubt in that truth wherein before they were persuaded and to hinder their coming hither which before they had purposed.'[1]

Having failed to gather in their fellow-exiles, the Frankfort exiles decided to have a permanent form of worship brought into use. Their first decision was to adopt the Genevan Order used in Calvin's Church, of which an English translation had been made by Huycke in 1550. This, however, Knox declined to use until they had consulted with their brethren elsewhere. But he also declined to use the 1552 Book since there were in it many things 'only by warrant of man's authority'. Calvin's advice was therefore sought on the 1552 Book, but he received only a 'platt' or brief description of the English Book. His reply included the famous depreciatory phrase, 'multas tolerabiles ineptias' (many foolish, tolerable things). Fortified by this opinion of the Book of Common Prayer, Knox, Whittingham, Gilby, Fox and Cole drew up a new order, which afterwards became known as John Knox's Genevan Service Book. Of this McMillan avers [2] that, while it did not differ greatly from Calvin's Genevan Order, 'the differences were more likely to offend those who wished the English book than to conciliate them'.

Even this new order did not prove completely satisfactory so that an eirenical liturgy was drafted. This has been termed the 'Liturgy of Compromise' by Dr G. W. Sprott.[3] This was approved and used by Knox and might have been permanently adopted but for the arrival of more of the exiles who, under the leadership of Cox, insisted upon the full use of the Anglican Book. The *Brief Discourse* asserts[4] that this order was used from the 6th of February until the 13th of March 'when D. Coxe and others with him came to Frankfort out of England, who broke the agreed order in answering alowde after the minister' and on the following Sunday 'one of his company entered the pulpit and read the Litany' and Cox and his company answered aloud.

As the opposition to Knox became too strong, he left for Geneva, where he acted as minister to the English congrega-

[1] *A Brief Discourse* (ed. cit.) p. xxiii [2] McMillan *op. cit.* p. 53

[3] This Liturgy is bound in the same volume of the *Church Service Society Series* as Wotherspoon's *Second Prayer Book of Edward VI*

[4] *A Brief Discourse* p. lv

tion there for a few weeks before he left for Scotland in August 1555. During the winter Whittingham and other exiles made their way to Geneva. In accordance with the Genevan laws the congregation chose two pastors, Goodman and Gilby (the latter to take the place of Knox until his return). When Knox left Frankfort he took with him the form of service which he and his colleagues had drawn up for use there. In 1556 this was formally adopted, while Knox was in Scotland, with the approval of Calvin. It was printed in Geneva and bore the title: *The Forme of Prayers and Ministrations of the Sacraments, etc., used in the English Congregation at Geneva: and approved by the famous and godly learned man, Iohn Caluyn.* We·now turn to a more detailed consideration of this Book as the parent of Puritan worship both in Scotland and in England. For this consideration the recent expository edition of Dr W. D. Maxwell is invaluable.

The Sunday Morning Service consists of the following items:[1]

A Confession of sins
A Prayer for pardon
A metrical Psalm
A Prayer for illumination
The Scripture Lection and Sermon
The Long Prayer and the Lord's Prayer
The Apostles' Creed (*said by the minister alone*)
A metrical Psalm
A Blessing (*either I Cor. or Numbers*)

The Lord's Supper was celebrated in the following order:[2]

A Psalm in metre while the elements were prepared
The Words of Institution
The Exhortation
The Consecration
The Fraction and Delivery
The Communion while Scripture is read
The Post-Communion Prayer
Psalm 103
The Blessing

These two orders, which will receive detailed treatment in

[1] Maxwell *John Knox's Genevan Service Book* (1931) p. 18
[2] *id.* p. 51

a later chapter,[1] suffice to show the essential characteristics of Puritan worship. These are: the Word of God as the sufficient basis of Divine worship, and the apostolic simplicity as its precedent. We notice that the Confession of sins is 'framed to our time out of the 9. chap. of Daniel'.[2] This beginning to the service is characteristically Calvinistic since it assumes the doctrine of man's inherent depravity and his need for pardon before he can worship his God aright. The phraseology of all prayers is Scriptural and it is equally significant that psalms are preferred to hymns since they are Scriptural. Similarly, the Lord's Prayer is used because of its Dominical authority. The centrality of the Sermon also testifies to the importance of the Word of God in worship. Man can only worship God aright, if he will heed the will of God in the Scriptures. Unscriptural worship is false worship since it imports human traditions. Similarly, the simplicity of the worship as shewn by the discarding of vestments and all unedifying and popish ceremonial, is based upon the simplicity of the worship of the Apostolic Church. These two Puritan positions are also illustrated by the Order of Communion. This commences with the words of Institution and expressly follows the pattern of our Lord's Last Supper in the Upper Room. It is therefore both Scriptural and Apostolic in character.

We may now summarise our consideration of the *Brief Discourse* and the *Forme of Prayers*. The narrative of the Frankfort Troubles proves the existence of two parties of English Puritans. The 'Knoxians' were prepared to approve of the Book of Common Prayer only in so far as it accorded with the Word of God and would have retained it in an amended form. Since the more conservative Puritans would not agree to such a liturgy of compromise, they set about producing their own which was Scriptural and Apostolic in basis. The 'Coxians', on the other hand, did not wish to accept a Calvinistic Prayer Book when there lay to hand a Prayer Book which had been revised by godly Englishmen and martyrs. This, they agreed, was not perfect but it was substantially sound and might be amended later. These two positions are clarified by the letter which Dean Sampson wrote to Calvin from Strassburg on February 25th 1555, concerning the state of the parties at Frankfort:[3]

[1] see below, Chapter IX [2] Maxwell *op. cit.* p. 85
[3] Laing *The Works of John Knox* iv 3

'While some desire the Book of the Reformation of the Church of England to be set aside altogether, others only deem some things in it to be objectionable, such as kneeling at the Lord's Supper, the linen surplice and other matters of the kind; but the rest of it, namely the prayers, Scripture lessons and the form of the administration of Baptism and the Lord's Supper, they wish to be retained. Some contend for retaining the form both because the Archbishop of Canterbury defends the doctrine as sound, and also the opposite party can assign no just reason why the form should be changed. They exclaim on the other hand that the sole object of these persons is the establishment of ceremonies.'

Each party was quite clearly working for the ultimate triumph of its own principles in England. Thus we shall expect to find in Elizabethan Puritanism one party that stands by the Book of Common Prayer but objects to its ceremonies, while another party rejects it and prefers to use the Genevan type of worship. This is in fact precisely the situation, as we shall shew.

### C. *The Genevan Service Book as used by the English Puritans*

Our first evidence of the use of the Genevan Book is in the year 1567; Strype records the existence of both Puritan parties in this year:[1]

'The refusers of the orders of the Church (who by this time were commonly called Puritans) were grown now into two factions. The one was of a more quiet and peaceable demeanour; who indeed would not use the habits, nor subscribe to the ceremonies enjoined; as kneeling at the sacrament, the Cross in Baptism, the ring in Marriage; but held to the Communion of the Church and willingly and devoutly joined with the common prayers. But another sort there was, that disliked the whole constitution of the Church lately reformed; charging upon it many gross remainders of Popery; and that it was still full of corruptions not to be borne with, and Anti-Christian; and especially the habits the clergy were enjoined to use in their ministration and conversation. Insomuch that these latter separated themselves into private assemblies, meeting together not in Churches, but in private houses, where they had ministers of their prayer, they used a Book of Prayers framed at Geneva, for the congregation of English exiles lately sojourning there. Which book had been overseen and allowed by Calvin and the rest of his divines there, and indeed was for the most part taken out of the Genevan form.'

[1] Strype *Grindal* (Oxford 1821) p. 168*f*

Confirmation of Strype's assertion will be found in the reprint of 'The examination of Certain Londoners before the Ecclesiastical Commissioners June 20, 1567'.[1] The Puritan Smith in answer to the Bishop of London, Grindal, declared that the displacing of good preachers was the cause of their assembling privately, and continues:

'and then were we troubled and commanded to your courts from day to day, for not coming to our parish churches:—then we bethought us what were best to do; and we remembered that there was a congregation of us in this city in Queen Mary's days; and a congregation at Geneva, which used a book and order of preaching, ministering of the sacraments and discipline, most agreeable to the word of God; which book is allowed by that godly and well-learned man, Master Calvin, and the preachers there; which book and order we now hold. And if you can reprove this book, or anything that we hold, by the word of God, we will yield to you and do open penance at Paul's Cross; if not, we will stand to it by the grace of God.'

It is significant that the description of the *Forme of Prayers* echoes verbally the 1556 edition printed by Crespin.

In the year 1571, Strype records,[2] the Puritans

'did still in their own or other churches, or in private houses, read prayers different from the established office of Common Prayer: using the Genevan Form or mangling the English book, and preached without licenses.'

'Mangling the English book': does this mean the use of the 'Liturgy of Compromise' or merely the exclusion of the Litany or of what the radical Puritans regarded as the popish remnants and dregs of the Book of Common Prayer? The answer is uncertain.

In 1584 there was a Puritan petition to Parliament for which, says Strype,[3] the Puritans

'had compiled and got in readiness a new platform of ecclesiastical government, agreeable to that of Geneva, and another form of prayer prescribed therein, in room of the old one, for the use of this Church.'

Such then is the direct evidence that the *Forme of Prayers* was used by the Puritans in the reign of Elizabeth.

[1] *The Remains of Edmund Grindal* (ed. Parker Soc. 1843) p. 203*f*
[2] Strype *Parker* (Oxford 1821) ii 65 [3] Strype *Whitgift* (Oxford 1817) i 348

## CHAPTER IV

# PURITAN WORSHIP AND THE CONTINENTAL REFORMED CHURCHES

The Westminster Divines in their Preface to the *Directory for the Publick Worship of God* affirm that they are at one with the Reformed Churches abroad in deploring the corruptions in the Book of Common Prayer:[1]

'. . . Long and sad experience hath made it manifest, that the Liturgy used in the Church of England (notwithstanding all the pains and religious intentions of the composers of it) hath proved an offence, not only to many of the godly at home, but also to the Reformed Churches abroad.'

It is clearly their intention to bring English worship into line with Reformed practice. It was also the custom of the earlier Puritans to appeal to the continental Reformed Churches for precedents to reformation in worship; whilst even the Separatists laid claim to a share in the Reformation heritage.

It is, therefore, surprising to find John Durel, the Minister of the French Church in the Savoy, confuting the claim that the Puritans were closer disciples of the Reformed Churches than were the Anglicans. He declares that the conceptions the Westminster Divines had of the Reformed Churches, were

'mere *Chimeras* and *Ideas;* which, like the *Utopia* of *Sir Thomas More,* never existed but in their brain.'[2]

It is the purpose of this chapter to examine the justice of Durel's accusation and to enumerate and explain the departures of the Puritans from the Reformed tradition.

In the first place it is clear that the Puritans did in fact regard themselves as the representatives of the Reformed tradition in England. The Puritan case-book of apologetics, *A Parte of a Register*, published at the end of the 16th century, abounds in references to the customs of Reformed Churches

[1] Sprott & Leishman *The Book of Common Order of the Church of Scotland, commonly known as John Knox's Liturgy, and the Directory for the Public Worship of God agreed upon by the Assembly of Divines at Westminster* (London 1868) p. 287

[2] Durel *A View of the Government and Publick Worship of God in the Reformed Churches beyond the Sea* (London 1662) p. 14

abroad as the precedents for their required reforms, and frequently cites the writings of the Reformed divines. A typical example is that of an author who offers 'Reasons against kneeling at Holy Communion'. His thesis is:

'What-soeuer churches rightly reformed vse not, is to be by vs not only suspected, but iustly reiected . . . But the right reformed churches vse not kneeling at the receit of the Supper: for proofe hereof, looke vpon all the churches of *France*, *Flanders*, *Hungarie*, *Polonia*, *Berna*, *Zurich*, *Sauoy*, *Scotland* . . . besides the presidents and practise wee haue heere at home before our owne eyes, in the French, Dutch, and Italian Churches at London, Norwitch, Sandwitch, and other places in this Realme: and besides the publike iudgements of particular persons of those Churches as *Bullinger* in his Decades, and *Beza* in his Epistle . . .'

The following personalities are cited as authorities in this Register: Calvin, Beza, Viret, Peter Martyr, Tremelius, Iunius, Knox, Bullinger and Melanchthon,[1] and the general customs of the Reformed Churches are as frequently mentioned as authorities. Even the Separatists claimed that their worship was substantially that of the Reformed Churches:[2]

'Lastlie, yf it be not thought convenient that wee her Maiesties naturall and louing subiectes shold haue the same libertie graunted vs in the Worship of God, wch her highnes giueth to strangers, French, Dutche, and Italian (sithe our practise is no other in every chiefe poinct, then that of theirs, and Geneua, and all other Reformed Churches) . . .'

This is no isolated case since Robinson, whilst a semi-Separatist, affirmed that his church at Leyden differed from the Dutch Reformed Churches on minor points, 'not at all in the substance of things'.[3]

On the other hand, although the Puritans were essentially in agreement with the Reformed Churches, they reserved the right to differ from them in certain matters. Whilst they listened attentively to the voice of Geneva, they would not hold that because 'Geneva locuta est' therefore 'causa finita'. Their criterion was the Word of God by which Geneva itself was to be judged. Their point of view is illustrated by the following conversation, which took place between the eccles-

[1] pp. 7, 32, 35, 37, 39, 303, 411, &c.

[2] *The Works of John Robinson, Pastor of the Pilgrim Fathers* (ed. Robert Ashton, London 1851) iii 48*f* [3] *ibid.*

iastical authorities of London and certain Puritans on the 20th of June 1567:[1]

'*W.Wh.* It is good to followe the best example: but we must follow them [*i.e. the Genevese*] as they follow Christ.

*Deane* All the learned in Europe are against you.

*Wattes* Ye will beleeue no man.

*Smith* Yes we reuerence the learned in *Geneua*, or in other places wheresoeuer they be: yet we buylde not on them our faith and religion.

*Bishop* Will you be iudged by the learned in Geneua? they are against you.

*Hawkins* We will be iudged by the words of God, whiche shall iudge vs all at the last day, therefore sufficient to iudge now.'

The question at issue in this debate was whether ecclesiastical authorities had a right to add to the ordinances of worship required by the Scriptures. The Puritans claimed that they had not any right to add to the minimum required by the Word of God, and they claimed Geneva as their authority. To which the Churchmen replied that in fact the Church of Geneva had made additions to the ordinances and requirements of the Scriptures. As an instance of this they cited the wafer cakes with which the Genevan Church communicated. The Puritans thereupon admitted that the Genevan Church itself was condemned by the Word of God in this.

The same right of appeal to the Scriptures against the Church, the central principle of the Reformation, was insisted upon by John Robinson in his memorable address to the parting Pilgrim Fathers. He declares:[2]

'I am verily persuaded the Lord hath more truth yet to break forth out of his holy word. For my part, I cannot sufficiently bewail the condition of those Reformed Churches which are come to a period in religion and will go, at present, no further than the instruments of their reformation. The Lutherans cannot be drawn to go beyond what Luther saw. Whatever part of his will our God has revealed to Calvin, they will rather die than embrace it; and the Calvinists, you see, stick fast where they were left by that great man of God, who yet saw not all things. This is a misery much to be lamented.'

[1] *A Parte of a Register* p. 29*f*

[2] Skeats & Miall *A History of the Free Churches in England* (London 1891) p. 34

Clearly the Puritans attached no sacrosanct authority to the Reformed tradition. But, at the same time, they recognised in the Reformed Churches overseas a close relationship to themselves. They would probably have been surprised had they realised the extent of their divergence from the customs of the Reformed Churches. They would have been even more amazed to learn that, in certain features of her worship, the Established Church in England approximated more closely to the Reformed tradition than they did themselves. The main difference between the Puritans and the upholders of the Book of Common Prayer was that the former disliked set and 'stinted' prayers, while the latter approved of a liturgy. Not all of the Puritans concurred in their disapproval of set prayers, as the case of Richard Baxter shows. Indeed, there is a letter extant which declares that two eminent Puritans did not object on principle to set prayers.[1] Generally, however, the Puritans felt that the restraint of a liturgy and its unsuitability for varying needs of varying congregations and times, made it undesirable. In this they departed from the Reformed tradition. Dr Robert Some, in a treatise directed against the views of Barrowe and Greenwood, was quick to point out that Calvin had approved of set forms of prayer:[2]

'Master Caluine writing to the Lord Protectour in the time of King Edward the sixt, hath these wordes: *Quod ad formulam precum & rituum Ecclesiasticorum, valde probo, ut certa illa extet, a qua pastoribus discedere in functione sua non liceat, tam ut consulatur quorundam simplicitati & imperitiae, quam ut certius ita constet omnium inter se Ecclesiarum consensus. Postremo etiam, ut obviam eatur desultoriae quorundam levitati, qui novationes quasdam affectant. Sic igitur statum esse catechismum oportet, statam sacramentorum administrationem, publicam item precum formulam. Calu. Epist.* 87.'

It should also be remembered that Calvin's Service Book, *La Manyere* . . ., while it provided for the need for extempore prayer at certain points of the service (particularly before the Sermon) yet prescribed all else in detail. Williston Walker sums up Calvin's practice in prayer thus:[3]

'As between a fixed liturgy and free prayer he evidently had none of the

[1] *A Parte of a Register* pp. 528*ff* (esp. p. 537)
[2] *A Godly Treatise &c.* (1589) p. 32; *cf.* Calvin *Opera* xiii 85
[3] *John Calvin* p. 224

scruples which later controversy was to develop among his spiritual disciples in England, Scotland, and America; and his Genevan form of worship, at least, was a happy combination of both.'

While this statement is true, it does not do justice to the emphasis which was weighted in favour of set prayers. In this respect, the Book of Common Prayer approximated more closely to the Reformed tradition than did the Puritan practice of extempore prayer. On the other hand, the Westminster Directory by defining the subject-matter of prayer, without suggesting the actual wording, brought the Puritan practice nearer to Calvin's. It is most probable that Calvin would have regarded the extreme Separatist insistence on extempore prayer as entitling them to the rebuke of 'novationes quasdam affectant'.

The Puritans also departed from Calvin in regarding unscriptural ceremonies, such as kneeling at the reception of communion, the ring in marriage, and the sign of the cross in Baptism, as intolerable. Whilst he did not approve of a multitude of ceremonies, he allowed them with the *caveat* that

'whatever observances we use are manifestly useful, and very few in number . . . Let us not imagine that the worship of God is improved by a multitude of ceremonies.'[1]

Moreover, he would have allowed each Church freedom to ordain its own ceremonies, which was the very point which the Puritans would not grant to the authorities of the Established Church. He wrote to the Bernese Council:[2]

'Touching ceremonies, since they are unimportant things, the churches can differ freely in their use of them. One would be well advised, and it would sometimes be useful, not to have too meticulous a uniformity, in order to show that faith and Christianity itself do not consist in that.'

One of the dignified and significant ceremonies which Calvin approved of was kneeling for prayer. To those who object that it is a human addition to the worship of God, not required by God, Calvin replies:[3]

'I say that it is so of men, that it is also of God. It is of God, in respect that it is part of that comeliness, the care and keeping whereof is commended unto us by the Apostle.'

[1] *Inst.* IV x 32 [2] *Opera* xv 538 [3] *Inst.* IV x 30

He also insists that ceremonies must be orderly for the avoidance of confusion or of barbarity. He instances some of such ceremonies 'which are in common use', such as 'that we pray kneeling and bare-headed' and 'that in the burial of the dead we use some honest shew'.[1] He would doubtless have forbidden the Puritan ministers to give up their ministry because the imposed ceremonies were offensive to them. In 1557 he wrote that the faithful must be prepared to tolerate enforced ceremonies with which they disagreed rather than disrupt the church:[2]

'For in such things it seems to me that it is enough to have secured, so far as it lies with us, what we know to be best. For even though what they wish to have accepted bring scandal or evil consequences, yet so long as it is not of itself repugnant to the Word of God, it can be granted.'

Durel[3] informs us that

'the Reformed Churches of the Confession of *Augsburgh* for the most part use the Cross in Baptism.'

But he has to admit that the other Reformed Churches do not sign the infants whom they baptize, with a cross. The nearest approach to Calvinistic recognition of the validity of the ceremony, is to assert that the Reformed ministers who officiate in Prussia to congregations partly Lutheran and partly Calvinist

'do make sometimes the sign of the Cross with their hand in the aire, when they give the blessing to the people . . .'[4]

It is clear, however, that Calvin regarded the practice of crossing in Baptism as a superstitious usage and omitted it from his Baptismal services.[5] This tradition was certainly maintained by the Churches of the Calvinist tradition, as the remark of Sir Andrew Weldon, a traveller to Scotland, shews: 'They Christen without the Cross'.[6] In this particular the Puritans, rather than the Anglicans, were the heirs of the Reformed tradition.

[1] T. Norton's translation (ed. 1611) of the *Institutes* IV x 29
[2] *Opera* (*Consilia*) x 279 [3] *op. cit.* p. 41 [4] *ibid.*
[5] Maxwell *John Knox's Genevan Service Book* p. 48
[6] McMillan *op. cit.* p. 261*n*

It also appears that it was not customary for the Reformed Churches to employ the ceremony of the ring in marriage. The forms of the Calvinist order are silent concerning it, and the Westminster Directory, which is in the direct line of descent, expressly directs that no further ceremony is to be used.[1] Apparently the custom was occasionally used in Scotland.[2] The Puritans must also in this respect claim to be more Reformed than the Established Church.

The Puritans, however, in their condemnation of the festivals of the Christian Year, appear to have moved far from Calvin. The Puritan attitude to fasts and festivals has been admirably stated thus:[3] 'The Sabbath retained its lonely splendour as the sole red-letter day of the Puritan calendar.' Durel makes great capital out of this departure from the Reformed tradition by the Puritans. He quotes the *Helvetic Confession:*[4]

'Every Church chuseth for her self a certain set time for Common-Prayers &c. And it is not lawful for any man to overthrow at his pleasure this Order of the Church . . . Besides if the Churches using their Christian liberty do religiously celebrate the commemoration of the Lords Nativity, Circumcision, Passion, and Resurrection, also of his Ascension into Heaven, and of the sending of the Holy Ghost upon his Disciples: we do approve of it exceedingly.'

In this and in other respects the Puritans were so afraid of superstitious abuse of a custom, that rather than erect it with safeguards, they avoided it altogether. They had not measured the wisdom of Luther's principle: 'Abusus non tollit usum'. In Scotland the Reformers were not easily able to eradicate the old customs to which the common people clung tenaciously, but that such was their intent appears from the exception taken by the General Assembly of the Scottish Church in 1566 to this one point in the Helvetic Confession cited above:[5]

'We dare not religiously celebrate any other feast day than what the Divine articles have prescribed.'

Both English and Scottish Puritans discarded the customs as they could not find warrant for them in the Word of God,

[1] Maxwell *op. cit.* p. 156 [2] McMillan *op. cit.* p. 268*f*
[3] A. G. Matthews in *Christian Worship* p. 173 [4] *op. cit.* p. 26*f*
[5] McMillan *op. cit.* p. 301

although this required a departure from the continental Reformed tradition.

The Established Church in one other particular preserved the Genevan heritage, whilst the Puritans relinquished it. Calvin writes plainly that he approves of the Pronouncement of Absolution by the Minister after the Confession of Sins:[1]

> 'There is none of us but must acknowledge it to be very useful that after the General Confession, some striking promise of Scripture should follow whereby sinners might be raised to the hope of pardon and reconciliation. And I would have introduced this custom from the beginning but some fearing the novelty of it would give offence, I was over easy in yielding to them. And so the matter was allowed to remain.'

Maxwell[2] points out that the Absolution used by Calvin in *La Manyere* . . . of 1542 is found in the Book of Common Prayer in the Order for the Visitation of the Sick, where it has been excellently translated by Cranmer.

Calvin would also have championed the Anglican retention of Confirmation. He declares in the *Institutes:*[3]

> 'This laying on of hands which is done simply by way of blessing, I commend and would like to see it restored to its pure use to-day.'

Moreover in the *Tracts* he says of Confirmation:[4]

> 'We should like to see that rite everywhere restored, by which the young people are presented to God, after giving forth the confession of their faith.'

The real value of this Confirmation, in Calvin's view,[5] was that it afforded an opportunity for catechising the adolescent members of the Church. In this respect, whilst the Puritans did not use the rite of Confirmation, they preserved Calvin's intention by the thoroughness of their catechising and by their horror of ignorant or unworthy reception of the Lord's Supper. Calvin, no doubt, would have deprecated the confining of the performance of the rite to a Bishop, but it is doubtful whether he would have accepted the Puritan claim that laying on of hands was intended only for ordination in the New Testament.

It cannot be doubted that the Puritans did not follow the lead of Calvin in emphasising the centrality and the dignity of

[1] *Opera* x 213 [2] art. in *Church Service Society Annual* (1929–30) p. 26
[3] IV xix 4; *cf.* 13 [4] *Tracts* iii 288 [5] *Inst.* IV xix 13

the Lord's Supper. It is true that the early Puritans regularly celebrated Communion every Lord's day. But monthly Communion became the rule for most of them in time and the Presbyterians communicated only four times a year. In one respect they, not the Anglicans,[1] obeyed his wishes. He maintained that the true administration of the Sacrament requires the preached Word, otherwise it becomes a 'dumb show'.[2] Hence the Puritans' preparation-services would have met with his approval. He would not, however, have allowed the Puritan tendency to exalt the Sermon to the depreciation of the Sacrament. They were equally important to his mind. He gives his description of the true relation of the Sermon to the Sacrament in the following passage:[3]

'It might thus have been most decently administered, if it were frequently and at least every week set before the church, but that they should first begin with public prayers, then a Sermon should be made; then the Minister having bread and wine set upon the table, should rehearse the institution of the Supper; and then should declare the promises that are left unto us in it, and then should excommunicate all those that by the Lord's forbidding are debarred from it . . .'.

From this account it would appear that the Established Church fulfilled Calvin's wish for frequent Communions, whilst in its laxity in administering excommunication, it would have earned his disapproval. The Puritans during the first half of the seventeenth century would have been approved by him for their weekly Communions, whilst they kept to the letter his desire to forbid unworthy receivers to partake of the Lord's Supper.

Calvin parted company with the Puritans in his desire for Communion to be given to the sick. This they regarded as superstitious. Calvin, however, was satisfied if the ordinance was administered by a Minister to the sick person in the presence of some members of the church. He says in a letter written to Fulger in 1558:[4]

'That the Communion is not distributed to the sick also displeases me; and it is not on my account that this consolation has not been accorded

[1] Whilst preaching or reading a homily was recommended as preparation for the Communion in the Book of Common Prayer, this was often ignored in practice. [2] *Inst.* IV xvii 39 [3] *Inst.* IV xvii 43

[4] cited by Maxwell in *Church Service Society Annual* (1929–30) p. 28

to those who are quitting this life. But because a different custom has prevailed, and because a change could not be brought about without great discussion, I have preferred peace . . . I should have wished, however, to witness to those who will come after us, what I should have desired.'

Communion was given to the sick in the Churches of Hungary, Transylvania, Poland, Lithuania, and Hessen, but apparently it was not the custom in the non-Lutheran Churches.[1] The Puritans followed the custom of the Calvinist Churches, whilst the Established Church in England followed the wishes of Calvin himself.

Calvin also approved of auricular Confession, and failing that, of a private interview with the Minister prior to each Communion. In a letter to Farel he writes:[2]

'I have often told you that I should have thought it unwise to abolish Confession in our Churches, unless the rite which I have lately introduced be established in its place.'

The 'rite' referred to is the private interview mentioned above. There is little doubt that the Puritans would have regarded the re-introduction of auricular Confession as a re-establishment of the prerogatives of the priesthood.

Perhaps the most striking departure from the Reformed tradition made by the Puritans concerns their acceptance of marriages and burials as civil and not ecclesiastical actions. Durel informs the Nonconformists without qualification:[3]

'In all the Reformed Churches Matrimony is celebrated in the publick Congregation, and by the Minister.'

The Genevan Church certainly used a form of Marriage, as did the Scottish Church. The Westminster Assembly in the Directory also provided instructions for 'the solemnization of Marriage'. It was the Independents who raised objections to the proposals. Goodwin and his fellows regarded marriage as a civil contract in which the minister acts only as the magistrate's delegate. Rutherford combines Independent views with Presbyterian custom in declaring:[4]

'I doubt it is not a mere civil contract. It is the commandment of God. A civil contract may be dissolved with the consent of parties.'

[1] Durel *op. cit.* p. 49 [2] Maxwell *loc. cit.* [3] Durel *op. cit.* p. 47
[4] Sprott & Leishman *op. cit.* p. 359

He also makes a distinction between marriage, of which the essence is consent, and solemnization to which belongs the vow. Cartwright had already set the precedent for this distinction in desiring that there might be two services: one of espousals and the other of nuptials. Ultimately the Independents were satisfied that the ecclesiastical authorities did not usurp the position of the civil magistrate in claiming to 'marry' the consenting parties. Hence the careful nomenclature: 'Of the Solemnization of Marriage'.[1] The extreme Independent and Separatist position is expressed by John Robinson:[2]

'We cannot assent to the received opinion and practise answerable in the reformed churches, by which the pastors thereof do celebrate marriage publicly, and by virtue of their office . . . neither ought the pastor's office to be stretched to any other acts than those of religion, and such as are peculiar to Christians: amongst which marriage, common to Gentiles as well as to them, hath no place.'

It is remarkable that the extreme Puritans who excommunicated any of their members who married members of other communions than their own, and hence stressed the importance of Marriage, should have been unwilling for their pastors to perform the ceremony.

The Puritans also held that Burial was essentially a civil action, and therefore did not fall within ecclesiastical rights. For this position they found some justification in the procedure of the Reformed Churches. Pullain, the Minister of the Church of the Strangers in Glastonbury in the time of King Edward VI and also of the French congregation meeting in the town of Frankfort, used prayers at the graveside, with readings and a short address, but it is extremely doubtful whether Calvin did so.[3] This was probably due to the aversion of the early Reformers to the superstitious accretions to the Roman burial service, with its prayers to the saints and for the soul of the departed. The same aversion characterized English Puritan thinking on the subject. The question occupied the Westminster Assembly for six days. Rutherford, one of the Scottish Commissioners, held the view that there was no more occasion for an act of worship at a man's leaving the world, than at his

[1] *id.* p. 358 [2] *Works* (ed. Ashton) iii 45

[3] Maxwell *John Knox's Genevan Service Book* p. 57

entering it.[1] The Directory enacted quite explicitly that neither in the house nor on the way to the grave should any religious office be performed. Apparently all that was allowed at the grave side, at the suggestion of Dr Temple, was that the Minister might say, 'We commit the body to the ground'.[2]

The Assembly also discussed the suitability of funeral sermons. Whilst the Independents approved of them, the Scottish Commissioners were loud in their denunciations of the abuses to which they were prone. Baillie, in particular, declaimed:[3] 'It is nothing but ane abuse of preaching to serve the humours of rich people only for a reward'. The English Puritans do not appear to have felt the same scruples, for many of them had their sermons published only after they had been delivered at a burial of some local worthy. So intense was the Scottish disapproval of them that the Commissioners refused to attend the burial of Pym, because a sermon was to be preached at it.[4] On this question the English Puritans were truer sons of Calvin than their Scottish brethren.

Finally, there remains to be considered the Puritan attitude to ecclesiastical vestments, compared with the view of the Reformed Churches. Durel asserts that it is the custom of the Reformed Ministers to wear ecclesiastical vestments both during divine service and out of doors:[5]

> 'The *Ministers of France*, in the towns where the greatest part are Protestant, and where they may freely appear for what they are . . . never go out of their houses into the open street without a long *Cassock* or narrow coat down to the very ground, and a *Gown* over it, with a *Girdle* upon the *Coat:* And it would be taken very ill if they should appear without this decent apparrel.'

He also informs us[6] that the Ministers of Hungary and Transylvania wear a long cloak and cassock when they go out of doors, whilst long cloaks are worn by German pastors, or 'a Gown and a long cap, as at *Basil*'. It is fairly certain that in the Genevan Church the Ministers wore the priest's outdoor habit, consisting of cassock, bands, black gown, scarf or tippet, and cap.[7] This is corroborated by a letter of Calvin's in which he tells how he confuted a woman who claimed that the 'long habits' (presumably cassocks) worn by the Genevan ministers,

[1] Sprott & Leishman *op. cit.* p. 361 [2] *id.* p. 361*f* [3] *id.* p. 362
[4] *ibid.* [5] *op. cit.* p. 21 [6] *ibid.* [7] Maxwell *op. cit.* p. 210

were disobeying our Lord's command to 'beware of the Scribes, which desire to walk in long robes'.[1] Calvin did not deny that the Ministers wore long robes, but he told her that her faulty exegesis was derived from the 'Gospel of the Manichaeans'.[2]

The English Puritans, however, objected strenuously to all vestments. In 1562 a request was made to Convocation to do away with copes and surplices 'so that all ministers in their ministry use a grave, comely, and side-garment, as they commonly do in preaching', whilst it petitioned 'that the ministers of the word and sacraments be not compelled to wear such gowns and caps, as the enemies of Christ's gospel have chosen to be the special array of their priesthood'.[3] Six years later the Puritans appealed to Beza, Calvin's successor at Geneva, to know his opinion of their being coerced into wearing gowns and vestments in England. Beza expressed regret at hearing that the vestments had been restored, 'yet since they are not of the nature of those things which are themselves ungodly, we think them not of so great moment, that therefore either the pastors should leave their ministry or that the flock should neglect their public food, rather than hear pastors so habited.'

In Scotland it appears to have been the regular custom for ministers to wear a gown when conducting divine service. The cassock also was in frequent use, but this is not surprising since it was not a liturgical vestment, but the usual out-of-doors dress of the ministry. In England, however, the Puritans appear to have discarded the cassock, whilst there is little evidence to show that the early Puritans wore gowns. This is the only possible interpretation of the following pamphlet-conversation:[4]

'*The Protestant* Well ouer-taken Sir, whither trauel you?

*The Puritane* I trauell towards the Parliament.

*The Protestant* What, are you one of the *Burgesses?*

*The Puritane* No, I am a Minister.

*The Protestant* Are you a Minister? why weare you not then a Priest-cloake with sleeues, as you are injoyned in the late *Booke of Cannons and constitutions Ecclesiasticall?* I tooke you for one of the Burgesses, because you differ not from them in habit.

[1] Luke xx 46 [2] Durel *op. cit.* p. 22*f*

[3] Strype *Annals* (Oxford 1824) I ii 501

[4] Ormerod *The Picture of a Puritan* (London 1605) p. 3 *verso*

*The Puritane* What reason is there, that the fashion and forme of Ministers attire should bee different from other mens?'

In this disapproval of any distinctive dress for the clergy, the English Puritans departed from the Reformed tradition.

In conclusion: are the Puritans or the Anglicans to be adjudged the more Reformed in their worship? The answer is that neither is in complete conformity with the Genevan tradition. Whilst the Established Church conformed to the mind of Calvin in several matters, such as the pronouncement of Absolution by the Minister, the giving of Communion to the sick, the rite of Confirmation, the employment of set prayers, the use of a few ceremonies; the Puritans held tenaciously to the accepted customs of the Reformed Churches in such matters as burial, ceremonies, and above all in the exercise of discipline. In the main, the Anglicans could claim Lutheran sanction for their usages, whilst the Puritans could claim Calvinist precedents for their customs. At the same time it is doubtful if the Puritans were aware of the cleavage between themselves and John Calvin. It is probable that in their departures from the Calvinist norm they were influenced more than they knew by the examples of the Separatists. As will be shewn, this alone explains their radical opposition to any set forms of prayer. It almost certainly explains their occasional Bibliolatry and their fear of risking the possibilities of abuse, which often resulted in sheer iconoclasticism in worship. The influence of the Separatists, with its constant emphasis on the danger of idolatry, is also probably responsible for the failure of the Puritans to distinguish between bareness and simplicity. Whilst they claimed to be true heirs of the Reformed Churches, in actual fact they had proceeded with a more radical reformation than their continental mentors. The impetus in this revolution, as well as the apparent unawareness of the radical nature of the changes, it is claimed, are the direct result of the doctrine and practice of Separatist worship, mediated by the Independents.

## CHAPTER V

## THE WORD OF GOD AS THE SUPREME LITURGICAL CRITERION

Puritanism, as we have seen, was born in Geneva, but it was christened in England. The lusty infant repudiated the name because of its associations. While the Nonconformists of the ejection of 1662 referred proudly to their spiritual ancestors as 'the good old Puritans', the ancestors themselves scorned the nickname. They were dubbed 'Puritans' or 'Precisians' as mere cavillers on the question of church government. Later the term implied a haughty ethical superiority which distinguished these new Pharisees who thanked God 'that they were not as other men' and who regarded the natural man's concern for sports and pastimes as trivial and unworthy of their high seriousness. But, whatever opprobrium was intended by the name, it had at least one justification. First and foremost the Puritans were the champions of the authority of the 'pure Word of God' as the criterion not only for church doctrine, but also for church worship and church government. In this sense the nickname was well-deserved and the Puritans lived up to it. If they stood for the pure Word of God, they stood out against all impurities which, by hypothesis, were the admixture of human traditions in doctrine and discipline. Their platform was based upon two tenets inherited from John Calvin.

The first was his doctrine of Scripture; the second, his reaffirmation of the doctrine of original sin in its most sombre colours. Following Calvin, they affirmed the sufficiency of Scripture as a directory of worship, as well as the repository of the saving knowledge of God. If the Scriptures were to Luther 'the cradle of Christ', they were to Calvin the declared will of God for every aspect of human life. If Luther deprecated the use of the Scriptures as a liturgical directory on the score of its being relegated to the position of a 'nova lex', a new Leviticus, Calvin asserted that the human ordering of the worship of God was mere presumptuousness, since God had already laid down how he was to be worshipped. In the second place, if man was by nature corrupt then he was utterly incapable of worshipping God aright, until God should lighten his darkness. To attempt to order his own worship was therefore futile, where it was not blasphemous.

The Puritans were the heirs of this legacy. It can be shewn that the extreme Puritans who wanted 'a reformation without tarrying for any' were more scrupulous in carrying out Calvin's doctrines to their logical conclusion than the logical Reformer himself. While Calvin, as his biographer Doumergue has shewn,[1] admitted a 'principle of accommodation' in inessential matters, his English disciples admitted of no compromise. Their all-sufficient manual for all liturgical matters was 'the Word of God'.

In their apologia their first position was inevitably the all-sufficiency and perfection of the Scriptures for the ordering of worship. William Bradshaw writes in 1605:[2]

'*IMPRIMIS* they hould and maintaine that the word of God contained in the writings of the Prophets and Apostles, is of absolute perfection, given by Christ the Head of the Churche, to bee unto the same, the sole Canon and rule of all matters of Religion, and the worship and service of God whatsoever. And that whatsoever done in the same service and worship cannot bee iustified by the said word, is unlawfull.'

Having stated their thesis in such bold terms, they proceed to justify it by quotations from the Scriptures. It is their invariable practice to find a warrant in Holy Writ for every postulate they make. Thus, believing themselves bound to the Word of God, they do not assert a mere opinion, or a reasonable conviction, but the declared will of God. What may appear as Bibliolatry to their successors or opponents is, in fact, their consistency.

The Scriptural citations warranting their main thesis are derived from both Testaments. Thus II Peter i 19–21 and II Timothy iii 15–17 urge the perfection of the Scriptures; while Matthew xv 9, 13, and Rev. xxii 19 are taken to forbid any man-made additions to the worship of God. Even more relevant and stronger proof-texts are found in the Old Testament. Exodus xx 4–6 (the Second Commandment), Joshua i 7, Deut. iv 2, xii 32, and Proverbs xxx 6 assert that God will not tolerate any additions to his worship since he is 'a jealous God'.

[1] *Jean Calvin* ii 499–502 [2] *English Puritanism &c.* (1605) p. 1

Once their thesis is established, the Puritans then diligently search the Scriptures for evidences of the worship which God demands from his people. Their norm is the Apostolic Church and their aim is to re-establish its purity and simplicity in their midst. They believe that the worship of this church is characterized by six ordinances: namely, (i) Prayer; (ii) Praise; (iii) the proclamation of the Word; (iv) the administration of the Sacraments of Baptism and the Lord's Supper; (v) catechising; and (vi) the exercise of Discipline. The source of their information as to the perpetual ordinances of the church is Acts ii 41–42:

'Then they that gladly received his word were baptized; and the same day there were added unto them about three thousand souls. And they continued stedfastly in the apostles' doctrine and fellowship, and in breaking of bread, and in prayers.'

This *locus classicus* of Apostolic worship omits other characteristic Puritan ordinances such as praise, catechising and excommunication. But these were found in other parts of the New Testament, as will be detailed later.

(i) *Prayer*

The types of prayer required are enumerated in I Tim. ii 1*ff*:

'I exhort therefore that, first of all, supplications, prayers, intercessions, and giving of thanks be made for all men; for kings and for all that are in authority; that we may lead a quiet and peaceable life in all godliness and honesty.'

In this rule of the Apostle the Puritans found their justification for commencing their services with prayer and for certain essential concerns in prayer: petition, thanksgiving and intercession. The other two main features of Puritan prayer, *viz.* invocation or adoration and confession, were learned from our Lord's model prayer. It is also to be noted that the characteristic prayer of Calvin for all in authority owes its presence to the apostolic injunction.

If the Puritans sought the types and the matter of true prayer in the Scriptures, they also sought there for the posture for prayer. The typical Puritan posture was to stand for prayer. For this they had the authoritative examples of Abraham

(Gen. xviii 22), the Levites, Priests and people (Heb. ix 2–5), and of our Lord (Luke xviii 10–11 and Mark xi 25). When Isaac Watts wished to persuade the Nonconformists of the eighteenth century to desist from their practice of sitting down at prayer, he assured his readers that there were three permissible attitudes for prayer warranted by the Scriptures: prostration, kneeling and standing; but that there was no divine sanction for sitting.[1] This was in the Puritan tradition. Further, the Scriptures also taught what part the people had to play in prayer. In criticising the responsive parts of the services in the Book of Common Prayer, they took their stand on Neh. viii 6 and I Cor. xiv 14–16. These references incontrovertibly declared the necessity for the pastor to pray audibly, the people following him silently and declaring their assent in a vocal *Amen*.[2]

Their concluding prayer, the benediction, was warranted by the examples of Num. vi 23–26 and II Cor. xiii 14.

(ii) *Praise*

The Puritans, under the leadership of Calvin, re-established the importance of the praises of the congregation. As the 'elect' of God, freely chosen by him and through no merit of theirs, they had good reason to praise God. Their warrant in the Word of God came from the Psalms and the New Testament injunctions to praise God with 'psalms and hymns and spiritual songs, singing and making melody in your heart to the Lord' (Eph. v 19).[3] It was also their invariable custom to conclude the ordinance of the Lord's Supper with a psalm, on the authority of Matt. xxvi 30.

(iii) *The Preaching of the Word*

This became the central feature of Puritan worship. For it was the declaration of God's message to his people, confirmed in their hearts by the operation of the Holy Spirit. Through it alone men came to a saving knowledge of God. No homily could adequately fulfil the task of expounding the Word and applying it to the hearts of the congregation. It was 'the power of God unto salvation'. Its importance was testified to by the

[1] *Guide to Prayer* (1716) sect. 7

[2] *cf.* John Robinson *A just and necessary Apology of certain Christians &c.*; *Works* iii 21

[3] *cf.* Col. iii 16; Jas. v 13; Rev. xiv 2–3

whole corpus of the Scriptures, but particularly by II Cor. i 12, ii 2, and in Rom. x 14–15.

(iv) *The Gospel Sacraments*

The Puritans accepted only two Sacraments as of Dominical institution: Baptism and the Lord's Supper. Their doctrine of the Sacraments, as their administration of them, rested upon the apostolic example. While always reciting the institution narrative in the Lord's Supper as their warrant for the ordinance, so they always prefaced Baptism with the recital of Matt. xxviii 19–20. Similarly they interpreted 'Do this in remembrance of me' as a command to repeat the original order of the manual and spiritual actions of the Lord. In the same way, as Jesus had received little children, so they also took them in their arms to baptize them. In both Sacraments they believed they were adhering rigidly to the original Dominical institution.

(v) *Catechising*

Whilst others might assume that catechising was a necessary part of the duty of all Christians to spread the saving knowledge of God (as an extension, so to speak, of the Sermon), the Puritans had to justify the particular method they used. As will become apparent later, the Puritans objected to set forms of prayer and of preaching (homilies), so that they had to justify their use of a set catechism. Their ingenuity did not fail them. They found the required proof-text in II Tim. i 13: 'Hold fast the *form of sound words*, which thou hast heard of me, in faith and love which is in Christ Jesus'. Another form of the declaration of the Word of God which has more affinity with the Catechism than with the Sermon, was Prophesying. This means of expounding the Scriptures and the answering of questions due to any difficulty experienced in comprehension, was a favourite 'holy exercise' amongst the Puritans. This was justified by verses 31 and 1 of I Cor. xiv, even to the purpose of prophesying and the plurality of prophets allowed.

(vi) *Ecclesiastical Censures*

The true marks of a Church were, the Puritans contended, preaching of the Word, the administration of the Gospel Sacraments, and the practice of Church Discipline. Only by a rigid use of discipline could the purity of the Church be maintained. They believed that St. Paul's warning to the unworthy not to partake of the Lord's Supper was but one instance of the necessity for Church discipline. The complete procedure for the admonishment, excommunication and reception of repentant offenders, was found in Matt. xviii 15–18; xviii 2; I Cor. v 3–5, 11; III John 10; whilst apostolic authority for the practice of censures was clearly proved by the excommunication of Simon Magus by St. Peter (Acts viii 13) and of the incestuous person by St. Paul (I Cor. v 1–7). As will be seen later,[1] both John Owen and Thomas Goodwin follow the Scriptural example in the smallest detail when describing the procedure for excommunication.

Besides discovering the pattern for their main liturgical ordinances in the Church of New Testament times, the Puritans also sought in the Apostolic Church the prototype of their occasional ordinances. For instance, if they held a day of humiliation either for the public repentance of the people after some great natural or political calamity or for the election of office-bearers in the church, the New Testament was their model. The unchangeable order for such occasions was: fasting, prayer and sermon (as in Acts xiii 1–3 and xiv 23). For some time, it was the custom of the exiled Puritans in Arnhem to anoint their sick with oil and to pray over them. Their precedent was taken from James v 14–15.

They even sought in the Scriptures for such details as when and how often they were to have services. That the Lord's day was to be sanctified by worship they proved from John xx 19–26; Luke xxiv 26; Matt. xviii 20; Acts xx 27; I Cor. iv 1; I Cor. xiv 37; Acts xx 7; Rev. i 10. They found as their sanction for two services on the Lord's day, one in the morning, the other in the afternoon, the double burnt-offering required in Num. xxviii 9;[2] whilst they found a Scriptural sanction for the necessity of the Lord's Supper being preceded by a sermon in Acts xx 27. They were even able to settle such a minor point as to who should collect the offerings of the people and when they should present them, from the evidence in Acts iv 36 and I Cor. xvi 2.

Text-scrutinizing, however, went to ridiculous extremes at the hands of Puritan exegetes. The argument from silence was

[1] see below, Chapter XIV [2] see Ames *The Marrow of Modern Divinity*

made use of to prove that the celebration of marriage was not the duty of a pastor, because it was not mentioned in the catalogue of pastoral duties given in II Tim. iv 2*ff*. Ingenuity, however, gives way occasionally to perversity as, for example, when sitting is claimed to be the only posture for the reception of the elements, since it signifies the rest that the Saviour promised to his disciples.[1] Equally perverse was Cartwright's argument for the retention of the same locality and posture in worship (as over against the Anglican 'movements' in the celebrating of divine service). The text chosen for fixity of posture and position was Acts i 15 ('Peter stood up in the midst of the disciples').

The Puritans, however, generally observed the spirit of the Scriptures rather than the letter and this is clearly seen in their controversies with the Anglicans. In the disputed questions of vestments, ceremonies and fixed or free forms of prayer, they, rather than their opponents, observe the general liturgical principles formulated in Scripture. Whilst their opponents appeal to isolated instances or strain the meaning of Scripture, the Puritans appeal to the consensus of the New Testament, and not infrequently seem to perceive the mind of Christ, as the Apostle enjoins them. They disapprove of the retention of vestments on the grounds that these are Aaronical and therefore unsuitable to the new dispensation of Christ, that they are badges of idolatry, that they do not edify and that they are a stumbling block to the weaker brethren. In this they follow respectively the purport of the Epistle to the Hebrews and Rom. xiv 15. Whilst on their side is our Lord's *caveat* against the Pharisees who wished to be esteemed for their long garments (Matt. xxiii 5–7), their opponents point to the tradition of the Church (an invalid criterion for the Puritans since tradition must be criticized for impurities by the canon of the Word of God) and lamely take Rev. xv 6 as their warrant.

On the question of ceremonies, the Anglicans urge tradition; against this the Puritans urge that the essence of freedom from the Law is that Christians should not be burdened by unnecessary additions, quoting Acts xv 28. Furthermore, on the question of the necessity urged by the Anglicans for the reception of the elements in the Lord's Supper kneeling, the

[1] Matt. xi 28: 'Come unto me, all ye that labour and are heavy laden, and I will give you rest'

Puritans would avoid 'the appearance of evil' (I Thess. v 22)[1], *i.e.* the suggestion of transubstantiation and the adoration of the elements.

Foremost amongst the controversies was the question whether set forms of prayer were allowed in the Scriptures or not. The Puritans held that they were not, while the Anglicans were able to adduce several examples of set forms of worship in the Scriptures. Amongst them were: Exodus xv 1; Num. vi 23–6; Deut. xxvi 4–12, 13–16; Hosea xiv 1–3; the Psalms; Matt. xxvi 44, xxvii 46 (quotation from Ps. xxii 1); Luke xi 2. The Puritans, however, preferred to rely upon the consensus of New Testament teaching which insisted that the Spirit 'helpeth our infirmities' (Rom. viii 26–27). A pneumatic and a legal worship were, they held, incompatible. They equated set forms of worship with the tutelage under the Law, and a pneumatic worship with free forms of prayer inspired by the Spirit with the liberty of the New Dispensation under Christ. They also supported their contention with Scriptural references (Gal. iii 14, Gal. iv 6; Eph. vi 18; Rom. viii 26; Luke xi 13; James v 16; Jude 20; I Pet. iv 10–11; I Tim. i 3). If the Anglicans could produce isolated examples of set forms of prayer, the Puritans could only affirm that this was to limit the operations of the Holy Spirit.

If Puritan exegesis was strained, Anglicans were not above forcing the Scriptures to reveal *their* meaning. A notable example of coercive exegesis is the frequent attempt to defend the gesture of prostration at the name of Jesus from the text 'that at the name of Jesus every knee should bow' (Phil. ii 10). Calderwood observes:[2]

'Cur magis ad titulos Filii quam Patris aut Spiritus Sancti?'

[1] cited in *A Parte of a Register* p. 113 [2] *Altare Damascenum* (1623) p. 623

## CHAPTER VI

# PURITANS AND THE BOOK OF COMMON PRAYER

If Mary's reign was a terrifying nightmare, then Elizabeth's coronation was hailed as the dawn by the Puritans. They believed that the blood of Protestant martyrs would prove to be the seed of a Reformed Church of England, tenderly cultivated by the Queen. The Continental exiles returned in the firm hope and belief that a reformation according to the Word of God, begun by Edward VI, would be consummated by Elizabeth. The Zurich letters[1] are the testimonies of this confidence. But they were doomed to disappointment.[2] The slow process of their disillusionment is explained both by the political astuteness of the Queen, and by the late emergence of a complete critique of the Book of Common Prayer. The Puritans resorted to literary attacks on the Prayer Book only when other methods had failed. Having found the Queen unsympathetic to their radical reforms, they then turned to Convocation. In 1563 they failed to carry their proposals by the narrow margin of one vote.[3] Finally they sought the desired remedy at the hands of Parliament (1571). Only when this stratagem was defeated, and the immediate likelihood of a constitutional reform of the Church appeared to be remote, did they attempt a root-and-branch criticism of the Book of Common Prayer. Obviously, while there was yet hope of internal reform, and it appeared that the Book of Common Prayer was being tolerated merely as a temporary expedient in its contemporary form, there was little point in launching a full-scale attack against it. Only when it was realized that the Book of Common Prayer with all its rubrics had come to stay, and the least infringement of it was visited with displeasure, did the Puritans write against it, openly or surreptitiously, and with a hearty dislike.

It is not, however, to be assumed that criticisms of the Book of Common Prayer did not originate until Elizabeth's time.

[1] ed. Parker Society, 2 vols. (1842 & 1845) [2] vol. i, pp. 11, 17, 63

[3] Cardwell *History of Conferences* p. 117

The Vestments controversy[1] had already arisen in the time of Edward VI, and Hooper had refused to become Bishop of Gloucester unless the rubric requiring sacerdotal and episcopal vestments were relaxed: whilst it is credibly reported that when Ridley came to the stake with Hooper, he renounced his former support of the ecclesiastical garments. Furthermore, as we have already seen, criticism of the Book of Common Prayer was at the root of the Frankfort troubles which agitated the Anglican exiles of that city. But it is not until Archbishop Parker enforced the vestments by his 'Advertisements' of 1566, with the threat of suspension for refusal to wear them, that criticism of the Book of Common Prayer becomes concerted or coherent. The vestments question forced upon the recusants the duty of re-examining the whole of the Prayer Book. In this examination other objectionable matters were also discovered. By the time of Field and Wilcox's *First Admonition to Parliament* in 1571, and with the *Second Admonition* of Cartwright, Puritan liturgical criticism was in full spate.

Hooker[2] enumerates the following as a convenient summary of the Puritan criticism of the Book of Common Prayer. It has

'too great affinity with the Form of the Church of Rome; it differeth too much from that which Churches elsewhere reformed allow and observe; our attire disgraceth it; it is not orderly read, nor gestured as beseemeth; it requireth nothing to be done which a child may not lawfully do; it hath a number of short cuts or shreddings, which may be better called wishes than Prayers; it intermingleth prayings and readings in such matter, as if suppliants should use in proposing their suits unto mortal Princes, all the world would judge them mad; it is too long, and by that mean abridgeth Preaching; it appointeth the people to say after the Minister; it spendeth time in singing and in reading the Psalms by course, from side to side; it useth the Lord's Prayer too oft; the Songs of *Magnificat*, *Benedictus*, and *Nunc Dimittis*, it might very well spare; it hath the Litany, the Creed of Athanasius, and *Gloria Patri*, which are superfluous; it craveth earthly things too much; for deliverance from those evils against which we pray it giveth no thanks; some things it asketh unseasonably, when they need not to be prayed for, as deliverance from thunder and tempest, when no danger nigh; some in too abject and

[1] The controversy was not primarily concerned with the Mass vestments, but with the surplice, the distinctive vesture of public worship

[2] *Eccl. Pol.* V xxvii 1

diffident manner, as that God would give us that which we for our unworthiness dare not ask; some which ought not to be desired, as the deliverance from sudden death, riddance from all adversity, and the extent of saving mercy towards all men. These and such like are the imperfections whereby our form of Common Prayer is thought to swerve from the Word of God.'

Such was the extent and the seriousness of the charges of the Puritans, and, had it not been for the reasonableness of Hooker in replying and even rebutting some of them, the Puritans might have emerged as victors in the controversial field.

### 1. *Vestments*

Whilst the Second Prayer Book of Edward VI required that a priest or a deacon need only wear a surplice, Elizabeth in 1559 reinstated the ornaments rubric of the second year of Edward VI's reign, requiring alb and vestment or cope. This was regarded by the Puritans as an intolerable turning back towards the old religion. The expected vehemence of Puritan opposition may be gauged from the fact that Parker was not able to obtain the Royal assent to his publication of the 'Advertisements'. Although the Queen approved of the policy, she would not openly commit herself to its support, and her Primate had to bear the brunt of the criticism.

The Vestments controversy was not an insignificant sartorial matter to be decided on purely æsthetic grounds. While the alb, cope and surplice might be defended on the grounds of decency and comeliness by the supporters of the Queen, the Puritans felt that their retention involved the sacrifice of cherished principles. The vestments, in the course of the controversy, became symbols of allegiance.

The radical Puritans stated their case for the abolition of vestments on the following grounds. First and foremost, they were regarded as an infringement of their Christian liberty; the Church which had been freed by Christ from the bondage of the Law was now attempting to infringe the crown rights of the Redeemer by introducing new burdens on the consciences of believers.[1] Moreover, these vestments were disliked

[1] *cf. A Parte of a Register* p. 41: 'if it be abolished and *Christ* bee come in steede, then a great injurie is done to Christ for manie causes. The one is, that those ceremonies which Christ by his passion did abolishe, should in contempt of him and his passion be taken agayne.'

because of their association with Romish superstition; they were 'badges of Anti-Christ' upholding the priesthood of the clergy and, by implication, denying the priesthood of all believers; they were, further, sacrificial vestments that had been associated in recent memory with the sacrifice of the Mass. Furthermore, they were symbols of pomp and grandeur, ill-befitting the humility with which all men should approach God, and contrary to the simplicity of the first disciples and apostles of Christ. Besides, these garments had a Jewish origin belonging to the Aaronic priesthood, not to the Christian ministry. And, the radical Puritans pleaded, even if they were indifferent matters, as their opponents held, it was inexpedient to retain them, for the sake of the weaker brethren who associated them with the old superstitious religion.[1] Finally, the abolition of vestments would bring the Church of England into line with the other Reformed Churches.

Those who were for retaining the vestments defended themselves with the following arguments. In the first place they repudiated the idea that the Church of England should abolish vestments because the other Reformed Churches had done so. The English Church as an autonomous body had the right to determine its own ceremonies, which it did.[2] Furthermore, by its teaching it had maintained evangelical doctrine, which prevented any superstition being attached to the vestments it retained. In themselves the vestments were neither forbidden nor commanded in the Scriptures. They were decent and becoming and there was no point in altering them for alteration's sake. Besides, the Early Church, long before the rise of popish corruptions, had favoured some distinctive habits for those who discharged a public and official function. The catechumens, moreover, in the earliest times wore white vestments as a modest sign of the purity they then professed. Similarly, the surplice had a long and dignified history and was retained not

[1] *id.* p. 43*f*: 'for foure causes ought the surplisse, the coape, the Tippet, and other popishe ceremonies to be taken away and removed out of God his Church.

'1. First, that Christ may more clearely shine and appear in his Gospell without the darkness of mans devyces.

'2. Secondly, that papistrie may appeare more to bee hated and detested.

'3. Thirdlie, that the offence of the weake may be taken away.

'4. Fourthlie, that contention amongst brethren might cease.'

[2] Hooker *Eccl. Pol.* V xxix

for superstition but for the sake of a uniform decency. As Grindal puts it: 'And neither good pastors nor pious laymen are offended at these things'. Briefly, the reply of those who upheld the vestments was: the vestments could mislead no one who had listened to the doctrinal teaching of the Church of England. The further reformation pleaded for by the Puritans was endangered by these persistent troubles about insignificant matters, such as vestments. It was expedient in the interests of reformation itself not to clamour for such changes at present.

The historical importance of this controversy lies in the fact that after refusal to wear the vestments was visited by suspension, the cleavage between conforming and non-conforming Puritans became apparent. This threat forced all conscientious Puritans to consider the question whether they were to witness to the truth by a rigid refusal to compromise in things that would offend their weaker brethren and hence to leave the Church's official ministry, as did Sampson and Humphrey, or whether they must compromise in these matters in order to continue to minister to their flocks, as was the view of Jewel and Pilkington. In their nonconformity the radical Puritans had to accept the alternative either of schism and separatism (following the examples of Penry, Barrow and Greenwood) or of suspension. As they could not bring themselves to deny that the Church of England was a true Church and were unwilling to become schismatics—the implications of Separatism—they remained within the fold of the Church hopefully waiting for a change of heart in their leaders. Their witness was now expended in writing against the vestments and ceremonies and in putting forward their claims in the exercises known as 'prophesyings'. Only a very small minority 'cut the painter' and became Separatists.

### 2. *The Ceremonies*

The Puritans were also agreed in their desire to abolish three ceremonies enforced by the Book of Common Prayer. These were: Kneeling for the reception of the elements in Holy Communion; the sign of the Cross in Baptism; and the use of the ring in Marriage. In brief, the kneeling at Communion was objected to as countenancing the adoration of the elements, and the doctrine of transubstantiation; the crossing of the child in Baptism was scrupled as teaching the *ex opere operato* functioning of the sacrament and priestly efficacy; while the ring in Marriage was held to be interpreted by the simple as effecting the union of the betrothed.

'A Survey of the Booke of Common Prayer by way of 197 Queres grounded upon 58 places'[1] refers to the Prayer Book as 'The *Helena of Greece*, and cause of all these controversies'. The ceremonies are regarded as the chief blemishes of 'Helena'. Query 61 asks:[2]

'Whither kneeling in the very act of receiving be lawefull by the word, seeing it is contrary to the example, not only of such reformed Churches as condemn consubstantiation as well as transubstantiation with whom there ought to be conformity, as well as amongst ourselves, but also of Christ himselfe, and his Apostles, who ministred and of purpose received sitting. Seeing it came from the Papists who thereby adore their breaden God.'

This ceremony was to be refused primarily to obey the apostolic injunction to 'avoid the appearance of evil'. Further reasons are adduced from 'Reasons against kneeling at the receit of the Communion'.[3] The practice is unapostolic, unprimitive and unreformed.

'What soeuer was not in use, whilest the Church continued in her puritie, after the Apostles times, is not now to bee vsed . . . But kneeling at the Communion was not used then, as may appeare by *Chrysostome* and some others, who make express mention of sitting at the receite thereof. . . . Whatsoeuer churches rightly reformed vse not, is to be by vs not only suspected, but iustly reiected . . . But the right reformed churches vse not kneeling at the receit of the Supper: for proofe hereof, looke vpon all the churches of *France*, *Flanders*, *Hungarie*, *Polonia*, *Berna*, *Zurich*, *Sauoy*, *Scotland* . . . besides the presidents and practise we haue heere at home before our owne eyes, in the French, Dutch, and Italian Churches at London, Norwitch, Sandwitch, and other places in this Realme: and besides the publike iudgements of particular persons of those Churches as *Bullinger* in his Decades, and *Beza* in his Epistle, *epist. duodecima*.'

If the Puritan objections to kneeling at the receipt of Holy Communion was due to the concern for the weaker brethren,

[1] Frere & Douglas *Puritan Manifestoes* (1907) [2] *id.* p. 71

[3] *A Parte of a Register* pp. 410*ff*

its argument from the posture of the Dominical institution was, to say the least of it, uncertain. While our Lord and his disciples certainly did not receive the bread and wine kneeling, neither did they receive it sitting. In all probability the disciples received it lying on couches. In combating the other two ceremonies the Puritans were upon firmer ground. Their objections rested upon the conviction that crossing in Baptism and the ring in Marriage were unwarrantable additions to the Dominical institutions, explicable alone in terms of the presumptuousness of human inventions.

A certain Master Nicholas Crane says of the sign of the Cross in Baptism:[1]

'if the brasen Serpent, which was by Gods commaundement set vp to a singular vse, was for the abuse thereof broken in pieces, is it not equal that the signe of the crosse, which hath no defence in the booke of God to be shrowded by, nor examples of the Apostles to rest upon, after so notable abuse, should be thrust cleane out of the Church?'

Furthermore, the insistence upon crossing was felt to be tantamount to instituting a new sacrament. Query 95 of 'A Survey of the Booke of Common Prayer' asks:[2]

'Whither the childe be not received againe by and with Crossing, and so may seeme to be a sacrament as well as Baptism for that cause . . . as if regeneration were by baptisme, and incorporation by crossing?'

The ring in Marriage was scrupled for similar reasons. This point is made in a plea for consistency in liturgical reform by a certain Robert Johnson of Northampton:[3]

'You must yeeld some reasons, why *the shauen crowne* is despised and *the square cappe* receyued: why the *Tippet* is commanded, and the *stole* forbidden; why the vestiment is put away, and the coape retayned: why the *Albe* is layd aside, and the Surplesse is vsed . . . Wee would knowe why you do reiect *hallowed beades*, and yet receyue *hallowed Ringes* . . ?'

He concludes:

'And of these things I say wee would haue and heare some reason taken and gathered out of the word of God, which if we shall heare, we shall be gladde to learn . . . If the conscience be perswaded, the hande shall straightway subscribe.'

[1] *id.* p. 121 [2] Frere & Douglas *op. cit.* p. 90
[3] *A Parte of a Register* p. 104

That is the authentic Puritan note: If God does not ordain these things in his worship, how can they either please him, or be edifying to his people?

### 3. *Homilies*

The conforming Anglicans were frequently caricatured by the Puritans as 'dumb dogs'. This description was applied to them not merely because they used set forms of prayer, as opposed to extempore utterance in prayer (for the Puritans did not, in the main, object to set forms as such); the term castigated the practice of reading Homilies, as a substitute for preaching Sermons. The writers of the *Admonition*[1] contrast the usage of the primitive Church and the contemporary practice, thus:

'In the old Church the ministers were preachers, now bare readers. And if any be so well disposed to preach in their own charges, they may not without my Lord's licence.'

The Church authorities had some measure of reason on their side. For the shortage of well-educated ministers made Homilies a wise alternative to wild and uneducated preaching. And the doctrines of the Homilies were, in the main, unexceptionable. Moreover, the 'Prophesyings' which had attempted to educate the ministry had frequently been used as platforms for the spreading of characteristically Puritan tenets, rather than for the proclamation of the Apostolic gospel.

On the Puritan side, however, there were real causes for criticism. As Cartwright says,[2]

'The Word is all one read and preached, but it pleaseth the Lord to work more effectually with the one than the other; thereby approving and authorizing that means and way which he especially ordained for us to be saved by.'

The Word of God, so the Puritans maintain, is vital in its operation only when it is applied to the hearts and consciences of believers by way of consolation and of rebuke. Cartwright says:[3]

'As the fire stirred giveth more heat, so the Word, as it were, blown by preaching, flameth more in the hearers than when it is read.'

[1] Whitgift quotes it in the *Answer* p. 52

[2] Hooker *Eccl. Pol.* (ed. Hanbury, 1830) vol. ii, p. 73*n* [3] *id.* p. 75*n*

The Archbishop, Grindal, in his historic letter to the Queen refusing to put down the 'Prophesyings', states the Puritan case with understanding:

'The Godly Preacher is termed in the Gospel a Faithful Servant, who knoweth how to give his Lord's family their apportioned food in season; who can apply his speech to the diversity of times, places and hearers; which cannot be done in Homilies: exhortations, reprehensions, and persuasions, are uttered with more affection, to the moving of the Hearers, in Sermons than in Homilies.'

Even Hooker, who is concerned to deny that Sermons are not the only avenues by which saving truth can enter the soul, grudgingly testifies to the efficacy of Puritan sermons:[1]

'Whereas the cause why Sermons only are observed to prevail so much, while all means else seem to sleep and do nothing, is in truth nothing but that singular affection and attention which the People sheweth everywhere towards the one, and their cold disposition to the other; the reason hereof being partly the art which our adversaries use for the credit of their Sermons, to bring men out of conceit with all other teaching besides; partly a custom which men have to let those things carelessly pass by their ears, which they have oftentimes heard before, or know they may hear again whensoever it pleaseth themselves; partly the especial advantages which Sermons naturally have to procure attention, both in that they come always new, and because by the hearer it is still presumed, that if they be let slip for the present, what good soever they contain is lost, and that without all hope of recovery.'

In effect the Puritans were pleading for a return to the prophetic conception of worship, in which the climax is the proclamation of the gospel of God declared by his prophet, conscious of an inner compulsion to speak the message. Prayer, the response of the people to the declared will of God, was less important than Preaching. For the people could add nothing to God's glory by their thanksgiving or praises, but without the saving knowledge of God declared in the gospel they would be in complete darkness. It is in this light that we can understand Cartwright's criticism that the prolixity of Anglican prayers necessitated the shortening of their sermons. Whereas the Reformed Churches spend about an hour and a

[1] *Eccl. Pol.* V xxii 20

half on their morning worship, it is claimed that the Anglican service takes an hour to be performed,

'whereunto also, if another hour at the least be added for the celebration of the holy communion, he may see, that either the preaching must be abridged, or not due regard had of men's infirmities.'[1]

The whole emphasis of the Prayer Book service was priestly, concerned rather with men's approach to God than with his speech to them. If the characteristic note of Hooker's defence of the existing practice is the need to consider the wants of men and their capacities, Cartwright's emphasis is on the demands of God. For the Puritan, 'Soli Deo gloria' was the lofty criterion.

### 4. *The Lections*

The chief objections to the Lectionary in the Book of Common Prayer were two: there was a rooted antipathy to the readings from the Apocrypha, as these writings were clearly not the canonical Scriptures, which alone enshrined the Word of God; and it was felt that such lessons from the Scriptures as were prescribed were too short.

The Puritans would not be satisfied with Hooker's defence of the Apocrypha as 'a list or marginal border unto the Old Testament'[2] for this would appear as a slight upon the all-sufficiency of the canonical Scriptures. Neither would the appeal, 'should the mixture of a little dross constrain the Church to deprive herself of so much gold?'[3] meet with any success: for these men stood for the pure Word of God. It is not surprising to find therefore that the offensive passages in the Apocrypha are detailed by Puritan critics. As, for instance, the authors of 'The Humble Petition of 22 Preachers in London and the Suburbes thereof'[4] who observe the following 'manifest untruthes' in the Apocrypha: Tobit xii 9, 12, 15; Ecclesiasticus xxiv 11–12; Judith ix 4, 10, 13; Tobit iii 8. Furthermore, as 'A Survey of the Booke of Common Prayer' asserts:[5]

'In place of 182 chapters canonical left unread, there be 134 out of the Apocrypha appointed by the Calendar to be read.'

[1] Hooker *Eccl. Pol.* (ed. Hanbury) vol. ii, p. 112*n* [2] *Eccl. Pol* V xx 10
[3] *id.* V xx 12 [4] section v, in Frere & Douglas *op. cit.*
[5] Frere & Douglas *op. cit.* p. 26

The Puritans also criticized what they termed contemptuously 'pistling and gospelling'. Query 44[1] asks appositely enough:

'Whither the reading of these Epistles and Gospels (so called) be not the same fault which is blamed as unorderly in the preface of the Communion Booke, *viz.* a breaking of one peece of Scripture from an other?'

The previous query doubts the veracity of the nomenclature of the 'epistles' since 'there be 23 out of the Prophets, Acts and Apocalypse'. They would not tolerate 'shreddings' of Scripture torn from their contexts. Furthermore, they wished to introduce the custom of the other Reformed Churches which read the Scriptures before the divine service was due to begin. The Puritans, at least, approved the truth of Chillingworth's famous dictum that 'The Bible is the Religion of Protestants'. And we might add, the Bible, the whole Bible, and nothing but the Bible, is the religion of Puritans.

## 5. *The Prayers*

The prayers, no less than the ceremonies and lections, were criticized. Both the form and the matter were carefully scrutinized. Whilst the Collects, the Litany and the repetitions of the Lord's Prayer came under the fire of Puritan criticism, their content was felt to be theologically inadequate.

*The Collects.* The Puritans[2] claimed that while the primitive and Reformed Churches used long prayers, the Anglican Church resorted to 'short cuts' in prayers. What they regarded as distracting, Hooker claimed to be their merit since these dart-like prayers had the effect of keeping the worshipper vigilant by a 'piercing kind of brevity'.[3] Collects were also criticized as being inaccurate in several cases. For instance, the Collect for the Sunday after Christmas reads: 'Almighty God who hast given us thy only begotten Sonne to take our nature upon him and *this day* to be borne of a pure Virgine, &c.'[4] The stylized endings, moreover, were characterized as 'vain repetitions'.

*The Litany* was censured by the Puritans in the main because

[1] from 'A Survey of the Booke of Common Prayer'

[2] *e.g.* Cartwright *Second Admonition* i 138; iii 210*f*

[3] *Eccl. Pol.* V xxxiii

[4] 'A Survey of the Booke of Common Prayer', in Frere & Douglas *op. cit.* p. 57

many of its petitions were unrealistic and *mutatis mutandis* inappropriate. Moreover, the responses of the people were stigmatized as 'vain repetitions' because of their reduplications. The Puritans frequently cited I Cor. xiv 16 as a proof that only one person should speak at once, which appeared to them to veto congregational responses, with the single exception of the word *Amen*. Query 30 asks:[1]

'Whither this confused speaking with a loud voice be according to the word which commandeth all things to be done in order, because God is not the author of confusion and sheweth what is order, *viz.* when men speak strange tongues, and prophecies one by one, and private men say Amen to prayer and thanksgiving.'

It was felt therefore that all responds or responsive reading ('the tossing to and fro of tennis balls') was prohibited by the Word of God.

The *content* of the prayers was also criticized. In particular the gravamen of the Puritan charge rested upon the preponderance of material blessings craved in the prayers. The Litany was cited as the example *par excellence*. Cartwright declares:[2]

'I can make no geometrical and exact measure, but verily I believe there shall be found more than a third part of the prayers, which are not Psalms, and Texts of Scripture, spent in praying for and praying against the (commodities and) incommodities of this life, which is contrary to all the arguments or contents of the Prayers of the Church set down in the Scripture, and especially of our Saviour Christ's Prayer, by the which ours ought to be directed.'

Objection was also taken to certain sentiments in the Collects, which were felt to be unevangelical. 'The Humble Petition of 22 Preachers'[3] takes exception to the Collect for the 12th Sunday after Trinity which contains the offensive petition, 'and giving unto us that that our prayer dare not presume to ask', and also to the post-offertory prayer in the Communion Order which contains the clause, 'and those things which for our unworthiness we dare not . . . ask'. Both those expressions, the Puritans declared, savoured more of popish fear than of Christian confidence.

The *repetition of the Lord's Prayer* several times in one Ser-

[1] *id.* p. 48 [2] *op. cit.* i 136 [3] section vii, Frere & Douglas *op. cit.*

vice proved to be another bone of liturgical contention. Cartwright can see nothing but tautology in the practice:

'What a reason is this we must repeat the Lord's Prayer oftentimes, therefore oftentimes in half an hour, and one in the neck of another.'[1]

The Lord's Prayer, it should be noticed, becomes the crux of the liturgical problem. Since both radicals and conservatives regarded it as the model prayer, it was all-important to determine whether it was intended as a set form of prayer or merely as a pattern to which prayers should conform. The Separatists, who dispensed entirely with all forms of prayer, maintained that the Lord's Prayer was a pattern; the supporters of the Prayer Book, on the contrary, held that it was a liturgical formula and the charter of set forms of prayer. This question, however, is not all-important at the present juncture of this study.

In summing up the opposing views on prayer, it may be said that the Puritans favoured long prayers said by the minister either from a book or extemporarily, to which the people added 'Amen'; whilst the Anglicans preferred many short prayers, some of them being responsive in character, all of them being set forms.

## 6. *The Sacraments*

(*a*) *Baptism.* The ceremony of crossing in Baptism, already dealt with, may here be omitted. The Puritans took exception to four other requirements in the Baptismal service: namely, private baptism, baptism by women, the interrogatories put to the child, and the custom of godparents standing as sponsors of the child.

The four objections quite clearly rest upon the Reformed doctrine of Baptism adumbrated by John Calvin,[2] which allowed none of the above practices. God seals his promises in the Church, therefore private baptism is unthinkable. Moreover, since women are forbidden to speak in the Church, it is unbecoming that any one other than the pastor set apart for the service of God, should perform the ceremony. Furthermore, as the promises of God are made to the faithful and their seed, children inherit them in virtue of the election to grace of

[1] *op. cit.* i 219  [2] *Inst.* IV xvi

their parents. These alone, therefore, must stand as sponsors for them, and not any godparents or other substitutes. The interrogatories to the infants themselves, of course, are not explicitly criticized by Calvin. It is doubtful if he could have envisaged such an unreasonable procedure. This was condemned by the Puritans as irrational.

Field and Wilcox in their *Admonition to Parliament* contrast the apostolic administration with the Anglican method:[1]

'And as for Baptisme, it is enough with them, if they had water and the partie to be baptised faith, and the minister to preach the word and minister the sacraments. Nowe we must have surplesses devised by Pope Adrian, interrogatories ministred to the infant, godfathers and godmothers brought in by Higinus, holy fonts invented by Pope Pius, crossing and such like peces of poperie, which the church of God in the Apostles times never knew (and therefore not to be used) nay (which we are sure of) were and are mannes devises broght in long after the puritie of the primative church.'

The remedy for these abuses, they continue, is to remove

'ignorant ministers, to take awai private Communions and baptismes, to enjoyne Deacons and Midwives not to meddle in ministers matters, if they do, to see them sharpelie punished.'[2]

It is of interest to reflect that the Puritans who here claim to rid the Anglican Baptismal Order of 'human traditions' and to return to the apostolic simplicity, are actually following the example of John Calvin. It is true, of course, that his practice may claim greater Scriptural warrant and that where it is not explicitly Scriptural, it is deduced from Scriptural principles. It is doubtful whether the Puritans realized that they were following Calvin and not the apostles.

(*b*) *The Lord's Supper.* The Puritan objection to the reception of the Communion kneeling, has already been touched upon. There were, however, other objections raised to the Order for Holy Communion in the Prayer Book.

The method of delivery, for instance, was criticized as contrary to the Dominical institution. Query 62 asks:[3]

[1] Frere & Douglas *op. cit.* p. 14

[2] see also *A viewe of Antichrist, his lawes and ceremonies, in our English Church vnreformed* in *A Parte of a Register* pp. 55*ff*

[3] 'A Survey of the Booke of Common Prayer'

'Whither the delivering of the Communion into the hands of the communicants be according to Christ, his institution. Seeing he said, and in the plural number said, Take ye, eate ye, drink ye all, &c.'

Individual participation, singly, appeared to contradict the corporate participation envisaged by our Lord's command.

Similarly, the Puritans saw no reason for substituting the original words of delivery recorded in the Scriptures by other unscriptural phrases. The second part of Query 62 demands:

'The body of our Lord Iesus Christ which was given for thee, preserve thy body and soul unto everlasting life, and, Take and eat this &c, Whither these versicles . . . be the verie pure word of God, or evidently grounded upon the same.'

Greatly as the Puritans regretted these departures from the original Scriptural order, they deprecated even more the cheapening of the Lord's Supper by unworthy reception of it. Field and Wilcox assert:[1]

'Ther was then, accustomed to be an examination of the communicants, which now is neglected.'

Moreover, it was felt to be a slight upon the importance of the Communion to insist upon attendance thrice in the year, as the bare minimum necessary. It was, the Puritans thought, particularly inappropriate to urge Easter communion as the only set time insisted upon during which one of the three minimal attendances must be made; since the Communion commemorates the Lord's death, while Easter celebrates his resurrection from the dead.

The authors of *An Admonition to Parliament* gather together all the Puritan criticisms by contrasting the primitive order of Communion with the Prayer Book order:[2]

'They had no introite . . . but we have borrowed a piece of one out of the masse booke. They read no fragments of the Epistle and Gospell: we use both. The Nicene Crede was not read in their Communion we have it in oures . . . (examination of communicants then, not now). Then they ministred the Sacrament with common and usual bread; now with wafer cakes . . . They received it sitting; we kneeling, according to Honorious decree. Then it was delivered generally and indefinitely, Take ye and eat ye: we particularly and singulerly, Take thou and eat

[1] *An Admonition to Parliament;* Frere & Douglas *op. cit.* p. 13 [2] *id.* p. 134

thou. They used no other wordes but such as Chryste left: we borrow from Papustes The body of our Lorde Iesus Chryste which was geven for thee, &c. They had no Gloria in excelsis in the ministerie of the Sacrament then, for it was put to afterward. We have now. They took it with conscience. We with custume. They thrust men by reason of their sinnes from the Lords Supper. We thrust them in their sinne to the Lordes Supper. They ministred the Sacrament plainely. We pompously, with singing, pyping, surplesse and cope wearyng. They simply as they receeved it from the Lorde. We, sinfullye, mixed with mannes inventions and devises.'

In this extract the characteristic Puritan pleas are all heard: simplicity, fidelity to the Word of God, the sacredness of God's ordinances, and a high seriousness. From this it may be gathered how strong and how consistent the Puritan attack upon the Prayer Book was. If it was over-scrupulous, it was detailed and precise; if it was narrow and literalistic in its exegesis of Scripture, it was also certain and confident in tone; if its opponents appealed to tradition where they could not find support in Scripture, the Puritan apologetic believed itself to rest on the bed-rock of Apostolic tradition, and hence on the Divine will.

### 7. *Marriages and Burials*

The general objection against these services was that they were in essence not religious but civil. The Church could not marry two persons, at the most it could only give its blessing on a solemn promise made by the contracting parties. Marriage was, therefore, the concern of the State, a civil contract enforced by society for its own protection and cohesion. As will be seen, the earliest Separatists had no graveside services. The committal was a silent one. This was however dictated by a fear of a recurrence of funeral excesses, such as praying to the saints for the soul of the deceased person.

(*a*) *Marriage*. The ring in Marriage, as has already been seen, was regarded as an unnecessary ceremony, a relic of the Roman Church which had no authority in the Word of God. Exception was also taken to the profession of the bridegroom, 'With my body I thee worship'. The offensive words did not merely overstress the physical aspect of the relationship, but degraded the worship of God by associating it with a dissimilar and inferior love in the use of the word 'worship'.

(*b*) *Burial.* Strong Puritan criticism was levelled against the words of committal in the Burial Service of the Book of Common Prayer: 'We commit his body to the ground in sure and certain hope of the resurrection to eternal life'. It was, said the Puritans, not charity but presumption which was the father of these sentiments. Certainty of eternal life was not assured even for the godly, but for the ungodly it was impossible. Hence, the Anglican words of committal were a flat contradiction of the Gospel which combined promises to the faithful with the most solemn warnings to the faithless. Query 173 of 'A Survey of the Booke of Common Prayer' makes this clear.[1] Referring to the words of committal, it continues:

'Whether this be a prayer of faith. Seeing we cannot be assured, that all, at whose buriall this prayer is to be said, depart in the true faith.'

The alternative suggested is the words of committal in the Second Prayer Book of King Edward VI (1552): 'We commend into thy handes of mercie the soule of this our brother departed.' The pure Word of God gave no sanction for an indiscriminate, 'free-for-all' hope of eternal life.

## 8. *The Churching of Women*

This form of service, in so far as it was a thanksgiving for safe delivery from child-birth, was approved of by the Puritans, though, no doubt, they would prefer it to have been a part of family worship rather than a portion of the public liturgy. Their objection to it was rather that it gave the appearance of being a service of Purification on the Jewish model. The Jewish dispensation had been abrogated by the arrival of Christ and therefore did not form a model for Christian imitation. Moreover they held an ethical conception of sin, not a materialistic one. It is rightly questioned (in Query 179)[2]

'Whither weake and superstitious womē may not be occasioned to thinke this Service rather a Purification (which were Iewish) than Thankes-giving . . . as if women were by childbirth uncleane, and therefore unfit to go about their business, until they be purified.'

[1] Frere & Douglas *op. cit.* p. 144 [2] *ibid.*

### 9. *Confirmation*

On a superficial view, the Puritan objection to Confirmation appears to be mere cavilling. Why should they, who insisted so strenuously on the necessity for educating communicants and on the evil of unworthy reception of the Lord's Supper, refuse to countenance a service which was designed to promote edification in the faith and reverence for Holy Communion? The Puritan answer would be threefold. Primarily, they would hold that the service of Confirmation was in effect the creation of a third Sacrament (Query 126).[1] Moreover, since it could only be performed by a Bishop, it was a derogation of the two Dominical Sacraments, which required no Bishop for their celebration. Secondly, if Baptism marked the commencement of the Christian life, the Lord's Supper itself added the completing grace of confirmation and thus rendered a separate Confirmation service superfluous. These two criticisms are succinctly put in Queries 124 and 125:[2]

> 'Whether the Lordes Supper doth not seale the confirmation of that grace.'
>
> 'Whither this sacramentall confirming of grace sufficiently sealed by the sacraments of the Holy One of Israell, be not derogatorie to those sacraments, and the rather, because this confirmation is said heere to be, not by Examination, but by imposition of hands, and those, not of a plaine minister, but only of a Lord Bishop, who is accounted an Apostolicall man, in the preface to the exhortation, in the time of visitation.'

Thirdly, the Puritans deprecated the practice of laying on of hands in an unapostolic manner, while claiming to follow the Apostolic model. We find as the basis to their objections the same rock-principles that were the foundation of all previous criticisms. God is a jealous God and has prescribed all that is necessary for the adequate honouring of himself in public worship in the Scriptures. To depart from them in the smallest practice is to disobey God and therefore to make all innovations futile.

[1] *id.* p. 117 [2] *id.* p. 116

### 10. *Ordination*

As heretofore, the criticisms are based upon the infidelity to Scripture of the Anglican usages. It is inopportune to enter here into a discussion of Anglican orders, but to the Puritan mind they were clearly not based upon the New Testament Order. The triple division of the ministry into bishops, priests and deacons seemed to them to be using Scriptural nomenclature without understanding the Scriptural significations of the names. Whilst all three orders of the Anglican ministry were clerical, the Puritans held that Bishops or Ministers (apart from Apostles and Prophets) were the sole order of the ministry recognized in the New Testament, whilst Elders and Deacons were lay officials, the former sharing with the Bishops the spiritual concerns of the Church, whilst the latter were busied with the temporal needs of the Church. It was inevitable that the Puritans with their different conception of Church Orders, should find the Ordinal unacceptable.

They also found fault with the words which the presiding bishop was required to say, whilst laying his hands upon the ordinand. 'Receive ye the Holy Ghost' was interpreted by them not as an optative or prayer, but as an imperative. It seemed to them to imply that the Holy Spirit was crudely conceived as being dependent upon the bidding of the presiding bishop. At best the phraseology was open to misinterpretation, whilst at worst it was blasphemous.

### 11. *Saints' Days and Festivals*

For the Puritan there was only one festival of the Church, and that a weekly one. The Lord's day was the single red-letter day in his calendar. The Lord had decreed that one day out of every seven should be spent in religious exercises. The Jewish Sabbath was the testimony to his command under the old dispensation; the Christian Lord's day, commemorating the Lord's resurrection from the dead, was the Divine imperative under the new dispensation. On this day every week the mighty acts of God in the creation, redemption and sanctification of man, through the life, death and resurrection of Christ, were celebrated. The whole drama of salvation was rehearsed each Sunday in its entirety. What need was there, then, for separate festivals which celebrated only one scene of the divine drama at once? But the Puritans did not merely regard the Saints' days and Festivals as superfluous. They regarded the Saints' days in particular as a diminution of the glory due to God alone, as well as a denial of the sole Mediatorship of Christ. That was the gravamen of their objection.

This is not to assert that Sunday services comprised all of the public religious services of the Puritans. On the contrary, they held Lectures and Prayers on week-days and frequently met for special Fasts and Prayers on days of national emergencies. But these were the foothills of their public devotion, whilst the Lord's day services were the peaks of their religious life.

It seemed to them that the uniqueness of the Lord's day could be retained only if Saints' days and Festivals were abolished.

The watchword of Calvin's heirs was 'Soli Deo gloria'. It was this that drove them to criticize the Book of Common Prayer, to aim at erasing all human inventions that had encrusted the original purity of Divine institutions. While it often made them over-scrupulous, it never made them inconsistent. And they were sustained in the task of reformation by the unquenchable conviction that the Word of God in Scripture was the only all-sufficient guide for the true and acceptable worship of God. What was unscriptural was false and to be eradicated. Their attack on the Book of Common Prayer was not the criticism of a clique of rebel innovators, nor the cavilling of precisians. It was aimed at the restoration of the primitive purity and simplicity of the Apostolic Church in England.

## CHAPTER VII

## THE WORSHIP OF THE ENGLISH SEPARATISTS

Whilst there is a radical difference between the Puritans and the Separatists, constituted by their relation to the State Church, there are also close resemblances. The Puritans remained within the State Church in the hope of reforming it from within. The Separatists, on the other hand, desired 'Reformation without tarrying for any'. The earliest Separatists may have believed that their self-exclusion from the National Church would hasten the process of reformation in the Church they left. But as Separatism became more rigid it regarded the Church from which it seceded as a 'false' Church. For the purpose of this study it is important to recollect that apart from this radical difference in the attitude towards the State Church, Separatists and Puritans were largely in agreement.

For this reason: both groups of reformers took as their criterion the Word of God, as declared in the Old and New Testaments. If the Independent Puritan, Henry Jacob, could declare:[1]

> 'For as much as wee are in conscience throughly perswaded, that Gods most holy word in the New Testament is absolutely perfect, for delivering the whole manner of Gods worship . . .'

his thoughts are anticipated by Richard Fitz, the Minister of the 'Privye Churche' in London, a Separatist who writes,[2] interpreting the thoughts of his Church members, of them as

> 'The myndes of them that . . . have set their hands and hartes, to the pure vnmingled and sincere worshippinge of God, according to his blessed and glorious worde in al things, onely abolishing all tradicions and inuentions of man . . .'.

Both parties asserted positively that only such ordinances as were warrantable by the Word of God should be tolerated in public worship. Alike they denied the validity of any tradition,

[1] Burrage *The Early English Dissenters* (Cambridge 1912) ii 162
[2] *The Trewe Markes of Christes Churches*, in Burrage *op. cit.* ii 13

other than the primitive Apostolic tradition, as a 'human devyce'.

Moreover, the Separatists provided the Puritans with practical illustrations of a divine worship modelled, as they believed, upon the New Testament. Whilst the Puritans denounced the impurities of the Established worship, the Separatists provided the living remedy. It is true that the Puritans anathematized the Separatists as schismatics, while the latter regarded the Puritans as time-servers. There was little community of sympathy between the contending parties. It is also clear that there was little direct influence upon the Puritans by the Separatists. On the other hand, contact between the two parties is seen in the persons of their members who crossed the frontierland between them. Separatism is seen to be the left-wing of Puritanism if the case of Francis Johnson is considered. He, who was the successor of Travers and Cartwright as Puritan Minister to the Church of the Merchant Adventurers in Holland, became an outstanding Barrowist Pastor. On the other hand, Puritanism appears to be the right-wing of Separatism in the case of John Robinson, who commenced as a Brownist and under the influence of Henry Jacob and Dr Ames became an Independent Puritan. It would not be rash to assert that Puritanism and Separatism aimed at the same end—a Church of England reformed; but they differed in the means which they would employ to attain it. As the Separatists demanded immediate action, they were in the position to furnish an existing pattern of reformed worship, whilst the Puritans were left theorizing, until the times should be ripe for action. This is not, of course, to imply that all Separatist worship was acceptable to the Puritans. Much of it appeared to them to be an arbitrary interpretation of the Biblical evidence. On the whole, however, Puritans and Separatists were agreed liturgically.

It is contended in this chapter that the term 'Separatists' cannot be legitimately applied to the Independents, but that it is more properly reserved for the Barrowists, Brownists and Anabaptists. It is also assumed, since all parties (even including the Moderate Separatists) agreed in denouncing such obscure and eccentric sects as the Seekers and the Family of Love, that the influence of the latter upon the development of Puritan worship is negligible. The first assumption requires evidence to substantiate it. It cannot be denied that the opponents of the Independents taunted them with their Barrowist and Brownist origins. It is equally certain that they would have rebutted the charge. Indeed the Independent members of the Westminster Assembly did so in their 'Apologeticall Narration'. The assertion that the Independents were not Separatists can be proved by an examination of the writings of two of its earliest leaders, Henry Jacob and John Robinson. Jacob was the Pastor of the first English Congregation of Independents founded in 1616. Among his papers was found a copy of 'A third humble Supplication' of the Puritans, addressed to the King in 1605, and corrected in Jacob's handwriting. He represents the views of the Puritans of the time who asked for toleration and permission

'to Assemble togeather somwhere publikly to the Service & Worship of God, to vse and enioye peacably among our selves alone the wholl exercyse of Gods worship and of Church Government . . . without any tradicion of men whatsoever, according only to the specification of Gods written word and no otherwise, which hitherto as yet in this our present State we could never enjoye.'[1]

Jacob and his fellow-Puritans append a guarantee that if this is allowed them they will

'before a Iustice of peace first take the oath of your Maiesties supremacy and royall authority as the Lawes of the Land at this present do set forth the same'

and promise to keep communion with other churches, to pay all ecclesiastical dues and to submit themselves, in any case of trespass, to the civil magistrate. Clearly Jacob was no Separatist. John Robinson, as we have seen, began as a Separatist and later became a Puritan. In 1610 his well-known work *A Iustification of Separation from the Church of England* proclaims his Separatism. But the same hand penned the following words after he was 'converted' to Puritanism by Jacob:[2]

'To conclude, For my selfe, thus I beleeue with my heart before God, and professe with my tongue, and haue before the world, that I haue one and the same faith, hope, spirit, baptism, and Lord which I had in the Church of England and none other: that I esteem so many in that

[1] Burrage *op. cit.* i 286

[2] *A Treatise of the Lawfulness of Hearing of the Ministers* (1634) p. 63*f*

church, of what state, or order soeuer, as are truly partakers of that faith (as I account many thousand to be) for my christian brethren: and my selfe a fellow-member with them of that one misticall body of Christ . . .'

The same viewpoint is expressed by Cotton Mather in the Preface of his *Magnalia Christi Americana:*[1]

'. . . the Little Daughter of *New-England* in *America*, may bow down herself to her Mother *England* in *Europe*, presenting this *Memorial* unto her; assuring her, that tho' by some of her *Angry* Brethren, she was forced to make a *Local Secession*, yet not a *Seperation*, but hath always retained a Dutiful Respect unto the *Church of God in* England.'

Thus both American and English Independents regarded themselves as Puritans and not Separatists. For this reason the worship of the English Independents will receive consideration as Puritan worship, and is therefore omitted from this chapter.

The worship of the Barrowist Separatists claims our attention first, because it was established in England before that of the Brownists, with whom it has affinities, or of the Anabaptists. The Barrowists are known to have flourished from 1587 to 1593. Their leaders, Barrowe himself, Greenwood and Penry, all died for their faith. Information concerning their practices is obtained from depositions made by Barrowists before being haled to prison.

A comprehensive account is given of their Meetings:

'In the somer tyme they mett together in the feilds a mile or more about London. there they sitt downe vppon A Banke & diuers of them expound out of the bible so long as they are there assembled.'[2]

It appears that they would arrange in advance where their next meeting was to be held on the following Sunday and they would assemble at the chosen rendezvous as early as five o'clock in the morning. Here they would probably remain all day, kept there partly by the prolixity of their Biblical 'exercises' and partly for fear of detection if they should leave while it was yet daylight. Here

'. . . they contynewe in there kinde of praier and exposicion of Scriptures all that daie. They dyne together, After dinner make collection to paie for there diet & what mony is left some one of them carrieth it to the prisons where any of there sect be committed.'[3]

[1] (London 1702) p. viii [2] Burrage *op. cit.* i 26 [3] *ibid*

Their form of prayer was not liturgical, but extempore in character. They would not even repeat the Lord's Prayer, which they regarded as the perfect model of prayer:

'. . . for thuse of set or stynted praier (as they terme it), this they teach that all stynted praiers and redd service is but Babling in ye Lord*es* sight'.[1]

Evidently they claimed Apostolic warrant for this practice:

'a forme of prayer not to bee vsed for the Apostles did not vse to saye it.'[2]

The Lord's Prayer, which many Puritans repeated, having Dominical warrant, as they believed, for it, was regarded by the Barrowists not as a liturgical form but as part of the Sermon on the Mount, illustrating the kind of prayer to be aimed at. Moreover the Barrowists believed that all liturgical forms, the Lord's Prayer included, were a hindrance to the operation of the Spirit of God. The most radical statement of this view is expressed by John Penry, the Barrowist martyr, answering the objection that Christ intended the Lord's Prayer to be repeated:[3]

'We answer first that the scrypture yt selfe sheweth his meaning herein to be, not that the disciples or others should be tyed to vse these very wordes, but that in prayer and geuing of thankes they should followe his direction and patterne which he had geuen them, that they might know to whom, with what affeccion and to what end to pray as yt is expresslie sett downe in these wordes. After this manner therfore pray ye, and not as men will now haue vs: Say ouer these very wordes. Secondly we doubt not but that we may vse anie of these wordes as others applying them to our seuerall necessyties as we see Christ himselfe did when he prayed. O my father yf this cupp cannot pass from me but that I must drinke yt, thy will be done where yt is plaine that Christ himselfe who gaue the rule doth shew vs how to vse yt, to weet . . . in praying according to that rule as our specyall necessyties shalbe, whether we vse any of these wordes or other, or pray with sighes & groanes that cannot be expressed.'

Thirdly he asks, how can his opponents reconcile a set form of prayer with Rom. viii 26? Fourthly, the Apostles kept to the meaning of Christ but not to the very words he used:

[1] *id.* ii 56 [2] *id.* ii 43 [3] cited Burrage *op. cit.* ii 74*f*

'they neuer in all their Epistles chardge them when they pray to say ouer the Lordes prayer . . . but they teach and exhort them according to their seuerall necessyties and occasyons in all things to shew their requests vnto God in all maner of prayer and supplycacion in the spryt with geuing of thankes . . .'

Fifthly, if Christ's words are an express commandment, 'When ye pray, Say,' then it is sinful to use any other form of words. 'But the Apostles used others and so may we.' Charismatic gifts and formularies were, to their minds, mutually inconsistent. In their insistence upon 'free prayer' the Separatists supplied a precedent for the extemporary prayers of Presbyterians and Independents.

As to their praise, it appears that the early Barrowists used neither psalms nor hymns. The documents do not, in fact, mention singing at all. We are informed by Henoch Clapham[1] that the Barrowists were first persuaded to sing in their assemblies by a man who urged its necessity, one Francis Johnson, the Barrowist Pastor of the congregation in Campen and Naarden:

'*Franc-Iohnson* (being advised by one that talked with him thereabouts in the *Clinke* at *London*) did presse the use of our singing Psalmes (neglected before of his people for Apocrypha;) wherevpon his Congregation publikely in their meetinges vsed them, till they could haue them translated into verse, by some of their Teachers . . .'

They administered the Sacraments of Baptism and the Lord's Supper. But, in the case of Baptism, they held it to be unlawful to baptise children in the churches of the Establishment, preferring to let them go unbaptised until a satisfactory Baptism could be administered by a true preacher of the Gospel. The method of administering the Baptism among the Barrowists is described in Daniel Bucke's deposition. Seven children were baptised by Johnson in 1592, as follows:[2]

'they [*the congregation*] had neither god fathers nor godmothers, and he tooke water and washed the faces of them that were baptised: the Children that were there baptised were the Children of Mr. Studley Mr. Lee with others beings of seuerall yeres of age, sayinge onely in the administracion of this sacrament I doe Baptise thee in the name of the

[1] *A Chronological Discourse* (London 1609) p. 36

[2] Harl. MS. 6849 fol. 216 *verso;* cited Burrage *op. cit.* i 142*f*

father of the sonne and of the holy gost withoute vsinge any other cerimony therein and is now vsually observed accordinge to the booke of Common praier . . .'

The same witness gives a most vivid picture of the Barrowist administration of the Lord's Supper:[1]

'Beinge further demaunded the manner of the lordes supper administred amongst them, he saith that fyve whight loves [*loaves*] or more were sett vppon the table and that the Pastor did breake the bread and then deliuered to the rest some of the said congregacion sittinge and some standinge aboute the table, and that the Pastor deliuered the Cupp vnto one and he to an other, and soe from one to an other till they had all dronken vsinge the words at the deliuerye thereof accordinge as it is sett downe in the eleventh of the Corinthes the xxiiijth verse.'

It will be noted that the Barrowist Lord's Supper is characterized by its simplicity and fidelity to the New Testament narrative. This is clearly seen in the repetition of the actions of our Lord, as well as in the words of delivery. This again was insisted upon by the Presbyterians and the Independents.

Chief amongst the other ordinances of the Barrowists is Excommunication, or, to use its Biblical name, 'the handing over to Satan'. This is described by Robert Aburne, the offenders being Robert Stokes and George Collier:[2]

'He saieth that they did vse to excommunicate amongst them, and that one Robert Stokes, and one George Collier, and one or twoe more whose names he Remembreth not, wear excommunicated, for that they discented from them in opinion but in what poynte he Remembreth not, and that the said Iohnson thelder did denounce thexcommunication against them, and concernynge the manner of proceadinges to excommunication he saieth, that they the said Stokes and the Rest beynge privatelye admonished of their pretended errors, and not conforming themselves, and by Witnes produced to their congregacion, then the said Iohnson, with the Consent of the whole Congregacion, did denounce the excommunication, and that sithence they weare excommunicated which was a halfe yere and somewhat more sithence, they wear not admitted into their Churche.'

The Separatists provided the Puritans with the example of a rigid and inflexible discipline. Both parties alike insisted upon

[1] *id.* fol. 217 *verso;* cited Burrage *op. cit.* i 143

[2] Harl. MS. 6848 fol. 41 *verso;* cited Burrage *loc. cit.*

the purity of the Church being kept. In the particular example cited, purity of doctrine was the aim of the excommunication. Normally, however, Puritan discipline was concerned with the purity of life and conduct. Thus both Puritans and Separatists plead for a three-fold reformation: Gospel-doctrine, Gospel-government, and Gospel-discipline. The doctrine of the 'gathered church' which plays such an important part in Puritan theory and practice, is seen to be exemplified in the Barrowist discipline.

Marriage was held by the Barrowists to be a purely civil ceremony, which did not require to be performed by a minister or in a church. Christopher Bowman, a Deacon in the church of which Francis Johnson was the Pastor declares roundly:[1]

> '. . . Mariage in a howse without a Mynister by Consent of the parties and frends is sufficient.'

The Anglican marriage ceremony was scrupled not only because it required the use of the ring, to them a ceremony for which there was no warrant in the Word of God, but also because the New Testament gave no example of a marriage being performed by our Lord or the Apostles. It seemed therefore to both Separatists and some of the Puritans that the Church had no right to exert its power in the civil sphere, in which marriage quite clearly fell.

It may also be assumed that all three groups of Separatists agreed in regarding burials as essentially civil in character. This is not entirely an *argumentum e silentio*, as the one recorded description of the funeral of a famous Separatist, Eaton, asserts that his many followers proceeded behind the corpse to the graveside and without prayers or exhortations or commendations thrust the body into the grave and stamped earth upon it.[2] We shall see that the Puritans in the Commonwealth period were averse to burial services. Their objection was the fear that superstition might attend the ceremony. It is not improbable that the Separatists were actuated by the same motives. In regarding marriages and burials as essentially civil ceremonies with which the Church had nothing to do, the Separatists again prepared the ground for the Puritans.

At first the Barrowists do not appear to have had any Or-

[1] *id.* fol. 70 *verso;* cited Burrage *op. cit.* i 144

[2] Burrage *op. cit.* ii 326*f*

dination to their church offices. Clapham informs us that Johnson and Greenwood were chosen as Pastor and Teacher, respectively, 'without any *Imposition of hands*'. However it seems that when Johnson came to Amsterdam some years later, he had a ceremony of the imposition of hands, this being performed by the lay members of his own congregation.[1]

We are also indebted to Clapham for an amusing description of the manner in which the offertory was taken at the Barrowist meetings:[2]

'And hereupon it was, that the *Separists* did at first in their Conventicles, appoynt their Deacons to stand at the Chamber dore, at the people's outgate, with their Hats in hand (much like after the fashion of a Play-house) into the which they put their voluntary. But comming beyonde seas, where a man might haue seauen Doyts for a penny, it fell out, howsoeuer their voluntary (at the casting in) did make a great clangor, the *Summa totalis* ouerseene, the maisters of Play came to haue but a few pence to their share. Whereupon, a broad Dish (reasonable flat) was placed in the middest of their conuention, that when the voluntarie was cast in, others might obserue the quantitie. But this way serued not the turne, for a few doyts rushing in upon the soddaine, could not easily be obserued, of what quantity it might be. Vpon this, the Pastor gaue out, that if (besides giftes from others abroad) they would not make him *Tenne pounds* yearely at least, he would leaue them, as unworthy the Gospell.'

In the general description of the Barrowist meetings, it was seen that the time was spent in prayer and the expounding of the Scriptures. All Barrowist sermons were expository, and it appears they were delivered in a homely, if not a rough, manner. Henoch Clapham styles these preachers 'Syncerians'. He complains[3] that they have degraded preaching by

'holding every howers talke, A Sermon: Insomuch as a number would not goe to meate (if a few were present of their faction) but there must be a kind of Sermon.'

In the same passage Clapham declares that Barrowe himself disliked this form of preaching,

'saying of that, and of some Pinsellers and Pedlers that then were put to preach in their Thursedayes Prophecie, that it would bring the Scriptures into mightie contempt.'

[1] Clapham *op. cit.* p. 31 [2] *id.* p. vi [3] *id.* p. vii

The exercise of 'Prophecie' mentioned above was regarded by Puritans and Separatists alike as a valuable means of inculcating doctrine. Various speakers would preach and expound the same passage of Scripture *seriatim*, allowing members of the congregation to state their difficulties, which the Church officers would attempt to resolve. Archbishop Grindal, it will be remembered, was sequestrated for refusing to execute an order by the Queen for the suppression of prophesying. In this as in other ways the Puritan heritage was carried over into Separatism.

Another parallel between Barrowists and Puritans is seen in their invariable custom of founding a church upon a Covenant subscribed by officers and members. For instance, Abraham Pulbery in 1592 admitted upon examination that (says the reporter)[1]

> 'hee hath made a promise to the Lord in the presence of his Congregacion when hee entred therevnto that hee would walke with them as they would walke with the Lorde.'

In almost similar words, another declared[2] that

> 'as longe as they did walke in the lawes of God hee would forsake all other assemblies and onely followe them.'

The use of Covenants was later to become a marked feature of Independency. Occasionally, ministers of Puritan leanings in the Established Church would enter into a Covenant with the members of their churches. There is little doubt that the Separatists provided the Puritans with this precedent.

The worship of the English Brownists now falls to be considered. Browne's company achieved complete separation in 1581 at Norwich. Therefore they emerged some years earlier than the Barrowists. But as Robert Browne removed with his followers to Holland in 1581 or 1582 their future history is to be sought at Middleburgh rather than in Norwich. The Barrowists (with whom they have great affinities and with whom they were often confused) made Separatism more widely known in practice than the Brownists, though Browne's writings gained a wide notoriety in this country.

The meetings of the Brownists resembled those of the

[1] Burrage *op. cit.* ii 34 [2] *id.* ii 45; *cf.* 60

Barrowists. The following description of them is given in *The Brownists Synagogue*:[1]

'In that house where they intend to meet, there is one appointed to keepe the doore, for the intent, to give notice if there should be any insurrection, warning may be given them. They doe not flocke all together, but come 2 or 3 in a company, any man may be admitted thither, and all being gathered together, the man appointed to teach, stands in the midst of the Roome, and his audience gather about him. He prayeth about the space of halfe an houre, and part of his prayer is, that those which come thither to scoffe and laugh, God would be pleased to turne their hearts, by which meanes they thinke to escape vndiscovered. His Sermon is about the space of an houre, and then doth another stand up to make the text more plaine, and at the latter end, he intreates them all to goe home severally, least the next meeting they be interrupted by those which are of the opinion of the wicked, they seeme very stedfast in their opinions, and say rather then they will turne, they will burne.'

Browne himself is the authority for a description of the order of his service in Middleburgh. He writes:[2]

'Likevvise an order vvas agreed on ffor their meetinges together, ffor their exercised therein, as for praier, thanckes giuing, reading of the scriptures, for exhortation and edifiing, ether by all men vvhich had the guift, or by those vvhich had a speciall charge before others. And for the lavvefulness off putting forth questions, to learne the trueth, as iff anie thing seemed doubtful & hard, to require some to shevve it more plainly, or for anie to shewe it him selfe & to cause the rest to vnderstand it.'

This informs us that 'prophesying' occupied a central place in the Brownist meetings, which appear to have been essentially didactic in character. The distinction recorded above between 'praier' and 'thanckes giuing' may mean quite simply that the services included petitionary prayers and prayers of thanksgiving. On the other hand, it is quite possible that Browne refers to special Days of Thanksgiving which they might hold to commemorate some signal mercy. Such days were not infrequently held, as also Days of Humiliation, in the history of the Commonwealth.

We may also assume that the Brownists took up collections from their members during divine service as one set of officers in the church are expressly named 'Receeuers'.[3]

[1] (ed. 1641) p. 5*f* [2] *A Trve and Short Declaration &c.* (1582) p. 19*f*
[3] *id.* p. 20

Discipline was also enforced. This is Browne's meaning in referring to 'separating cleane from vncleane'.[1]

From an autobiographical passage in *A Booke which Sheweth &c.* . . . it may be inferred that Browne regarded marriage as a civil custom which did not require ecclesiastical sanction.[2]

For the other ordinances practised by the Brownists we have no evidence. Since Browne aimed at producing a Church on New Testament lines, it is most probable that the Sacraments of Baptism and the Lord's Supper were observed. There is no reason to suppose that the worship of the Brownists differed materially from that of the Barrowists or indeed departed from the liturgical convictions held in common by Puritans and Separatists. Browne's innovations were in the sphere of church government and not, it would appear, in church worship. Like the Barrowists, his Church was founded upon a Covenant. As his writings appeared five years before the rise of the Barrowists, they were no doubt debtors to him, as the Puritans were to both groups of Separatists.

The third group of Separatists who flourished at this time were the Anabaptists. They appear to have had no organized existence in this country before 1612. In the latter years of the reign of King Edward VI several publications appeared criticizing the 'pestilent' opinions of the Continental Anabaptists. In 1560 there was issued 'A proclamation for the banishment of Anabaptistes that refused to be reconciled, 22 Septembris'.[3] But throughout the sixteenth century Anabaptists are encountered not as organized societies, but sporadically as individuals or families. Indeed there is from 1589 a twenty years' silence in references to them. This was broken only when William Sayer was imprisoned as an Anabaptist in the Norfolk County Gaol in 1612. Hence Elizabethan Separatism was almost exclusively the contribution of the Barrowists and Brownists. The origin of English Anabaptism is to be sought in Holland. Francis Johnson, the Barrowist Minister, states[4] that there were 'divers' Anabaptists in his congregation, who ultimately were excommunicated. The first Baptist congregation to be settled in England was that over which

[1] *A Booke which Sheweth &c.* (1582) sig. K2 *verso*

[2] *ibid.* [3] Burrage *op. cit.* i 62

[4] *An Inqvirie and Ansvver of Thomas White* (1606) p. 63

Thomas Helwys presided with Thomas Murton. This withdrew from John Smyth's congregation in Amsterdam and returned to England about 1612.

The characteristic difference between the Anabaptists and the other Separatists concerned the mode of administering the Sacrament of Baptism. Helwys made believer's baptism, either by sprinkling or by pouring, a necessity for salvation. So dogmatic was he on this point that he insisted that the contrary doctrine of infant baptism was sufficient to warrant the penalty of eternal damnation being inflicted on those who held it:[1]

'. . . if you had no other sin amongst you al, but this, you perish everie man off you from the highest to the lowest, iff you repent not.'

The following description of the Church at Amsterdam and its public worship in 1608 is comprehensive:[2]

'The order of the worshippe and government of oure church is 1. we begynne with a prayer, after reade some one or tow chapters of the bible gyve the sence thereof, and confer vpon the same, that done we lay aside oure bookes, and after a solemne prayer made by the 1. speaker, he propoundeth some text out of the Scripture, and prophecieth owt of the same, by the space of one hower, or thre Quarters of an hower. After him standeth vp a 2. speaker and prophecieth owt of the said text the like time and space, some tyme more some tyme lesse. After him the 3. the 4. the 5. &c as the tyme will geve leave, Then the 1. speaker concludeth with prayer as he began wth prayer, wth an exhortation to contribution to the poore, wch collection being made is also concluded wth prayer. This morning exercise begynes at eight of the clock and continueth vnto twelve of the clocke the like course of exercise is observed in the aftnwne from 2. of the clocke vnto 5. or 6. of the Clocke. last of all the execution of the government of the church is handled.'

This description shows how opposed the Anabaptists were to the use of set forms in their worship. They were logical enough in their attempt at attaining a pneumatic worship to put away the Bible early in their service, as a form of words. The second feature in their daily worship which is unusual is the special offertory prayer that they made.

John Smyth, their minister, began as a Puritan within the

[1] Burrage *op. cit.* i 253

[2] *Letter of the Bromheedes to Sir Wm. Hammerton* (Harl. MS. 360 fol. 71 *recto*)

Established Church and his famous treatise on the Lord's Prayer, *A Patterne of true Prayer*, is the fairest consideration of the claims of liturgical prayer made by a Puritan. His conclusion concerning the legitimacy or otherwise of repeating the Lord's Prayer is:[1]

'. . . Christ leaveth it arbitrie vnto vs, as a thing indifferent when we pray to say this prayer, or not to say it, so be that we say it in faith and feeling; or if wee say it not, yet to pray according vnto it.'

These were his opinions in 1605, but three years later Smyth had decided unreservedly in favour of the more pneumatic type of worship. In *The Differences of the Churches of the Separation*[2] he declares:

'Wee hould that the worship of the new testament properly so called is spirituall proceeding originally from the hart: & that reading out of a booke (though a lawfull eclesiastical action) is no part of spirit*n*all worship, but rather the invention of the man of synne it beeing substituted for a part of spirituall worship. Wee hould that seeing prophesiing is a parte of spirituall worship; therefore in time of prophesjng it is vnlawfull to have the booke as a helpe before the eye wee hould that seeing singinging [*sic*] a psalme is a parte of spirituall worship therefore it is vnlawfull to have the booke before the eye in time of singinge a psalme.'

The rejection of forms in worship was so complete that one stage further would have led to Quakerism. This 'spiritual worship' while it does not altogether do away with the use of books, regards the part of the service in which they are used as a mere preparation for the pure worship, which proceeds without them. Helwys contrasting the worship of his church with that of the Johnsonians, also in Amsterdam, declares:[3]

'They as partes or meanes of worship read Chapters, Textes to preache on & Psalmes out of the translacion, we alreddy as in prayinge, so in prophesiinge & singinge Psalmes laye aside the translacion, & we suppose yt will prove the truth, that All bookes even the originalles themselves must be layed aside in the tyme of spirituall worshipp, yet still retayninge the readinge & interpretinge of the Scriptures in the Churche for the preparinge to worshipp, Iudginge of doctrine, decidinge of Controversies as the grounde of o^r^ faithe & of o^r^ whole profession.'

[1] *The Works of John Smyth* (ed. Whitley, Cambridge 1915) i 81

[2] (ed. 1608) p. v [3] Letter of Sept. 20, 1608: cited Burrage *op. cit.* ii 166

This is clearly shown by the following extract from Edward Draper's *Gospel-Glory proclaimed before the Sonnes of Men:*[1]

'To singe Psalmes in the Gospel is a speciall gift given to some particular member in the church, whereby he doth blesse, praise, or magnifie the Lord through the mighty operation of the spirit. Ep. 5, 18.19 which is to be performed I say, by one alone, at one time to the edification one of another and therefore it is an ordinance flowing from a cheerfulle heart . . .'

This information assures us that singing in unison was not a feature of early Anabaptist praise. Indeed this precedent was so rigidly followed by succeeding Baptist congregations that even in 1690 Benjamin Keach had great difficulty in persuading his own congregation to sing in unison.

The Sermons, we may surmize from the importance of the exercise of 'prophesying' in their worship, were long expositions of Scripture. These were of three quarters of an hour to an hour's duration.

The Sacrament of Baptism was, as has been seen, dispensed only to believers, that is to those

'which heere, beleeve and with penitent hartes receave ye doctrine of ye holy gospell: for such hath ye Lord Iesus commaunded to be baptized, and no vn-speaking children.'[2]

Whilst Helwys did not insist that the mode of administration should be either sprinkling or dipping, immersion appears to have been insisted upon by the London Baptists in 1633. This Church, under the leadership of Jessey and Blunt, used immersion as the only legitimate method of administration,

'being convinced of Baptism, yt also it ought to be by diping ye Body into ye Water, resembling Burial & riseing again.'[3]

There are no early accounts of Baptist celebrations of the Lord's Supper. Again, since the statement of their Eucharistic doctrine is strongly Calvinist in character, it is probable that their service resembled that of the other Separatists in its simplicity, its fidelity to the account of the Dominical institution in I Cor. xi 23*ff*, repeating not only the words of delivery but also the manual acts.[4]

[1] (ed. 1649) p. 163 [2] Burrage *op. cit.* ii 196 [3] *id.* ii 303
[4] *cf.* para. 32 of the *Short Confession;* cited Burrage *op. cit.* ii 106

The ordinance of the Lord's Supper was almost certainly practised every Lord's day. In this respect the Barrowists of Amsterdam were at one with the Anabaptist congregation of that city. Johnson asks:[1]

'Whether it be not best to celebrate the Lords supper where it can be every Lords day; this the Apostles used to do; by so doing we shall return to the intire practise of the Churches in former ages;'

whereas the Anabaptist Confession of Faith declares:[2]

'Oblata iusta occasione impedimenti, affirmamus caenam dominicam omitti posse donec tollantur impedimenta: aut aliter non audemus omittere quoque die sabbati quum convenimus ad praestandum caetera Dei publici Ministerii . . .'

Moreover, the Anabaptists, as the same Confession asserts, did not permit the lay celebration of the Sacraments:[3]

'Ministrationem sanctorum sacramentorum inseparatim cum ministerio verbi, coniunctam esse agnoscimus et cuique membro corporis administrare sacramenta non licere.'

In this matter also they concurred with the other Separatists. John Robinson, for instance, was unwilling to allow his godly ruling elder, Brewster, to celebrate the Lord's Supper.

Marriage was sanctioned by the Anabaptists only if the uniting parties belonged to their own communion. If this rule was broken, it was visited by ecclesiastical censure, often leading to excommunication. The *Short Confession of Faith* declares:[4]

'Wee permitt none of our communion to marry godles, vnbeleeuing, fleshly persons out of ye church, but wee censure such (as other synnes) according to the disposition & desert of ye cause.'

This practice continued to be enforced in Anabaptist and Independent congregations until the end of the seventeenth century.[5]

The election to church offices was performed, on the New Testament model, by setting the candidates apart with fasting and prayer and the imposition of hands:[6]

[1] Johnson's *Plea; id.* ii 293 [2] *id.* ii 235 [3] *ibid.* [4] *id.* ii 198*f*

[5] For Baptist practice, *cf. Fenstanton, Warboys & Hexham Records* (ed. Underhill, London 1854); for Congregational practice, *cf.* N. Glass *The Early History of the Independent Church at Rothwell* (1871) p. 75*f*

[6] Burrage *op. cit.* ii 195

'And although ye Election and vocation be performed by ye foresaid meanes yet nevertheless ye investing into ye said service is accomplished by ye Elders of ye church, through laying on of hands.'

It is also probable that the Anabaptists held love-feasts. This was certainly a feature of the church life of the early Separatists. In 1568 we are informed:[1]

'About a week ago they discovered here a newly invented sect, called by those who belong to it "the pure or stainless religion"; they met to the number of 150 in a house where their preacher used a half of a tub for a pulpit, and was girded with a white cloth. Each one brought with him whatever food he had to eat, and the leaders divided money amongst those who were poorer, saying that they imitated the life of the apostles and refused to enter the temples to partake of the Lord's supper, as it was a papistical ceremony.'

It is improbable that these were Baptists. On the other hand there is definite evidence that love-feasts were practised by the English Anabaptists, as a general feature in their communities. The Church Record of the Warboys Congregation has this entry for the year 1655:[2]

'The order of love-feast agreed upon, to be before the Lord's Supper; because the ancient churches did practise it, and for unity with other churches near to us.'

Another ordinance which seems to have been used exclusively by the Baptists was that of Feet-washing. Their warrant for it was the practice of our Lord's humility in performing this menial service for his disciples, as recorded in the Fourth Gospel.[3] The Assembly of the General Baptists

'had long agreed that the practise of washing the feet of the saints, urged in Lincolnshire by Robert Wright in 1653, and in Kent by William Jeffrey in 1659, should be left optional as not specified in Hebrews VI.'[4]

The practice of ecclesiastical censures was rigidly enforced by the Baptists, in common with all Puritans and Separatists.

[1] *A Calendar of Letters & State Papers relating to English Affairs, preserved principally in the Archives of Simancos* (London 1894) ii 7

[2] *Fenstanton......Records* p. 272 [3] John xiii 5

[4] *Transactions of the Baptist Historical Society* (1908–09) i 129*ff;* art. 'Original Sin, Feet-washing and the New Connexion'

Helwys's church proceeded to this every Sunday afternoon after the completion of the day's worship. Following the Separatists and Puritans, they also adopted Church Covenants as the basis of the membership of the church. The fullest description of the foundation of a church by covenant is that of the first Congregational or Independent Church formed in England in 1616 by Henry Jacob. This was probably characteristic and for that reason is cited here. The contracting individuals appointed a day

'to Seek ye Face of ye Lord in fasting & Prayer, wherein that particular of their Union togeather as a Church was mainly commended to ye Lord: in ye ending of ye Day were United, Thus, Those who minded this present Union & so joyning togeather joyned both hands each wth other Brother and stood in a Ringwise: their intent being declared, H. Jacob and each of the Rest made some Confession or Profession of their Faith & Repentance, some ware longer some ware briefer, Then they Covenanted togeather to walk in all Gods Ways as he had revealed or should make known to them.'[1]

The form of this Covenant is not unlike that which was probably used by the Barrowist church under Johnson, as contained in the deposition of Daniel Bucke. When he was asked as to

'what promise hee made when he came first to yt Societie he annswereth & sayth that he made ys Protestation: that he wold walke with the rest of ym so longe as they did walke in the way of the Lorde, & so farr as might be warranted by the Word of God.'[2]

There was, however, some opposition amongst the Baptists to the adoption of a Covenant. This was voiced by Hanserd Knollys. He challenged any one to demonstrate that covenants had any basis in Scripture and insisted that it had been the practice of the London Church to admit members on the conditions of faith, repentance and baptism, and no other.[3] As a result of this, covenants were less popular amongst Baptists than among the other Dissenting bodies. Certain churches of the Baptist order did, however, adopt covenants, as the congregation at Hitchin to whom Bunyan often preached; and the

[1] Hanbury *Historical Memorials* (London 1841) i 292*f*

[2] Williston Walker *The Creeds and Platforms of Congregationalism* (New York 1893) p. 116*n*

[3] W. T. Whitley, art. 'Church Covenants' in *The Baptist Quarterly* vii (1934–5) 228

Baptist Church of Great Ellingham in Norfolk followed suit in 1699.[1] The paucity of references to covenants and the late adoption of them demonstrates that they were not as regular a feature of Baptist life as of Independent Church order.

The peculiar contributions made by the Baptists to the worship of the English Separatists were three. They practised believers' baptism by immersion. This was their most distinctive custom. In the second place, they went further than the other Separatists in their opposition to forms in worship. This position is most radically expressed by John Smyth:[2]

> 'That the reading out of a Book is no part of spiritual worship, but the invention of the man of sin; that Books and writings are in the nature of Pictures and Images; that it is unlawful to have the Book before the eyes in singing of a Psalm.'

The third influence exerted by the Baptists was to become a regular feature of Puritan worship. This was the method of running exposition or interpolated comment during public reading of the Scriptures. This was the practice of the old General Baptists, as Grantham's survey of their church life, made in 1678, clearly demonstrates and it was certainly the method used by the New Englanders. For this it appears that John Smyth was responsible.[3]

It now remains to consider other influences upon Separatist and Puritan congregations, which derive from certain obscure congregations in England and the Continent. As their relation to the Established Church is in some doubt, they are not treated as Separatists, although their worship was Separatist in character, if their church government was not. The first in point of time and in importance as a precedent is, of course, the 'Privye Churche' that met in London during Queen Mary's time.[4] This, however, used the Second Prayer Book of King Edward VI. Its importance lies in the fact that it was organized worship under persecution, and provided later Separatists with a precedent for gathering secretly to worship in defiance of the rules of the land, according to their own conscience.

[1] *ibid.*

[2] *The Differences of the Churches of the Separation* p. 4; cited Baillie *A Dissuasive from the Errours of the Time &c.* (1645) p. 29*n*

[3] *Works* (ed. cit.) I lxxxvii*f*

[4] For details see Foxe *Acts and Monuments* (ed. Pratt, 1877) viii 458*ff*, 558*f*

The Plumber's Hall Congregation was of the lineage of the Marian secret church, as they themselves assert:[1]

'we bethought us what were best to doe, and we remembered that there was a congregation of us in this Citie in Queene Maries dayes: And a Congregation at *Geneva*, which used a booke and order of preaching, ministring of the Sacraments and Discipline, most agreeable to the worde of God: which booke is alowed by that godly & well learned man, Maister *Calvin*, and the preachers there, which booke and order we nowe holde.'

This congregation may be considered as the progenitor of the English Presbyterian movement, seeing that it is more Puritan than Separatist in its worship. It was discovered in 1567.

A similar congregation is that known as the 'Privye Churche' of Richard Fitz which the London authorities discovered in the same year as they unearthed the Plumber's Hall congregation. Their minister makes the three cardinal Puritan demands. He declares that the 'trewe markes of Christs churche' consist in

'Fyrste and formoste, the Glorious worde and Evangell preached, not in bondage and subjection, but freely, and purely. Secondly to have the Sacraments mynistred purely, onely and all together accordinge to the institution and good worde of the Lord Jesus, without any tradicion or invention of man. And laste of all, to have, not the fylthye Cannon lawe, but dissiplyne onelye, and all together agreable to the same heavenlye and almighty worde of oure good Lorde, Jesus Chryste.'[2]

The discipline so strongly insisted upon was practised, not after the second diet of worship on the Lord's Day, as was the Baptist custom, but

'on the fourth day in the weke we meet and cum together weekely to use prayer & exercyse disciplyne on them whiche do deserve it, by the strength and sure warrant of the lordes good word as in Mt.xviii.15–18 and I Cor.v.'[3]

The close affinities of this congregation with Independency are seen in their adoption of a covenant. Indeed Dr Peel claims[4] that on this account 'there is no valid reason for moderns to deny to Fitz's congregation, and probably to others contemporary with it, the title of "the first Congregational Churches".' In our view it may fitly be regarded as a predecessor of either

[1] Albert Peel *The First Congregational Churches* (Cambridge 1920) p. 7
[2] *id.* p. 32 [3] *id.* p. 33 [4] *id.* p. 47

the Brownists or Barrowists, but because it was strictly Separatist it cannot claim to be the progenitor of the Congregational or Independent Churches.

Two conclusions follow from this study of Separatist worship. The first is that the Separatists put into practice a 'reformation without tarrying for any', whilst the Puritans resolved to attain the liturgical achievements of the Separatists within the Establishment. For this reason the Separatists have a profound influence on the Puritans in providing the latter with definite instances of liturgical innovation which gave concreteness to Puritan theoretical considerations. The second influence of the Separatists lay in the radical opposition to any set forms in worship. It is this, probably more than any other factor, which accounts for the Puritan departure from the liturgical customs of the Continental Reformed Churches. This departure requires an explanation since the Puritans themselves claimed to be nearer to the Reformed Churches abroad than the defenders of the Establishment. Whilst their contention is relatively true, the Puritans were further away from the general practice of the Reformed Churches than they knew. This question, however, will be reserved for later treatment.

## CHAPTER VIII

## SET FORMS OR EXTEMPORARY PRAYERS?

If the main theological difference between Puritan and Anglican worship consists in the attempt of the Puritans to model their worship more closely on the Biblical criterion, this resolved itself practically in the Puritan emphasis on free prayer over against the 'stinted forms' of the Establishment. This is not to ignore the fact that the upholders of the liturgy defended their practice by an appeal to the Scriptures. Furthermore the Puritans defended their practice by an appeal to the worship of the early Church of the first three centuries of the Christian era; whilst the Anglicans appealed to a more uniform and comprehensive, if later tradition.

The appeal to the Scriptures was apparently inconclusive. For whilst the Old Testament yielded set forms of praise (for example, the Psalms) and the Aaronic Blessing (Num. vi 24*ff*), these were not to be imitated by Christians. For they were given under the Old Dispensation and moreover they were 'immediately and infallibly guided by the Spirit of Christ'.[1] The same could not be said of the Anglican hierarchy. Moreover the New Testament has given explicit instructions that in prayer only the pastor's voice is to be heard, to which the people are to add their 'Amen' to show concurrence (I Cor. xiv 14, 16). Furthermore the use of read prayers would seem to be a 'quenching of the Spirit' for 'the Spirit helpeth our infirmities for we know not what to pray as we ought' (Rom. viii 26). John Robinson adds ironically, commenting on this verse:[2]

> 'Yes, Paul, with your leave, right well; for we have in our prayer-book what we ought to pray, word for word, whether the Spirit be present or not.'

Thus there appear to be Old Testament examples for set forms of prayer, whilst the New Testament seems to be in favour of extemporary prayer. Had the New Testament been uniformly and unambiguously on the side of extemporary prayer, Puritan apologists would have had a simple task. In practice, however,

[1] John Robinson *A just and necessary Apology; Works* iii 21*f* [2] *id.* iii 28

they had to rebut the charge that the Lord's Prayer was intended as a set form not only for the first disciples but for all subsequent disciples.

In the hotly disputed controversy, the teaching of our Lord was the centre of operations. Apologists chiefly determined their views or sought confirmation for them in their interpretation of St. Matthew's words: 'After this manner therefore pray ye' (Matt. vi 9). Was this Dominical imperative to be interpreted as giving the disciples a set form of prayer? Or was it simply a model on which they were to build their individual prayers? The history of the discussion tends to show that the more radical Puritans and Separatists regarded the Lord's Prayer as a pattern and held that it was not intended that it should be repeated. The Anglicans interpreted it as a literal command for the repetition of that particular prayer. The Presbyterians combined both views and therefore held themselves free to repeat it and to model their extemporary prayers on it.

The Barrowists, the Brownists and the early Independents decided against repetition of the Lord's Prayer. The Barrowists in their deposition of 1587 declare that it is

'a forme of prayer not to bee vsed for the Apostles did not vse to saye it'.[1]

John Penry, one of their leaders, states his views with greater precision. The meaning of Christ was

'not that the disciples or others should be tyed to vse these very wordes, but that in prayer and geuing of thankes they should follow his direction and patterne which he had geuen them, that they might know to whom, with what affeccion and to what end to pray . . .'.[2]

The same author uses the *argumentum e silentio* assuming that as the Lord's Prayer was not explicitly commanded by the Apostles, this gives support to the plea that it was intended as a model, not as a set form of prayer. The Brownists followed the Barrowists in their disuse of the Lord's Prayer in public worship. In their Confession of 1596 they complain[3]

'. . . we are much slandered, as if we denyed or misliked that forme of prayer commonly called the Lord's Prayer.'

They declare it to be such an

[1] Burrage *op. cit.* i 56 [2] *ibid.* [3] Walker *op. cit.* p. 61

'absolute and most excellent forme of prayer such as no men or Angells can set downe the like.'[1]

It is infallibly inspired and therefore inimitable. The real intention of our Lord was

'not that wee should bee tyed to the use of those very words, but that wee should according to that rule make all our requests and thanksgyuing unto God, forasmuch as it is a perfect forme and patterne conteyning in it playne and sufficient directions of prayer for all occasions and necessities that haue been, are, or shalbee to the Church of God, or anie member thereof to the end of the world.'[2]

The early and late Independents, in the persons of John Robinson and of Isaac Watts, maintained the Barrowist and Brownist traditions. John Robinson decides that the Lord's Prayer was not intended to be exactly repeated word for word because,

'The two Evangelists, Matthew and Luke . . . do not precisely keep the same words.'[3]

He continues by claiming that it is absurd to imagine that the disciples were commanded to use no other prayers and concludes that the absence of Apostolic testimony to this prayer demands that it be regarded as a pattern, not as a prescribed form. This apparently was the general Independent view in 1625. Almost a century later the Independents held the same convictions. Isaac Watts, writing in 1715, grants rather reluctantly:[4]

'Christ himself seems to have indulged it [*a set form*] to his disciples in their infant state of Christianity.'

This was not the consistently held view of the Independents, for Baillie informs us that at the Westminster Assembly they agreed with the Presbyterian Divines to recommend its regular use in public worship.

'To that part of the Directory which recommends the use of the Lord's Prayer they did enter no dissent.'[5]

Further they are even prepared to use other Scriptural forms

[1] *ibid.* [2] *ibid.* [3] *Works* i 23
[4] *Guide to Prayer; Works* (ed. 1810) iii 125
[5] Baillie *A Dissuasive &c.* p. 148

as prayers. During the Commonwealth it appears that both Presbyterians and Independents agreed to use the Lord's Prayer regularly in public worship, but that after the Ejection of 1662 they had become definitely opposed to the use of any set prayers. Indeed, as Calamy informs us,[1] not all the Presbyterians in the early eighteenth century used the Lord's Prayer.

'Some ministers use the Lord's Prayer constantly, others frequently, others seldom or never, as reckoning it rather given for a Directory, than to be used as a Form.'

The Puritan position may be summed up as follows: while they valued the Lord's Prayer as a directory or pattern for prayer, they were certain that it was not intended to be repeated by the Christians of to-day, even if it was indulgently granted to the disciples in the 'infant state of Christianity'. They were positive, however, in declaring that it would be presumption for human authorities to claim to produce set forms of prayer on the analogy of our Saviour. That would be both an infringement of the Second Commandment and a denial of the crown rights of the Redeemer who was the only law-giver in his Church. Thus they concluded that the New Testament supported their conception of free prayer.

It was suggested earlier that neither of the contesting parties confined its appeal to the Scriptures, each also invoked the support of tradition. If the Anglicans claimed the aid of the undivided mediæval Church and the earlier tradition of the patristic period, the Puritans were not slow to urge that there was no uniformly imposed liturgy in the first three centuries of the Christian era. John Robinson, for instance, in his plea for extemporary prayer produces Tertullian as a witness. He cites the *Adversus Gentes:*[2]

'We pray, saith he, without any to prompt us, because we pray from the heart.'

Richard Baxter has to face the objection: 'But Antiquity is for set forms and therefore Novelty must not be permitted to exclude them.' He meets this by declaring that the Scripture is the truest criterion to judge antiquity by. He adds:[3]

[1] Edmund Calamy *A Letter to a Divine in Germany* (London 1717) p. 9
[2] *Works* iii 28
[3] *Five Disputations of Church Government and Worship* (London 1659) p. 391

'Forms were at first introduced in variety and not as necessary to the Churches Unity to agree in one: and they were left to the Pastors' Liberty and none were forced to any forms of other men's composing.'

This judgment is confirmed by recourse to the practice of St. Basil of Caesarea:[1]

'When Basil set us his new forms of Psalmodie and other worship, which the Church at Neocaesarea were so offended at, he did not for all that impose it on them but was content to use it in his church at Caesarea.'

Similarly, John Owen, the most learned defender of Independency, appeals to the purest primitive usages:[2]

'I do acknowledge that the general prevalency of the use of set forms of prayer of human invention in Christian assemblies, for many ages (more than any other argument that is urged for their necessity) requires a tenderness in judgment as unto the whole nature of them, and the acceptance of their persons in the duty of prayer by whom they are used. Yet no consideration of this usage, seeing it is not warranted by the Scriptures nor is of apostolical example, nor is countenanced by the practice of the primitive churches, ought to hinder us from discerning and judging of the evils and inconveniences that have ensued thereon; nor from discovering how far they are unwarrantable as unto their imposition.'

He regards the imposition of liturgies as

'the gilding of the poisonous pill, whose operation when it was swallowed, was to bereave men of their sense, reason, and faith.'[3]

It meant the perpetuation of errors. He does not, however, offer the same criticism of Reformed liturgies, but he regards the principle as dangerous.[4] In short, the Puritans claimed that tradition must itself be judged by the Word of God. The result of such a comparison was, they claimed, a demonstration that extemporary prayer was the usage of the Apostolical Church; whilst, if later centuries allowed the use of set forms of prayer, they at least did not impose them upon other churches. Thus they believed that Scripture and the primitive Church gave added support to their conviction.

[1] *ibid.*

[2] *A Discourse of the Work of the Holy Spirit in Prayer* (1682); *Works* (ed. Russell, London 1826) iv 12

[3] *id.* iv 15 [4] *id.* iv 18

Having considered the claims of the Puritans to base their technique of public prayer upon the Scriptural directions and upon the uncorrupted practice of the primitive Church, it remains to consider in detail their defence of extemporary prayer and their attack upon 'stinted forms'. The gravamen of the Puritan objection to read prayers was, of course, their belief that this practice was directly contrary to the Epistle to the Romans (viii 26): 'Likewise the Spirit also helpeth our infirmities; for we know not what we should pray for as we ought; but the Spirit itself maketh intercession for us with groanings which cannot be uttered.' Indeed John Owen's *A Discourse of the Work of the Holy Spirit in Prayer* is an extended sermon upon that text. Owen reminds his readers that

'to know our temporal wants so as to make them the matter of prayer according to the mind of God, requires more wisdom than of ourselves we are furnished withal.'[1]

In that sentence there can be detected the sombre hues of Calvinism with its emphasis upon original sin and utter dependence of the creature upon God. Man could not reach to God; God first must reach to him. Read prayers seemed to emphasize the self-sufficiency of man. Owen repudiates them for that reason also:[2]

'And indeed in the poverty, or rather misery of devised aids to prayer, this is not the least pernicious effect or consequent, that they keep men off from searching the promises of God, whereby they might know what to pray for.'

If the fundamental objection was theological in character, there were other practical objections of far-reaching character.

(i) First and foremost among these was the belief that a constant use of set forms of prayer deprived both minister and people of the gift of prayer. John Owen urges that as a result of the imposition of liturgies,

'we daily see men napkining their talents until they are taken from them.'[3]

When urged that this atrophy of spiritual capacities is necessitated by the insufficiency of adequately trained ministers, he replies:[4]

[1] *id.* iv 55 [2] *ibid.*

[3] *A Discourse concerning Liturgies and their Imposition* (1662); *Works* (ed. Goold, Edinburgh 1862) xv 52 [4] *Works* (ed. cit.) xv 53

'The necessity pretended from the insufficiency of ministers for the discharge of that which is their proper work, hath in great part been caused by this imposition, and where it hath not, some men's sin is not to be made other men's punishment.'

This point is put more roundly by the anonymous author of *The Anatomy of the Service Book* (1641) who asks:

'What, we pray you, is the procreant and conservant cause of dumb dogges that cannot barke; idle Shepheards, saying Sir Johns; mere Surplice and Service-Book men, such as cannot doe so much as a Porter in his frocke; for he doth Service, and the Priest onely sayes service: is it not the Service-Book?'[1]

Baxter, whilst allowing the use of set forms of prayer for those ministers who wrong the Church and dishonour the work of God 'by their erroneous or over-rude defective management', maintains that set forms do not edify the Church as free prayer can.[2] The ejected Ministers of 1662 declared:[3]

'We cannot believe that it is lawful for us at all times, by submitting ourselves to a Form of Prayer, to smother the Gift of Prayer, given (we hope) to some of us, or to cool the heat and fervency of our hearts in Prayer, or the Affections of them that hear us.'

John Owen speaks for all the Puritans in claiming that liturgical prayers tend to make the Christian satisfied in hearing prayers instead of encouraging him to pray for himself.

'But those who will never enter the water but with flags or bladders under them, will scarce ever learn to swim. And it cannot be denied, that the constant and unvaried use of set forms of prayer may become a great occasion of quenching the Spirit, and hindering all progress or growth in gifts or graces.'[4]

To vary the metaphor, the Christian who rests satisfied with read prayers is like a man who, having used crutches when he was lame, prefers to go on using them when his legs are sound. Set forms of prayer hinder the progress of the individual in the gift and grace of prayer; whilst they maintain a remiss and negligent Ministry.

[1] cited from 2nd edition (1652) p. 47 [2] *Five Disputations &c.* p. 47

[3] *A Sober and Temperate Discourse concerning the Interest of Words in Prayer* by H.D.M.A. (London 1661) p. 96

[4] *A Discourse of the Work of the Holy Spirit in Prayer; Works* (ed. Russell) iv 92

(ii) The second charge against set forms of prayer was that they could not meet the varied needs of differing congregations and occasions. Whilst the Book of Common Prayer was comprehensive in its appeal, it lacked the particularity and intimacy of free prayer. This argument is what convinces Isaac Watts that extemporary prayer is preferable to set forms:[1]

'I mention the most usual, most evident and most convincing argument against the perpetual confinement of ourselves to a form; and that is, because it renders our converse with God very imperfect: For it is not possible that forms of prayer should be composed, that are perfectly suited to all our occasions in the things of this life and the life to come. Our circumstances are always altering in this frail and mutable state. We have new sins to be confessed, new temptations and sorrows to be represented, new wants to be supplied. Every change of providence in the affairs of a nation, a family, or a person, requires suitable petitions and acknowledgments. And all these can never be well provided for in any prescribed composition.'

The two different types of prayer, liturgical and free, appear to reflect in this respect two differing conceptions of the Church. The former stresses the corporate nature of the Church in 'Common Prayer', the latter emphasizes the need of individuals in a family Church. If liturgical prayer adequately reflects what is held in common in its Creeds, its General Confession, its abstract Collects praying for graces required by all Christians, then free prayer meets the individual's particular requirements. And, moreover, liturgical prayer does not demand that the minister should know the members of his congregation; whereas free prayer implies a smaller, more compact community all of whom, theoretically, are known to the minister. Indeed these two varieties of prayer would seem to bear out Troeltsch's demarcation between the 'church' type and the 'sect' type of Christian life. Liturgical prayer would therefore require a parish as a background, with the wider horizon of the nation; free prayer suggests not Israel but the remnant, *i.e.* the compact unit of the congregation as a worshipping family. The differing conceptions of worship derive, therefore, to a considerable extent from differing ecclesiologies.

Precisely because the Book of Common Prayer is a national

[1] *Guide to Prayer; Works* iv 127

formulary of worship, it lends itself to the charge of being impersonal, because general. It is not surprising to find, therefore, that it is criticized both by John Owen and Isaac Watts as unable to impress the affections of the worshippers. In a memorable phrase, Owen refers to 'a recoiling of efficacy' resulting from the extemporary prayers of Ministers who have thought devoutly on the grace and majesty of God and of the needs of their congregations.[1] While Watts lays his finger on the weakness of set prayers, when he says[2]

'. . . but generals are cold and do not affect us, nor affect persons that join with us, and whose case he that speaks in prayer should represent before God.'

(iii) The third Puritan objection to set forms of prayer was that because they were regularly prescribed they persuaded the people that they were a necessity and that God could not be worshipped in any other way. John Owen regards their very uniformity as a danger. As they were prescribed to be repeated at each diet of worship, they appear to the unlearned, he says, to be as indispensable as the Scriptures. Indeed they have been equally with the Scriptures the rule of faith, the repository of Christian doctrine. Far from being the guarantors of uniformity

'. . . the present various liturgies that are amongst the several sorts of Christians in the world, are of little other use than to establish their minds in their particular errors, which by this means they adhere unto as articles of their faith.'[3]

Owen even ascribes the multiplication of ceremonies in the mediæval Church to an attempt on the part of the priesthood to set off their 'dead forms' by 'adventitious ornaments'.[4]

Richard Baxter makes the less fanciful deduction that congregations must not overvalue set forms as necessities of worship lest

'they offer God a blind kind of service, while they place his worship in that which is no part of worship (as forms are not, as such) but an indifferent circumstance.'[5]

Moreover, as Baxter insists, such uniform imposition of set forms would lead the people to uncharitable censures upon

[1] *Works* (ed. Russell) iv 92 [2] *Works* iv 127 [3] *Works* (ed. Russell) iv 16
[4] *id.* iv 20 [5] *Five Disputations &c.* p. 383

Churches that did not use them. To insist upon set forms as the only acceptable way of worshipping God was to equate human decisions with Divine imperatives.

'It is a grievous plague to our people's souls to be led into these mistakes, and to think that Circumstances and things indifferent are matters of Necessity.'[1]

Whilst many Puritans were prepared to accept the occasional use of set forms of prayer, they conscientiously refused to submit to the imposition of the Book of Common Prayer as the only adequate way of worshipping God. The illogicality and manifest unfairness of the imposition of the Prayer Book by Charles II is condemned by Vavasor Powell, a leader amongst the Baptists:[2]

'Either such Liturgies or Common Prayers are indifferent, or not indifferent; if indifferent, then they are not to be imposed upon Christians, but they are to be left to their liberty, as Christians were left by the Apostles; but if it be not indifferent, then unless a *Prescript* can be shewed from God (it being in his Worship) it is no less than Will-Worship, forbidden *Col.*2.23.'

Thus the Puritans protested against raising a Prayer Book, composed originally for the convenience of English Christians in corporate worship, to the dignity of an essential in the worship of God. Only the Divine ordinances were essential to the worship of God, said the Puritans, who were careful to differentiate the commands of the Divine Majesty from the prescriptions of men. It seemed to them that such an imposition of set forms of prayer was both an infringement of their liberty as Christians as well as a trespassing upon the Divine preserves. Whilst the Establishment under the influence of the Monarchy sought to impose a particular technique of prayer upon the whole Church in a national rather than in a religious interest, the Puritans protested, not in the interests of a different technique, but as the proud preservers of the rights of Christ, infringed by the earthly monarch. It was a point of principle for the Puritans, a matter of technique for the majority of the Established clergy. The Puritans chose to be rebels to a terrestrial potentate that they might serve the celestial King according to their conscience.

[1] *ibid.* [2] *Common Prayer-Book No Divine Service* (1661) p. 7

(iv) A further criticism of the constant use of set prayers was that they conduce to hypocrisy. Either familiarity breeds contempt, or it simulates an attitude which is not really felt. It produces a mere lip-service. As Watts expresses it,[1]

'Sometimes we shall be tempted to express those things which are not the very thoughts of our own souls, and so use words that are not suited to our present wants, or sorrows, or requests; because those words are put together and made ready before hand.'

(v) The final charge against set forms of prayer is that their imposition has brought persecution in its train. John Owen accuses the imposers of liturgies of bringing 'fire and faggot into the Christian religion'.[2] The same point is made by the anonymous author of a pamphlet entitled, *A Reasonable Account of . . . the Prescribed Forms of others*, who claims that the result of imposition has been 'a floud of iniquity'. Among these iniquities he mentions[3] 'suspensions, silencings, imprisonments, ruins of God's servants' and the divided Christian communions.

Together this array of five charges appears formidable: the deprivation of the gifts of minister and people; the unsuitability for varied needs and occasions; the obsession produced that they were essential to the worship of God; the production of hypocrisy in divine service; and the persecution that appeared to be consequent upon their imposition. They appear to constitute an invincible defence of free prayer. It is not, however, to be supposed that the upholders of the Prayer Book had no counter-criticisms to offer.

The chief critic of extemporizing in prayer was Jeremy Taylor. He characterized this type of prayer in the second of *Two Discourses*[4] as 'Prayer ex tempore, or By pretence of the Spirit'. His chief objection was that this type of prayer was produced by mental laziness:[5]

'I consider that the true state of the Question is only this, Whether it is better to pray to God with consideration, or without? Whether is the wiser men of the two, hee who thinks, and deliberates what to say, or he that utters his mind as fast as it comes?'

[1] *Guide to Prayer; Works* iv 127

[2] *A Discourse of the Work of the Holy Spirit in Prayer; Works* (ed. Russell) iv 23

[3] (London 1679) p. 129*f* [4] (London 1682) p. 1 [5] *ibid.*

This very facility of extempore prayer laid itself open to great abuse and Jeremy Taylor anticipated Isaac Watts in this criticism. The latter demanded that extempore prayer should only be used after intensive preparation. Otherwise it would be 'an entire dependence on sudden motions and suggestions of thought'.[1]

Jeremy Taylor makes the further point that extempore prayer may tend more to ostentation than to edification. Watts is also aware of this defect, which often issues in extravagant expressions calculated rather to glorify the one praying than to produce reverence towards the Divine Majesty. He divides such improper expressions under the following categories: foreign, obsolete, over-Latinized, philosophical.[2]

A third objection to free prayers is that the people cannot give their free assent to such prayers until they have carefully considered them. Jeremy Taylor asserts:[3]

'I am sure if the people be intelligent and can disern, they are hindered in their Devotion, for they dare not say *Amen* till they have considered; and many such cases will occurre in *ex tempore* prayers that need much considering before we can attest them.'

A fourth criticism is made by Dr Hammond in his *View of the New Directory*[4]. He claims that the ability for 'praying in public without any premeditation, discreetly and reverently' is not given to every Minister,

'some men of very excellent abilities wanting that suddaine promptnesse of elocution, and choice of words for all their conceptions, others being modest and bashfull, and not endued with this charisma of boldnesse, which is a great part, a speciall ingredient of that which is here called the gift of prayer.'[5]

It was a weakness in the Puritan plea for free prayer that it assumed as a matter of course that all ministers could express themselves felicitously, fluently and publicly.

The charges against extempore prayer are put comprehensively by Hooker:[6]

'To him which considereth the grievous and scandalous inconveniences whereunto they make themselves daily subject, with whom any blind and secret corner is judged a fit house of Common Prayer; the manifold

[1] *Works* iv 125 [2] *id.* iv 145 [3] *id.* iv. 26
[4] (Oxford 1646) p. 84*f* [5] *ibid.* [6] *Eccl. Pol.* V xxv 5

confusions they fall into, where every man's private spirit and gift (as they term it) is the only Bishop that ordaineth him to this Ministry; the irksome deformities whereby, through endless and senseless effusions of indigested Prayers, they oftentimes disgrace in most insufferable manner the worthiest part of Christian duty towards God, who herein are subject to no certain order, but pray both what and how they list; to him, I say, which weigheth duly all these things, the reasons cannot be obscure why God doth in public Prayer so much respect the solemnity of places where, the authority and calling of persons by whom, and the precise appointment even with what words or sentences his name should be called on amongst his people.'

The above citation, whilst laying bare the abuses of Puritan prayers, also succeeds in adumbrating the Anglican conception of prayer.

It is significant that neither the Puritans nor the Established clergy had unworthy conceptions of prayer. Their definitions prove this. Hooker describes prayer and doctrine as

'these two ghostly exercises . . . His heavenly inspirations and our holy desires are as so many angels of intercourse and commerce between God and us.'[1]

This definition of prayer is similar to that of Isaac Watts:[2]

'It is that converse, which God hath allowed us to maintain with himself above, while we are here below. It is that language, wherein a creature holds correspondence with his Creator; and wherein the soul of a saint gets near to God, is entertained with great delight, and, as it were, dwells with his Heavenly Father for a short season before he comes to heaven.'

If the end of prayer was conceived alike by both parties, how are we to explain their differences? They were confident that only their means could achieve the end desired. As is common in the most hotly disputed controversies, they were each aware of the weaknesses of their opponents, but unaware of the advantages of their type of prayer. If the Anglicans are to be charged with insensitivity towards the Puritan values, the Puritans were for the most part unwilling to recognize any worth in set forms of prayer. If the Anglican missed the spontaneity, simplicity, intimacy and purity of free prayer, the Puritan equally overlooked the uniformity, dignity, catholicity and order of the Book of Common Prayer. The modern reader

[1] *id.* V xxiii [2] *Works* iv 111

is perplexed that both types of prayer were regarded as mutually exclusive, rather than complementary. The reason is to be found in the obstinacy with which the Anglicans pleaded for tradition and the obduracy with which the Puritans claimed the sanction of the New Testament. Controversy, far from producing an accommodation, resulted in an acrimonious consolidation of positions and, after the Ejection of 1662, in petrifaction.

The history of this controversy shows, however, that at various points set prayers and extempore prayers were not regarded as mutually exclusive. Hooker, for instance, is quick to point out that not all Puritans were in opposition to set prayers:[1]

'Now, albeit the Admonitioners did seem at the first to allow no prescript form of Prayer at all, but thought it the best that their Minister should always be left at liberty to pray as his discretion did serve; yet because this opinion upon better advice they afterwards retracted, their defender and his associates have sithence proposed to the world a form such as themselves like.'

This form of Prayer proposed by the Puritans was *A Book of the Form of Common Prayers tendered to the Parliament*. It was preferred to the Book of Common Prayer since it was 'agreeable to Gods Word and the use of the Reformed Churches'. The very title shows that it was Presbyterian in character and derived originally from John Knox's Genevan Service Book. This was probably the book which was published by Waldegrave in 1584 or 1585. Suffice it for the present to note that the Puritans of the right wing were not in opposition to the Prayer Book in principle, but simply because of the corruptions in the particular 'Book of Common Prayer' established for national use in England.

Indeed the Puritan tradition, which originated from the practice of the Church at Geneva under John Calvin, made use of set forms of prayer. Calvin himself had written to the Lord Protector in the reign of King Edward VI:

'Quod ad formulam precum & rituum Ecclesiasticorum, valde probo, ut certe illa extet, a qua pastoribus discedere in functione sua non liceat, tam ut consulatur quorundam simplicitati & imperitiae, quam ut certius ita constet omnium inter se Ecclesiarum consensus. Postremo etiam, ut

[1] *Eccl. Pol.* V xxvii 1

obviam eatur desultoriae quorundam levitati, qui novationes quasdam affectant. Sic igitur statum esse catechismum oportet, statam sacramentorum administrationem, publicam item precum formulam.'[1]

The earlier Puritans were perfectly true to the Calvinist tradition in using their own form of liturgy, as also in deploring the corruptions of the Book of Common Prayer. Calvin had written to Knox in this vein of the 'multas tolerabiles ineptias' in the Book of Common Prayer.[2]

The Reforming Puritans amongst the Frankfort exiles were in favour of a reformed liturgy; the Presbyterians of Elizabeth's time, as we have seen, presented a liturgy to Parliament for acceptance; the same reformed liturgy was in use in Scotland for the year 1566; a reformed liturgy was also in regular use in the Puritan Church at Middleburgh; it was also proposed as the Prayer Book of the Commonwealth.[3] Moreover at the Westminster Assembly when the Parliamentary Directory was produced, the Divines allowed set forms as well as free prayer. Finally, Baxter's 'Savoy Liturgy' proves that the Puritans had not abandoned in 1661 the idea that formularies might be an acceptable way of worshipping God. If this tradition was still operative as late as the Restoration, how is the suspicion with which the set forms of prayer were regarded to be explained?

Undoubtedly because the right-wing and left-wing Puritans were thrown together in a common attack against the Established Book in the days of the Commonwealth. In this emergency the views of the Independents preponderated and they stood uncompromisingly for extempore prayer. As a modern Independent has shown, their intransigeance rested upon Bibliolatry. John Owen must take the chief responsibility for this reverence for the very silences of Scripture which prevented the Independents from any participation in liturgical worship. This is contained in Owen's tract, 'Twelve arguments against any conformity of members of separate churches to the national church' which was passed round in MS. before 1684. There the cardinal proposition reads:[4]

[1] cited in *A Godly Treatise &c.* p. 32

[2] *A Brief Discourse of the Troubles begun at Frankfort* (ed. cit.) p. 51

[3] McMillan *The Worship of the Scottish Reformed Church* p. 71

[4] cited by F. J. Powicke in *Essays Congregational and Catholic* (ed. Peel, London 1931) p. 300

'. . . that God's worship hath no accidentals, that all that is in it and belonging to it, and the manner of it, is false worship, if it have not a divine institution in particular; that all liturgies, as such, are such false worship (and not the English only)—used to defeat Christ's promise of gifts and God's spirit.'

Such a dogmatic statement by the leader of the Independents made accommodation impossible, whilst also rendering any negotiations entered upon by Presbyterians with Anglicans, liable to the charge of desertion. The intractability of the Independents, coupled with the Act of Uniformity, made a divergence between the streams of Anglican and Puritan worship even wider, and rendered all hopes of their ultimate confluence vain for well over two centuries. Baxter's was the last attempt at comprehension and, whilst the Independents frowned upon it and the Established Church refused to receive it, it did not sacrifice the essential Puritan ideals in worship. For it fulfilled the following conditions: it was agreeable to the Word of God; it was intended for the edification of the worshippers; it was consonant with the liturgies of the Reformed Churches; it was not to be imposed so rigorously as to exclude the extempore prayers of the Ministers. It was admittedly produced in fourteen days, but the main parts of it had been already in use in Baxter's Church in Kidderminster.[1] It was a valiant attempt to combine the virtues of both traditions but it was neither Puritan nor Anglican in pedigree but a mongrel; with the inevitable result that it was disowned by both parents.

This controversy was not entirely unproductive of good, however. For it prompted later Nonconformists to reconsider the abuses to which extempore prayer was prone. Indirectly it produced two valuable Puritan manuals of prayer, which attempted to save Puritan prayer from its two chief dangers, infelicity of phraseology and disordered rambling, by stressing the need for preparation and consideration. The two authors, whose work remains to be considered, were Matthew Henry and Isaac Watts. The former produced in 1710 *A Method of Prayer with Scripture Expressions Proper to be Us'd under each Head*, whilst the latter produced the classic Independent manual, *A Guide to Prayer*, in 1716. These two writers did much to re-invigorate Puritan prayer and they had learned

[1] F. J. Powicke *A Life of the Reverend Richard Baxter* (London 1924) p. 95

from the controversies of their predecessors. Matthew Henry had departed from the radical views of the left-wing Puritans to a just recognition of the need for ordering prayers according to plan:

'And it is requisite to the decent Performance of the Duty, that some proper Method be observ'd, not only that what is said be good, but that it be said in its proper Place and Time; and that we offer not any thing to the Glorious Majesty of Heaven and Earth, which is confus'd, impertinent, and indigested.'[1]

The same author cautions his readers to 'observe a Decorum in our Words, that they be well-chosen, well-weighed, well-placed'.[2] The sounds of the earlier controversy were muffled, but the Puritans, at least, had learned valuable lessons from the interchange of views.

[1] *A Method of Prayer &c.* (London 1710) p. A4 *recto* [2] *ibid.*

## CHAPTER IX

## PURITAN PRAYER-BOOKS

It will have been seen that whilst Puritans preferred extemporary prayers to liturgies, they did not condemn the moderate use of set forms of prayer. Indeed the opposition of the more radical Puritans was only to the Established liturgy—the Book of Common Prayer, to the exclusion of free prayer. Even then, it appears, it was the principle of subscription, rather than the formulary to be subscribed, that prevented the Puritans from remaining in the Established Church. The Puritan tradition in fact even recommended the use of formularies of prayer. Chapter III has already shown that the 'Frankfort Troubles' originated as a clash between two liturgical parties, each of which was firmly convinced of the need of a formulary for public worship. They disagreed as to which of the two formularies of prayer was to be authoritative. At no point in the discussion was it suggested that free prayer was to take the place of a formulary. The point at issue was: which prayer-book was to be accepted? The Coxians were in favour of the retention of the Second Prayer Book of King Edward VI, whilst the Knoxians (the Puritans) favoured a formulary which approximated more closely to Calvin's *Forme of Prayers*.

The moderate Puritans, made up mainly of Presbyterians, did not cease to hope that a prayer-book more in accordance with Scriptural directions might be produced which would prove acceptable to the Established Church. Indeed they made three attempts to produce such a prayer-book. Thomas Cartwright proposed in 1582 to obtain Parliament's approval for a prayer-book on the Genevan model; in 1644 the Westminster Assembly of Divines produced *A Directory for the Public Worship of God*, which was more of a manual than a formulary, but which contained model prayers for worship. The final attempt at an eirenical prayer-book was made in 1661 by Richard Baxter in the 'Savoy Liturgy', or, to give it its original title, *The Reformation of the Liturgy, as it was presented to the Right Reverend Bishops by the Divines appointed by His Majesties Commission to treat with them about the alteration of it.* These documents, as also the prayer-book used by English

Puritans in Middleburgh, prove conclusively that the main stream of the Puritan tradition was in favour of liturgical prayer, provided that this did not exclude free prayer. In this they were faithfully following their leader Calvin, and the very prayer-books they produced give evidence in form and in content of their Calvinist inspiration. A careful survey of the Appendix on Reformed Liturgies[1] demonstrates this conclusively. The parent work is Calvin's *La Forme* originating in Geneva in 1542; the transmission of this tradition is effected mainly through John Knox's Genevan Service Book; the liturgical offspring are:[2] *A Book of the Forme of Common Prayers &c* published by Waldegrave in London about the year 1584, *A Book of the Form of Common Prayers &c* of Middleburgh (editions in 1586, 1587 and 1602), the Parliamentary Directory of 1644 and the Savoy Liturgy of 1661. These now fall to be considered in turn.

## I

The first entirely Puritan prayer-book to be printed was *The Forme of Prayers and Ministrations of the Sacraments, etc., used in the English Congregation at Geneva: and approved by the famous and godly learned man, Iohn Caluyn.* This appeared in 1556 and was printed in Geneva. Its more common description of 'John Knox's Genevan Service Book' provides the clue to its authorship, although it was actually produced by a committee under the direction of Knox. Its genesis is described in detail in 'The Troubles at Frankfort'[3] and has been summarized in an earlier chapter.[4] The Marian exiles at Frankfort were all zealous for the reformation of the Church of England. They consisted of two parties: one, the more conservative, regarded the Second Prayer Book of King Edward VI as the highwater mark of the English Reformation and, since martyrs had died in its defence, resolved to honour their memory by a faithful retention of it. Others, more radical Puritans, regarded it as a step in the right direction but felt that the exiles now had the opportunity of proceeding further in the way of a more complete reformation according to the Word of God.

[1] see below, Appendix A

[2] reprinted by Peter Hall in *Reliquiæ Liturgicæ* (1847) (vol. i, Middleburgh Liturgy; vol. iii, The Directory; vol. iv, The Savoy Liturgy) and in *Fragmenta Liturgica* (1848) vol. i: Puritan (containing the Waldegrave Liturgy)

[3] ed. cit. [4] see above, Chapter III

The 'Troubles at Frankfort' describes the unsuccessful but zealous attempts to reach comprehension. In all, four such attempts were made. The Anglicans and Calvinists first agreed on an interim order of worship which was to be used until such time as they should have prepared a permanent prayer-book. This consisted of: Scripture Sentences and Exhortation; a Confession of sins; a metrical Psalm; a Prayer for the Holy Spirit; a Scripture Reading and Sermon; a General Prayer to be followed by the Lord's Prayer; the recitation of the Apostles' Creed; a metrical Psalm and the Blessing: 'The peace of God, etc.'. It was agreed that the Litany and responses, as well as the surplice, should be discarded. The result was an order of service which was Calvinist not Anglican in structure. Indeed, the only specifically Anglican item in the order was the form of the concluding Blessing.

Six months later, in December 1554, when Knox had accepted the invitation to become Minister, a second proposal was made: namely, that Huycke's translation of Calvin's orders of service should be used. This was not agreed to by Knox who first required the sanction of the other Marian exiles in other cities and who yet refused on principle to celebrate Communion according to the Second Prayer-Book. This resulted in an impasse.

The third proposal was made by Lever who came from Zurich as associate Minister with Knox. He proposed to end a difficult situation by drawing up an entirely independent order, based neither upon the Book of Common Prayer nor on the Genevan order. The suggestion was at first rejected. But after Calvin's opinion of the Anglican order had been sought, another attempt was made to find an order agreeable to all the Frankfort exiles. In January 1555 a committee, consisting of Calvinists, was appointed to produce the new order. The members of that committee were: Knox, Whittingham, Gilby, Fox and Cole. This was rejected by the congregation and appears never to have been used in Frankfort.

The fourth proposal was made a month later. The committee this time consisted of two Anglicans (Parry and Lever) and two Calvinists (Knox and Whittingham). They produced 'The Liturgy of Compromise'.[1] This was accepted and was in

[1] Sprott *The Liturgy of Compromise* (Church Service Society publication of 1905)

use for almost three months, when the arrival of a new contingent of uncompromising Anglicans headed by Dr Cox succeeded in rejecting the 'compromise' order and in banishing Knox from Frankfort.

Knox was received most amicably in Geneva by Calvin and he was joined there by the most extreme Calvinists from Frankfort. Here the Council granted the English exiles the use of the Church of Marie la Nove; this they were to share with the Italian refugees. While the decision of the Council was pending, the English congregation organized itself under the leadership of Christopher Goodman and Anthony Gilby as Ministers. Knox was the obvious choice as Minister but at the time he was out of Geneva. On his return, early in 1556, he became Minister. He has left on record a testimony to the happy tranquillity that reigned in this congregation during his ministry:[1]

> 'This place . . . is the maist perfyt schoole of Chryst that ever was in the erth since the dayis of the Apostillis.'

The primary task of the congregation was to frame a suitable order of service. This time no compromise was necessary since there were no Anglicans to placate. Moreover they already had to hand the form which the Calvinist committee had drawn up in Frankfort.[2] With little alteration this was taken, a Preface was added, together with fifty metrical psalms translated into English and an English translation of Calvin's Catechism. It was published on the 10th of February 1556 as *The Forme of Prayers and Ministration of the Sacraments, etc., used in the English Congregation at Geneva: and approved by the famous and godly learned man, Iohn Caluyn.*

This English congregation at Geneva which had produced the new order was the cradle of English Puritanism and its liturgy is of paramount importance as an influence on Puritan worship. The exiles who returned to England were so devoted to the book that they brought copies of it with them. These, with the minimum of adaptation, were printed in England for the worship of Puritan congregations in England and in exile on the Continent. They were superseded only by the introduc-

[1] *Works* (ed. Laing, 1855) iv 240

[2] *viz.* the third proposal mentioned above

tion of the Parliamentary Directory of 1644, which was itself modelled upon the Genevan Service Book.

The origin and importance of 'The Forme of Prayers' has been sufficiently treated. Its dependence upon Calvin has been conclusively shown by W. D. Maxwell.[1] It now remains to describe the contents. The Sunday Morning Service consists of the following items:

1. A Confession of sins
2. A Prayer for pardon
3. A metrical Psalm
4. A Prayer for illumination
5. Scripture Reading
6. Sermon
(7. Baptisms and publication of Banns)
8. Long Prayer and Lord's Prayer
9. Apostles' Creed (*recited by the Minister*)
10. A metrical Psalm
11. The Blessing (Aaronic or Apostolic)

This form of service is Calvinist in three main characteristics. It is Biblical, didactic and congregational. Its Biblical basis is seen in the opening Confession of Sins, based largely on the 9th chapter of the Book of Daniel; in the use of metrical psalms; and in the preference for Biblical Blessings as compared with the Anglican Blessing ('The peace of God . . .') which was used in the original interim order at Frankfort. It is didactic in that the climax of the service is approached by a prayer for Illumination, and reached in the reading and exposition of the Word of God; whilst the Apostles' Creed immediately precedes the closing acts of worship. Its congregational character is shown by the singing of two metrical psalms and by the particular intercessions for the members of the mystical Body of Christ in the Intercessory prayer, as also in the personal and intimate petition with which this prayer opens. The clearest indication of Calvinism is, of course, the extreme statement of the doctrine of original sin so dominant in the Confession with which the service begins.

The Order for the Lord's Supper contains the following items:

[1] *The Liturgical Portions of the Genevan Service Book* (Edinburgh & London 1931)

1. Words of Institution and Exhortation
2. The Eucharistic Prayer (containing Adoration, Thanksgiving for Creation and Redemption, Anamnesis, Doxology)
3. Fraction
4. Delivery
5. People's Communion whilst Scripture is read
6. Post-communion Thanksgiving
7. Psalm 103 in metre
8. Blessing (Aaronic or Apostolic)

This order is also simple in character but, except on the grounds of the omission of an epiclesis, it cannot be accused of incompleteness. The 'Sursum Corda', as W. D. Maxwell notes,[1] is paraphrased in the last paragraph of the Exhortation. Communion was received sitting by the congregation who remained in their pews. The Sacrament was celebrated monthly.

The Order for Baptism consisted of the six following items:

1. The Interrogation (immediately following the Sermon)
2. Lengthy Exhortation and Explanation
3. Recitation of the Apostles' Creed by the father or (in his absence) by the godfather
4. Prayer for grace and the reception of the child into Christ's kingdom, and the Lord's Prayer
5. Baptism in the Triune Name
6. Concluding Thanksgiving

Here, again, the didactic element predominates. The Exhortation appears to have Anabaptists in mind in its disclaimer:[2]

'Neither is it requisite that all those that receyve this sacramente haue the vse of vnderstanding and faythe but chiefelye that they be conteyned vnder the name of gods people.'

The responsibility of both parents and the Church in providing for the nurture of the child in the faith is made much of in the Interrogation, the Exhortation and the recitation of the Creed and in the repeating of the Lord's Prayer. But whilst the importance of Baptism is declared, it is not assumed that unbaptized children are damned. The following disclaimer is

[1] *op. cit.* p. 132 [2] *op. cit.* p. 106

ostensibly aimed at the Roman Catholic conception of Baptism:

'Neither yet is this owteward action of suche necessitie, that the lacke thereof shuld be prejudiciall to their saluation, yf that preuented by deathe thei may not conueniently be presented to the church.'[1]

This service is both solemn and simple.

The Marriage Service, whilst Calvinist in character, has more affinity with the Edwardian Prayer Book. It contains the following parts:

1. Exhortation
2. Charge to confess any impediments
3. Mutual declaration of acceptance by contracting persons
4. Exhortation on the permanence of marriage with Gospel lection from the 19th chapter of St. Matthew, with charge to live in holiness to God and fidelity to one another
5. Commendation in prayer
6. Psalm 128

Marriage took place in the church in the presence of the congregation. The ring was not used by the early Reformers. It was regarded as superstition and was one of the 'nocent ceremonies' which Puritans complained against in the successive criticisms they made of the Book of Common Prayer.

No order for a Burial Service is provided. The following directions, however, are given:[2]

'OF BVRIALL. The Corps is reuerently brought to the graue, accompagnied with the congregation, with owte any further ceremonies, which beyng buriede, the minister goeth to the churche, if it be not farre of, and maketh some comfortable exhortacion to the people, towchyng deathe, and the resurrection.'

These brief directions may be filled out by the following description of a funeral given by the Calvinist Pullain:[3]

'Funus effertur a certis hominibus extra urbem in coemiterium. Sequuntur proximi ac tota Ecclesia magna cum modestia, preeunte Pastore, vel aliquo ministro. Vbi ad locum ventum est, condito humi cadauere, habetur breuis concio de morte ac resurrectione mortuorum, cum com-

[1] *ibid.* [2] *op. cit.* p. 161 [3] cited by Maxwell *op. cit.* p. 163

mendatione defuncti, si quas habuerit virtutes, quarum exemplis possit Ecclesia aedificari. Tum facta oratione pro Ecclesia, vt Deus det sic vitam hanc transigere, vt per mortem transeamus in regnum ipsius, ac tandem in ultimo die per Christum omnes resurgamus ad beatam immortalitatem, dimittitur populus cum admonitione, vt eleemosynam aliquam conferat in vsus pauperum.'

The brief, bare service allowed by the Genevan Service Book was dictated by fear of superstition. The English compilers wished to avoid any recurrence of prayers offered to the dead or on their behalf. The same fear dictated the directions for burial in the Westminster Directory. Hence the burial rite is the barest of forms in this book.

## II

The Genevan Service Book, it has been claimed, had a profound influence upon the worship of the English Puritans. Evidence of the use of it has been shown in an earlier chapter.[1] Two versions of it, with relatively unimportant changes, were current among English Puritan congregations. The first of these was used in England, the second by the Puritan exiles in Middleburgh.

The first of these was published by Waldegrave and entitled *A booke of the forme of common prayers, administration of the Sacraments, &c. agreeable to Gods Worde, and the vse of the reformed Churches*. The frontispiece bears no date. It is conjectured by Dr W. D. Maxwell[2] that it was printed about 1584 or 1585. Little is known of the history of the Waldegrave Liturgy, except that it was published in London. Its publication was not, however, unnoticed by the Elizabethan ecclesiastical authorities. Both Bancroft and Hooker refer to it. From Bancroft we learn that the book was presented to Parliament in 1584 and that, prior to its introduction to the Low Countries in 1587, its use was almost exclusively confined to Northamptonshire, under the direction of a certain Edmund Snape, a notorious Puritan. Bancroft alludes to the formulary to substantiate his criticism that the Puritans, who claimed liberty to worship God according to their consciences and the Word of God, yet proposed, should Parliament give consent,

[1] see above, Chapter III [2] *op. cit.* p. 75

to make the book exclusively authoritative in public worship. He writes:[1]

'In the Parliament (27 of her Majesty, as I remember) the Brethren, having made another Book, termed at that time "A Booke of the Forme of Common Prayers, &c." and containing in it the effect of their whole pretended Discipline; the same book was penned, altogether statute and law-like, and their petition in the behalf of it was, *viz.* "May it therefore please your Majesty, &c. that it may be enacted, &c. that the Book hereunto annexed, &c. intitled, A Booke of the Forme of Common Prayers, Administration of the Sacraments, &c. and everything therein contained, may be from henceforth authorized, put in use, and practised throughout all your Majesty's dominions." See here, when they hoped to have attained to their purposes by law, and to have had the same accordingly established, they offered to the Parliament a book of their own, for the "Form of Common Prayers, &c." and thought it (as it seemeth) altogether inconvenient to leave every Minister to his own choice to use what form he list, other than such as were allowed in some church which had received the Discipline: for any such they liked of indefinitely.'

Hooker refers to the Waldegrave Liturgy in Section xxvii of Book V of *The Laws of Ecclesiastical Polity:* 'Of them who allowing a set Form of Prayer, yet allow not ours'. He claims that the Puritans originally proposed to leave the ordering of public prayer to the discretion of the individual Minister, but that later they came to see the value of a formulary.

'Now, albeit the Admonitioners did seem at the first to allow no prescript form of Prayer at all, but thought it the best that their Minister should always be left at liberty to pray as his own discretion did serve; yet because this opinion upon better advice they afterwards retracted, their defender and his associates have sithence proposed to the world a form such as themselves like.'[2]

The evidence of Bancroft, corroborated by Hooker, is of considerable interest for two reasons. Firstly, it shows the moderate Puritans moving in a direction towards prescribed forms of prayer and away from free prayer. Perhaps the license (as they would conceive it) of the Brownists or other groups of Dissenters had confirmed them in this view. The second suggestion of interest is that the 'Admonitioners' were responsible for the issuing of the Waldegrave Liturgy, as of the Middle-

[1] *Dangerous Positions* (1595) III x 96*f* [2] xxvii 1

burgh Liturgy. Waldegrave was undoubtedly the publisher for the Puritans and, as he had issued in 1584 the 'Brief and Plain Declaration concerning the Desires of all those Faithful Ministers that have and do seek for the Discipline and Reformation of the Church of England', it would be the natural sequel to publish in the same or the following year the desiderated form of worship for a reformed Church of England. It seems more than likely that Cartwright, who issued the first *Admonition to Parliament* was responsible for the Waldegrave Liturgy and for the subsequent editions of it which were printed in Middleburgh, after the Star Chamber had prohibited a second issue to be printed in 1585.

Two lines of evidence point to the conclusion that Cartwright or his sympathizers, Travers or Dudley Fenner, were responsible for the Waldegrave Liturgy. In the first place, as we have seen, the prohibition of the printing of a second edition of the Waldegrave Liturgy by the Star Chamber, necessitated a reprint being issued in Middleburgh. Cartwright himself had ministered to the English congregation there and his friend, Dudley Fenner, was at Middleburgh in 1586. The second line of evidence is Cartwright's 'A Directory of Church Government anciently contended for, and, as far as the times would suffer, practised by the first Nonconformists in the days of Queen Elizabeth, found in the study of the most accomplished divine Mr Thomas Cartwright, after his decease'.[1] Under the heading: 'Of the Office of the Ministers of the Word; and first of the Order of Liturgy or Common Prayer', he gives an outline of the proposed service. Its plan is as follows:

1. Psalm
2. Exhortation to Worship
3. Prayer of General Confession and Prayer of Pardon
4. Lord's Prayer
5. (Reading and) Sermon
6. Prayers of Petition and Intercession for the Church
7. Lord's Prayer
8. Psalm
9. Aaronic or Apostolic Blessing

A comparison of this order with the Sunday Morning order of

[1] Neal *History of the Puritans* (1822) vol. V, appendix 4

the Waldegrave Liturgy shows an essential similarity of structure. Three alterations only can be detected. In the Cartwright order the first Psalm introduces the service, in the Waldegrave order it follows the Confession; in the Cartwright order the Decalogue and the Apostles' Creed are omitted, although the petition for grace which precedes the Intercessions begs 'for grace to profit by the doctrine delivered, the principal heads thereof being remembered';[1] and, thirdly, the Cartwright order introduces an exhortation for preparing the minds of the worshippers to pray to God. The essential similarity of the two orders is shown in the introductory prayer which begins with a confession of sin both original and actual and which ends with a prayer for pardon. Similarly, in both orders the Long Prayer begins with a petition for grace and opens out into an intercession for the Universal Church and for all estates and degrees of the people. The ending with Lord's Prayer, Psalm and Blessing is the same in each case. There can, therefore, be little doubt that Cartwright's order is based upon the Waldegrave order and that he or another of the 'Admonitioners' was responsible for issuing the Waldegrave Liturgy and the reprints of it made in Middleburgh.

The Waldegrave and Middleburgh orders are based literally upon *The Forme of Prayers* which Whittingham and Knox had published in Geneva in 1556. The structural similarity of all three may easily be discerned in the Appendix on this subject.[2] In the Sunday Morning Service the Waldegrave and Middleburgh orders make one alteration in the Genevan order. They both commence their service with Scripture sentences inviting to worship; whereas the Genevan order began with the prayer of Confession. Furthermore, both allow alternative prescribed prayers of Intercession and even (if desired) an extempore prayer of Intercession. The Waldegrave order adds to the Apostles' Creed in the Genevan order the recitation of the Decalogue; the Middleburgh order omits both. Apart from these minor alterations, all three orders agree in their order of worship on the Lord's day. In their orders for Baptism and the Lord's Supper, all three agree exactly; as also in their orders for a Marriage service. The Waldegrave and Middleburgh orders make no religious provision for burials, whilst the Genevan book reduces the burial service to its barest essentials.

[1] Hall *Reliquiæ Liturgicæ* p. xv [2] see below, Appendix A

The only other difference between the Genevan book and the Waldegrave and Middleburgh orders is that the latter orders manifest the Scriptural warrant of their forms of worship by marginal references to substantiate each statement contained in their exhortations and confessions of faith. The spirit of all three orders is summarized in the appended comment in all three to the order for the Lord's Supper.[1] Their aim has been

'that Christ might witness to our faith, as it were with his own mouth ... so that, without his word and warrant, there is nothing in this holy action attempted.'

In ethos, in structure and verbally the three orders are agreed. The few and unimportant verbal changes made by the Waldegrave and Middleburgh orders are in the interests of clarity and solemnity. As an instance of the former, the archaism 'the Sacrament is a *singular* medicine for all poor sick creatures' in the Genevan Book is altered to 'excellent medicine'. A small instance of a verbal change in the interests of a greater seriousness is seen in the addition of the adjective 'heavy' to qualify 'wrath' in the following citation from the Genevan order: 'we kindle God's wrath against us' (in unworthy reception of the Lord's Supper). A polemical insertion into the list of those anathematized in the 'fencing' of the Lord's Table, in both the Waldegrave and Middleburgh Liturgies, reads: 'a maintainer of images, or man's inventions, in the service of God'. No other verbal changes are of any consequence.

If the Waldegrave and Middleburgh orders keep close to the Genevan original, the Middleburgh order is a word-for-word copy of the Waldegrave, as might be expected on the hypothesis that they are different editions of the same work. One significant addition is, however, made in the 1602 Middleburgh order. This includes the only complete Ordination order used in Puritan worship.

A consideration of the three liturgies, the *Forme of Prayers*, the Waldegrave and the Middleburgh, shews conclusively the Calvinistic basis of Puritanism and maintains its demand for a worship with Scriptural warrant. The association of Cartwright or other Presbyterian leaders with the Waldegrave and

[1] Maxwell *op. cit.* p. 128; Waldegrave: Hall *Fragmenta Liturgica* i 68; Middleburgh: Hall *Reliquiæ Liturgicæ* i 61

Middleburgh Liturgies, shews conclusively the preference of the moderate Puritans for a liturgical, rather than a charismatic, type of worship. This in itself, while not excluding but severely restricting free prayers, would tend to suggest that the Parliamentary Directory of 1644 was a compromise urged on the Presbyterians by the Independents. The natural development of Presbyterianism was towards a prescribed form of prayers, with alternatives and occasional opportunity for extemporary prayers. That the next prayer-book issued by the Presbyterians was a manual rather than a liturgy is conclusive proof that they were persuaded by the Independents, the heirs of the Brownists and Barrowists, to move in the direction of unprescribed prayer.

## III

The Parliamentary Directory shares with the Book of Common Prayer the distinction of being an officially recognized devotional manual, sanctioned by Parliament. In the summer of 1643 an ordinance of Cromwell was passed through both Houses of Parliament, directing that a Synod of divines and laymen should be convened to settle the church government and Liturgy of England. Accordingly the Westminster Assembly met. They provided a *Directory for the Public Worship of God in the three Kingdoms*. This Assembly was elected by Parliament. The representation was on a county basis; but the members also included ten peers, twenty members of the House of Commons and deputies from the Church of Scotland. The Episcopal clergy were invited but declined. Hence the business of the Assembly was left exclusively in the hands of Presbyterians and Independents. The Assembly numbered sixty-nine members in all, who first met in the year 1644.

It appears that at first nothing more than a revision of the existing Prayer Book was contemplated. This is confirmed by a declaration of Parliament made on April 9th, 1642, to the effect

> 'that they intend a due and necessary reformation and liturgy of the church, and to take away nothing in the one or the other but what shall be evil and justly offensive, or at least unnecessary and burdensome.'[1]

[1] Sprott & Leishman *The Book of Common Order &c.* p. 261

The existence of the Genevan Book, the Waldegrave and Middleburgh Liturgies, is proof positive that the Puritans did not object to a prayer-book on principle. Moreover, about half of the Presbyterian commissioners who attended the Savoy meeting with the Bishops in 1661, had been delegates to the Westminster Assembly. Even then, seventeen years later, they had not ceased to believe in the value of a liturgy. As we shall see later, the direction away from prescribed prayers was due to the influence of the small but vigorous group of Independents in the Assembly.

The preparation of the rough draft of a Directory was in the hands of a small sub-committee, consisting of Marshall (the Chairman), Palmer, Goodwin, Young, Herle and the Scots Commissioners. The composition of the sub-committee, which included only one Independent, Goodwin, accounts for the predominating Scottish character of the Directory, which is structurally based upon the Book of Common Order, a close relative of John Knox's Genevan Service Book, whilst Goodwin's presence is responsible for the many alternatives allowed and the variations from the Genevan Book.

The aims of the compilers of the Directory are sufficiently set forth in the Preface. They begin with a generous tribute to the Book of Common Prayer as the product of 'our wise and pious ancestors' who advanced the reformation of public worship according to the word of God by 'redress of many things which they then, by the word, discovered to be vain, erroneous, superstitious, and idolatrous in the public worship of God'.[1] Now the time has come to take another step in the same direction, especially as the Book of Common Prayer has 'proved an offence' to the other Reformed Churches, and by its insistence upon 'many unprofitable and burdensome ceremonies' has debarred many conscientious pastors from the discharge of their duties, since they could not conform to its requirements. It has had the further disadvantage of producing a negligent ministry, while its similarity to the Roman order of service has encouraged even Papists in their superstition and idolatry. It is therefore opportune for the compilers to 'answer the gracious providence of God, which at this time calleth upon us for further reformation'.[2] In conclusion they claim:

[1] Hall *Reliquiæ Liturgicæ* iii 13 [2] *id.* iii 17

'our care hath been to hold forth such things as are of Divine institution in every ordinance: and other things we have endeavoured to set forth according to the rules of Christian prudence, agreeable to the general rules of the word of God.'[1]

If their first aim is the divine sanction for their ordering of worship, the second is to achieve uniformity in worship:

'Our meaning therein being only that, the general heads, the sense and scope for the prayers, and other parts of worship being known to all, there may be a consent of all the Churches in those things that contain the substance of the service and worship of God.'[2]

The third aim is to provide, not an invariable prayer-book, but a general directory that 'the ministers may be hereby directed in their administrations to keep like soundness in doctrine and prayer' and that they may be provided with helps for prayer. It is therefore a manual rather than a prescribed liturgy. By it the ministers may

'if need be, have some help and furniture, and yet so as they become not hereby slothful and negligent in stirring up the gifts of Christ in them: but that each one, by meditation, by taking heed to himself and the flock of God committed to him, and by wise observing of the ways of Divine Providence, may be careful to furnish his heart and tongue with further or other materials of prayer and exhortation, as shall be needful upon all occasions.'[3]

The Directory, therefore, aimed at the merits of a prayer-book without its attendant disadvantages. It was to be Scriptural, comprehensive, orderly. But these merits in a prayer-book were not to be obtained by the suppression of the minister's gifts for extemporary prayer. It aimed at a marriage between order and liberty, which hitherto had been estranged.

The outstanding variations were those directed against previous usages. The majority of them had already been raised in Puritan apologetics and were therefore to be expected. These included the rejection of the Apocrypha in the Scripture lections, the discontinuance of private baptism and of godparents, the abolition of the sign of the cross and of the marriage-ring, as of the administration of the Lord's Supper to the sick. The Communion table was removed into the body

[1] *id.* iii 18 [2] *ibid.* [3] *id.* iii 18*f*

of the church, whilst sitting or standing were preferred to kneeling, as postures for the reception of the elements. All Saints' days were discarded, as were liturgical vestments. No service was appointed for the dead. No Creed is recited, nor are the Ten Commandments repeated in public worship. But both the Creed and the Decalogue were added to the Confession of Faith a year or two afterwards. These were the innovations that Puritans had contended for since the earliest days of Queen Elizabeth's reign.

All the Puritans, it appears, were agreed on the *delenda* but not on the *agenda*. Edwards of *Gangræna* fame informs us that some sectaries held that 'a Directory or Order to help in the way of worship is a breach of the second commandment'.[1] Indeed, Goodwin, a member of the sub-committee, was not far removed from this position. Criticism also came from another quarter. Dr Henry Hammond, a representative of the Episcopalians, in his *View of the New Directory*, makes much of its omissions. The chief amongst these are the absence of a service for the 'churching' of women and an inadequate burial rite.

The disagreement amongst the Puritans as to what items should be included in the Directory most probably accounts for the variety permitted and for the varying degrees of compulsion shown in various rubrics. Some things are urged peremptorily. Other rubrics are no more than recommendations, whilst others are mere permissions. As Leishman remarks:[2] 'In most cases the language used is sufficiently precise to show the force of each injunction. The obligation to a practice is not the same when it is called *necessary*, *requisite*, *expedient*, *convenient*, or *sufficient;* or when in one place the minister *is to*, or *shall*, in another *may*, do such and such things.'

The Lord's day services show an exact structural similarity to the Genevan *Form of Prayers*, as can be seen in the Appendix.[3] The service is to commence with the minister's 'solemn calling on them to the worshipping of the great name of God'. This custom of 'prefacing' was common both to the Book of Common Prayer and to the Book of Common Order. The introductory prayer begins, in characteristically Calvinist fashion, by lauding the majesty of God and declaring the

[1] *Gangræna* pt. i 31 [2] Sprott & Leishman *op. cit.* p. 238
[3] see below, Appendix A

'vileness and the unworthiness' of the worshippers to approach to him. The explicit inclusion of a confession of actual and original sin was made by the sub-committee as a corrective to its omission in the Book of Common Prayer.[1] In the Directory the opening prayer also includes a petition 'for a blessing on that particular portion of his word then to be read'. This was made the subject of a separate prayer in the *Forme of Prayers*. The alteration was made as a concession to the Independents, who, according to Baillie,[2] claimed the authority of I Tim. ii 1 for commencing with a comprehensive prayer.

Scripture readings are expressly confined to excerpts from the Canonical Writings. This was a departure from the lectionary of the Book of Common Prayer, which included passages from the Apocrypha. Moreover, in opposition to the short 'Epistle' and 'Gospel' read in the Book of Common Prayer it was judged convenient that at least one chapter from each of the Testaments should be read whilst even more might be added if either of the chapters was short. Also, that the people might learn the Scriptures thoroughly, it was prescribed that 'where the reading in either Testament endeth on one Lord's-day, it is to begin the next'. A running commentary upon Scripture is forbidden. Where it is desired to expound the Scriptures after reading them, it is insisted that this shall be done only after the complete passage has been read. The permission to expound the Scriptures was another concession made to the Independents.[3] The centrality and importance of the Scriptures in the service is clearly seen in the attempt to make the people acquainted with the whole of the Scriptures, in opposition to the 'anthologizing' tendency of the Anglican lectionary. Moreover the ministers are to exhort their charges to read the Scriptures privately and to possess a Bible.

After the lections and the succeeding psalm, a larger confession of sin is to be made. The aim is that the minister is

> 'to get his own and his hearers' hearts to be rightly affected with their sins, that they may all mourn in sense thereof before the Lord, and hunger and thirst after the grace of God in Jesus Christ . . .'[4]

The generalizations of the prayer of Confession in the Book of Common Prayer are replaced by the particularizations of the

[1] Sprott & Leishman *op. cit.* p. 332
[2] *A Dissuasive &c.* p. 118
[3] Sprott & Leishman *op. cit.* p. 333
[4] Hall *Rel. Lit.* iii 25

Parliamentary Directory. The same prayer then moves from confession and petition to intercession. This part of the prayer prays for the propagation of the Gospel to all nations, the conversion of the Jews, for all distressed Christians and for the Reformed Churches. It intercedes on behalf of the King, for the conversion of the Queen, for ministers, universities, schools and religious seminaries, for the particular city and congregation, and for the civil government, for those in distress and for seasonable weather and the averting of the judgments of God in famine, pestilence or sword. It concludes with the dedication of pastor and people to the Christian life. It is not regarded as necessary that the minister shall include all these petitions in the prayer preceding the sermon. Some of them may be deferred until the prayer after the sermon. The inclusion of all these petitions in one prayer was, apparently, another concession to the Independents; Baillie calls the long prayer

> 'a new fancy of the Independents, grounded on no solid reason, and contrair to all the practice of the Church, old or late, who divided always their prayers in more small parts, and did not have any one of a disproportionable length.'[1]

The directions 'Of the Preaching of the Word' presupposes not only a conscientious but a learned ministry, conversant with Hebrew and Greek and 'in such arts and sciences as are handmaids unto divinity'. Equally important are the requisite spiritual qualifications: he must know and believe in the Scriptures 'above the common sort of believers'. The construction of the sermon is to be perspicuous and based on the three-fold mode then current, of Doctrine, Reason and Use. The sermon, therefore, is to begin by an exposition of a text or passage of Scripture. Then follow the reasons why the doctrine is to be held, and finally an application of the doctrine to the practical exigencies of life, manifesting the practical advantages to be obtained from believing it. These directions are recommended, but not prescribed as necessary. The following general directions are given for the 'performance' of a minister's whole duty. It must be done 'painfully' (*i.e.* carefully), 'plainly', 'faithfully', 'wisely', 'gravely', 'with loving affection', and 'as taught of God'.[2] No directions are given on the vexed question as to whether sermons should be read or not. Apparently,

[1] cited Sprott & Leishman *op. cit.* p. 332 [2] Hall *op. cit.* iii 41*f*

however, sermons were not read in Scotland, but the practice was not unknown in England. Baillie, for instance, informs us that the Independent Nye was unpopular with his Scottish congregation in his Edinburgh visit because he had read a large part of his sermon.[1]

The sermon ended, a prayer of Thanksgiving ensues. This includes an acknowledgment of the benefits brought by the Gospel, 'as namely, election, vocation, adoption, justification, sanctification, and hope of glory'.[2] The advice is also offered 'to turn the chief and most useful heads of the sermon into some few petitions'. This, with the foregoing doctrinal acknowledgment, points to one of the weaknesses of Puritan prayer. It was excessively edifying. Adoration is too often forgotten in exhortation. Praying over the sermon again is the most acute instance of this defect. The prayer concludes with a petition for forgiveness. The Lord's Prayer is recommended not only as 'a pattern of prayer' (the Independent conception of it) but as 'itself a most comprehensive prayer'. It is, therefore, to be assumed that the prayer after the sermon concluded with the Lord's Prayer, although it could, no doubt, be used earlier in the service if desired. The fact that the Lord's Prayer is recommended, but not prescribed as a necessity, is further evidence of the compromise between the Presbyterian and Independent viewpoints. The freedom of extemporary prayer is guaranteed for the minister at the administration of the Sacrament and on days of thanksgiving and of humiliation. The service concludes with a psalm and a blessing.

There is no reference to the *Gloria Patri* with which the psalm up to this period usually ended. In the Assembly of 1645 Calderwood defended the usage as primitive and tried to dissuade the Assembly from abolishing it, exclaiming 'Let that alone, for I hope to sing it in glory'.[3] But his protest was unavailing. It is not surprising that the usage was abolished, since from early days the more radical Reformers had taken exception to it as an unscriptural practice.[4]

The Directory then proceeds to outline the order for the Sacrament of Baptism. This must be performed neither by a private person, nor in a private place. The Committee had in mind what they regarded as two current abuses of the Sacra-

[1] Sprott & Leishman *op. cit.* p. 338
[2] Hall *op. cit.* iii 43
[3] Sprott & Leishman *op. cit.* p. 339
[4] *cf. Zurich Letters* i 283

ment, which they were determined at all costs to avoid. In cases of extreme necessity, according to Anglican and Roman usage, a child might be baptized by a midwife in a private house. This practice originated from the belief that unbaptized children, still polluted by the stains of original sin, were damned. The Puritans, however, rejected the belief explicitly in the exhortation that the minister was required to give at Baptism:

'. . . outward baptism is not so necessary, that through the want thereof the infant is in danger of damnation, or the parents guilty, if they do not contemn or neglect the ordinance of Christ, when and where it may be had.'[1]

The rejection of the belief that unbaptized infants were damned made the practices of baptism by a midwife and in the home unnecessary.

It was also regarded as unwarrantable that god-parents, as in the Book of Common Prayer, should make the vows on behalf of the child being baptized. The duties of sponsorship are laid upon the father in the first instance and a substitute is allowed only in the event of his necessary absence. The Puritan emphasis on edification is again seen in the words of instruction given by the Minister before Baptism. He is to

'use some words of instructions, touching the institution, nature, use and ends of this Sacrament.'[2]

It is described as 'a seal of the covenant of grace' which clearly points to the Calvinist origin of the order. Any *ex opere operato* suggestion is disclaimed:

'. . . the inward grace and virtue of baptism is not tied to that very moment of time wherein it is administered.'[3]

The general instruction on the meaning of Baptism is to be followed by an admonition to the whole gathered Church and a particular exhortation to the parent

'to bring up the child in the knowledge of the grounds of the Christian religion, and in the nurture and admonition of the Lord . . . requiring his solemn promise for the performance of his duty.'[4]

Then follows a prayer 'for sanctifying the water to this spiritual use'. The name of the child is demanded, the Minister then

[1] Hall *op. cit.* iii 48 [2] *id.* iii 46 [3] *id.* iii 47 [4] *id.* iii 48*f*

baptizes the child by name in the Triune formula. The order concludes with a prayer that 'the Lord would so teach him by his word and Spirit, and make his baptism effectual to him . . .', so linking this formal reception of the child into the Church to the time when it is hoped he shall make his own confession of the faith. Sprinkling or pouring the water is prescribed as the method of Baptism. The administration of the Sacrament follows the general line of the Knox, Waldegrave and Middleburgh Liturgies, with one exception. The Apostles' Creed is not required to be recited by the parent. It appears that the Puritans disliked the custom, whilst some of the Independents objected to the Creed itself.[1] The most striking difference between the Directory order for Baptism and the order provided in the Book of Common Prayer is the absence in the former of the signing of the cross on the child's forehead, as a token of admission into the 'congregation of Christ's flock'. Both English and Scottish Puritans regarded this as one of the most objectionable requirements of the English Liturgy. It will be noted that the Directory contains no order for the 'Churching of Women'. This apparent defect was noted by Hammond in his strictures on the Directory. In this connection Leishman remarks that a possible order of thanksgiving for safe delivery from childbirth was contemplated, but finally laid aside. He adds that the post-Baptismal prayer 'makes a thanksgiving on behalf of the mother'.[2] A careful study of the post-Baptismal prayer will prove that this is not the case. No mention is made of the mother, whilst the thanksgiving that the Lord 'is pleased to bestow upon our children this singular token and badge of his love in Christ' is made on behalf of the Church rather than on behalf of the parents. Thus the Directory makes no provision for the valuable elements included in the Prayer-Book service for the Churching of Women. Hammond's criticism is therefore justified.

The order for the celebration of the Lord's Supper occupied eighteen out of the seventy-five sittings of the Committee. Both Scots and Independents keenly contested every point, particularly when each party believed that its own distinctive principles were at stake. The all-important question of the

[1] *cf.* Baillie *A Dissuasive &c.* p. 30: 'The Apostles' Creed they detest, as an old Patchery of evil stuff; Christ's descent into hell, they count a blasphemous Article.'

[2] Sprott & Leishman *op. cit.* p. 346

frequency of the celebration of Communion was not settled. It was left to the discretion of the ministers and officers of each congregation to arrange. The Scottish Presbyterians, it appears, were in favour of a quarterly Communion, while the Independents preferred a weekly or monthly celebration. It is not to be assumed that the Assembly, in allowing this question of frequency to be settled by particular congregations, did not set a high value on this Sacrament. On the contrary, two rubrics in the Directory show that the importance of the Sacrament was realized. The first directs that, when the Sacrament cannot be conveniently celebrated at frequent intervals, either on the preceding Sunday or on a day in the preceding week,

'something concerning that ordinance, and the due preparation thereunto, and participation thereof, be taught; that, by the diligent use of all means sanctified of God to that end, both in public and in private, all may come better prepared to that heavenly feast.'[1]

Secondly, it is strenuously urged that 'the ignorant and scandalous are not fit to receive this Sacrament of the Lord's Supper'.[2] Moreover, the table is 'fenced' by a lengthy exhortation at the commencement of the order for the Lord's Supper, which forbids

'all such as are ignorant, scandalous, profane, or that live in any sin or offence against their knowledge or conscience, that they presume not to come to that holy table.'[3]

The following is the plan of the Communion order:

1. Exhortation
2. Fencing of the Table
3. Words of Institution and Exhortation
4. Eucharistic Prayer
5. Fraction
6. Delivery
7. Minister communicates himself, then the officers, then the people
8. Exhortation to a worthy life
9. Post-Communion Prayer
10. Metrical Psalm
11. Blessing

The rite is comprehensive, but prolix. It is clearly modelled

[1] Hall *op. cit.* iii 52 [2] *ibid.* [3] *id.* iii 53

in structure on the Calvinist liturgies. Its most impressive feature is the Eucharistic Prayer, which, although short, is composed of the following parts: Prayer of Access; Thanksgiving for Creation and Redemption, the Word and the Sacraments; the Anamnesis and the Epiclesis.

Two features in the administration of the Sacrament call for attention. A rubric states that the table is to be 'conveniently placed that the communicants may orderly sit about it, or at it'.[1] The concluding words of this rubric were arrived at only after an obstinate contest between the Scots and the Independents. Apparently, there are three possible ways in which communion may be received. The people may either receive the elements kneeling, at the communion rail (the Anglican custom); or they may receive the elements in their pews from the hands of the Minister (the Puritan and Independent custom); or again, they may sit at the table, which is specially brought into the nave of the church and sufficiently large to accommodate a large number of communicants (the Scottish custom). Both Independents and Scots disliked the first custom, which Laud had newly introduced into the English Church. But the Presbyterians were determined that their members should 'sit at' the table, whilst the Independents were equally insistent that the communicants should 'sit about' the table in their pews. The Scottish Presbyterians believed that only by sitting at the table could they express the great evangelical truth that they were guests at Christ's table. The Independents objected to this procedure because it was seldom possible to receive all the communicants in a congregation at one table and hence they had to be received either at another service or in successive companies at the same table. It was the custom of the Independents to receive the elements together, presumably to symbolize their unity. The rubric allowed either method of administration.

The Scots, however, differed from the Independents in another detail. It was their custom for the Minister to communicate himself first, the rest of the communicants distributing the elements from hand to hand. Their aim seems to have been to imitate the distribution of the elements at the Last Supper of our Lord. This is the only possible interpretation of the words of delivery:[2]

[1] *id.* iii 54 [2] *id.* iii 57 (italicised in the original edition)

'According to the holy institution, command, and example of our blessed Saviour Jesus Christ, I take this bread; and, having given thanks, I break it, and give it unto you.'

Both parties appear to have rejected kneeling as the posture for reception since they feared that this attitude might in time revive the doctrine of a material presence. Sitting appears to have been the usual posture, although standing was a permissible alternative. The Directory does not prescribe a posture for reception. The order for Communion is thus seen to be a compromise between the Independents and the Scottish Presbyterians. Where both parties were agreed the rubrics are imperative, where they differed the language is permissive. Only in one particular do the Independents appear to have yielded. It was their custom, according to Baillie, to have 'two short graces', that is, a double consecration for the bread and the wine respectively. This originated from a desire to imitate our Lord, who at his Last Supper prayed prior to the distribution of each element.[1] They were not allowed to retain this custom in the Directory. But it is also to be noticed that no language suggestive of successive tables at the Lord's Supper was allowed to remain in the Directory. The Scottish Presbyterians also had to make concessions. The orders for worship in the Directory are a *via media* between Independency and Scottish Presbyterianism.

The order for the Solemnization of Marriage was produced only after a prolonged dispute between the Independents and the Scottish Presbyterians. Goodwin and his fellow-Independents held marriage to be merely a civil contract in which the Minister acted only as the delegate of the magistrate. The Presbyterians, represented by Rutherford, made a distinction between marriage, of which the essence is consent, and solemnization which is concerned with the making of vows.[2] The same party further maintained that marriage is a command of God and is therefore worthy of religious solemnization. The Presbyterians gained their point. The service consists of the following parts: a prayer of confession and petition for God's blessing on the couple; an exhortation, based upon Scripture, reminding them of their duties to one another and to God; then the man and woman in turn promise faithfulness to one

[1] Sprott & Leishman *op. cit.* p. 356 [2] *id.* p. 359

another; the Minister pronounces them man and wife and concludes with a prayer of blessing.

The passages of Scripture upon which the Minister bases his exhortation are unspecified. The opening exhortations in both the Book of Common Prayer and the *Forme of Prayers* are founded upon the fifth chapter of St. Paul's Epistle to the Ephesians. The omission of a reference to this chapter in the Directory calls for explanation. It seems most probable that the Puritans feared that this passage might lend colour to the view that marriage is a sacrament. The other notable omission is that of the ring. This was one of the noxious ceremonies, without Scriptural warrant, which the Puritans had objected to in the Book of Common Prayer.

The directions for the Burial of the Dead were also hotly disputed in the Committee and in the Assembly. The Independents, it might be imagined, had even more reason to regard burial as a civil concern than marriage. This time, however, they were joined by some of the Presbyterians. Rutherford, for one, saw no more occasion for an act of worship at a man's leaving the world than at his entering it.[1] The result of these protests was that only the briefest and simplest offices were permitted. Praying, singing and reading on the way to or at the grave are expressly prohibited. The Assembly, however, allowed the Minister to put the mourners 'in remembrance of their duty'. Lightfoot implies that the Assembly would allow more than this however. He maintains that Dr Temple, who moved that some such formula of interment as 'We commit the body to the ground . . .'[2] might be allowed, won the approval of the Assembly. Funeral sermons, according to Lightfoot, were also permitted by the Assembly. This suggestion was vehemently opposed by Baillie in the words:[3] 'it is nothing but ane abuse of preaching to serve the humours of rich people only for a reward'. The Scottish feeling was so averse to funeral orations that they refused to attend Pym's funeral on account of the sermon that they knew would be preached on that occasion. The Puritans, it will be remembered, disapproved of the wearing of funeral garments.[4] Their offices to the dead were equally unadorned.

The Directory also issues instructions for the keeping of public solemn Fasts. These were, apart from Sundays, the only

[1] *id.* p. 361 [2] *id.* p. 362 [3] *ibid.* [4] Strype *Whitgift* i 368*f*

red-letter days in the Puritan Calendar. The peculiarly Calvinistic doctrine of providence, devoutly accepted by the Puritans, made them susceptible to interpreting great calamities or notable national successes as directly due to the hand of God. They therefore marked such occasions by religious services. As the Directory phrases it,[1]

'When some great and notable judgments are either inflicted upon a people, or apparently imminent, or by some extraordinary provocations notoriously deserved; as also, when some special blessing is to be sought and obtained, public solemn fasting (which is to continue the whole day) is a duty that God expecteth from that nation or people.'

These days were to be spent in reading and preaching the Word and in singing penitential psalms. Special lections were chosen for these occasions, probably, as Henderson and the Book of Common Order direct,[2] from the Law. Detailed directions are given for the prayer or prayers which must be included: Adoration, Thanksgiving and Confession; an intercession for the King and all in authority and for all others for whom Christians are bound to pray 'with more special importunity and enlargement than at other times'; a petition for pardon follows with a dedication of the people to the Lord. Private fasts are also encouraged.

The Directory concludes with directions on the singing of Psalms and an Appendix 'touching Days and Places for Public Worship'. The Calendar of the traditional Church was abolished. The reason being:[3]

'There is no day commanded in scripture to be kept holy under the gospel, but the Lord's day, which is the Christian Sabbath.'

Hence

'festival-days, vulgarly called holy-days, having no warrant in the word of God, are not to be continued.'[4]

It is most fitting that this Directory should conclude with a reference to its criterion, the warrant of the Word of God. For the authors in their preface averred that

'our care hath been to hold forth such things as are of Divine institution in every ordinance.'[5]

[1] Hall *op. cit.* iii 74*f* [2] Sprott & Leishman *op. cit.* p. 365
[3] Hall *op. cit.* iii 82 [4] *ibid.* [5] *id.* iii 18

The importance of the Parliamentary Directory in the history of Puritan Worship is threefold. It is the first comprehensive attempt to find an order of worship which would prove acceptable to the whole body of Puritans, Presbyterian and Independent. Since hitherto, apart from the Waldegrave and Middleburgh Liturgies, Puritan worship appears to have varied in each congregation, the importance of this agreed formulary cannot be over-estimated. Apart from this, our knowledge of Puritan worship could be gleaned only from critiques of the Prayer Book made by the Puritan polemical writers, or from occasional references to local gatherings for worship made in diaries or church minute-books. Such information would, of course, be of value but deficient in two respects: it would be a mere outline or sketch of the worship and, furthermore, it would be evidence not for Puritan worship in general but only for local usage. Therefore the Directory is invaluable in presenting a complete picture of seventeenth-century Puritan worship.

In the second place, its character is unique as a *via media* between the apparently unpremeditated and extempore worship of the Separatists and the prescribed liturgical order of the Establishment. This is, it would seem, the first publication of a Manual, as distinct from a Liturgy. It is a notable attempt to combine the spontaneity of free prayer with the advantages of an ordered context or framework of worship. It aimed at avoiding the deadening effect of a reiterated liturgy as also the pitfall of extempore prayer—the disorderly meanderings of the minister. This is the experimental importance of the Directory.

Thirdly, the Directory destroys the contention that Puritan prayer was necessarily and always extempore. This order allows for both types of prayer and is itself in the direct lineage of the Calvinist liturgies. The last fact shows that the Puritans who threw off the manacles of the Prayer Book yet accepted the bonds of Geneva. The very fact that it was possible for Independents and Presbyterians to arrive at an agreed syllabus for worship is sufficient indication that they held a common tradition in public worship and that there were not as many varieties of Puritan worship as there were conventicles. It should be remembered that the Puritans at no time claimed liberty to worship God as they pleased; their demand was rather that they should worship God according as he desired to be worshipped in his Word. The Calvinist orders of worship were acceptable to them because they believed these to be true to the criterion they demanded. The unanimity of the Westminster Assembly is itself a clear testimony to the existence of an ordered tradition amongst the Puritans. It must, of course, be granted that there were differences between the Independents and the Presbyterians: such differences are to be assumed when the rubrics of the Directory are framed in permissive language. But, on the other hand, the directions in the main are framed in imperative language and in these there was complete agreement between all sections of the Puritans. For all these reasons the Parliamentary Directory is a milestone in the history of Puritan worship.

## IV

The Parliamentary Directory remained in use for sixteen years, until the Restoration. The religious situation, in which the Episcopal clergy returned to official favour, had entirely changed. The Prayer Book once again became the established formulary of worship. But a notable attempt was made to supersede this by a Scriptural liturgy which should prove acceptable both to the Established clergy and the Dissenting ministers. This was known by several names, either as 'The Savoy Liturgy', since it was the outcome of the conference of Anglican Bishops and Dissenting Ministers meeting at the Savoy, or as Baxter's 'Reformed Liturgy', since it was the product of the famous Presbyterian of that name, whose aim it was to produce a liturgy completely conformable to the Word of God.

The Independents refused to play any part in the negotiations. Their objection was twofold: they disapproved of the Erastianism of the Presbyterians and they were by now convinced that Scripture gave no warrant for set forms of prayer.[1] This left the Presbyterians free to discuss liturgical comprehension with the Anglicans. The English Presbyterians were, it should be remembered, more akin to the Established Church than their Scottish brethren. They were more willing to admit the value of a modified liturgy and had no objection to a primitive episcopacy. Moreover, they were not jealous of the

[1] *cf.* F. J. Powicke, art. cit. *Essays Congregational and Catholic* p. 296

interference of the secular arm in religious affairs. Hence the way lay open to them to enter into negotiations with the Anglicans with a view to comprehension in a new national Church with wider boundaries. This they did with unbridled hopes.

Before, however, they could present their 'Reformed Liturgy', they were involved in a lengthy controversy which is of great value in elucidating the aims of the successors of the Puritans in worship. The proposals and counter-proposals of the Ministers, with the objections of the Bishops, together make an illuminating commentary and critique of both Puritan and Anglican techniques of worship. For this reason, and also because they provide an introduction to the 'Savoy Liturgy', they will receive detailed consideration.

Before returning to England Charles II prepared the way for religious unity by his Declaration of Breda on the 4th April, 1660. The Presbyterian Ministers were granted an interview with the King at Breda. Believing in His Majesty's favour, they drew up 'The first Address and Proposals of the Ministers'. This document is prefaced by four demands, which they consider essential for comprehension. If these points are not granted, then Presbyterian co-operation must be withheld. They are requests that the various congregations may have 'liberty for edification and mutual provoking to godliness'; that each congregation may have 'a learned, orthodox and godly pastor residing amongst them'; 'that none may be admitted to the Lord's Supper, till they completely understand the principles of Christian religion and do personally and publicly own their baptismal covenant, by a credible profession of faith and obedience . . . and that unto such only confirmation (if continued in the church) may be administered'; and 'that an effectual course be taken for the sanctification of the Lord's day, appropriating the same to holy exercises both in public and private without unnecessary divertisements'.[1]

The rest of the 'Proposals' are concerned with church government, the liturgy in general and ceremonies in particular. The Ministers approve of a liturgy in principle,

'provided that it be for the matter agreeable unto the word of God, and fitly suited to the nature of the several ordinances, and necessities of the

[1] Bayne *Puritan Documents &c.* pp. 14*ff*

church; neither too tedious in the whole, nor composed of too short prayers, unmeet repetitions or responsals: not to be dissonant from the liturgies of other reformed churches; nor too rigorously imposed; nor the minister so confined thereunto, but that he may also make use of those gifts of prayer and exhortation, which Christ hath given him for the service and edification of the church.'[1]

The next paragraph contains the genesis of the idea of a comprehensive Scriptural liturgy to be agreed upon by a conference of Anglican and Dissenting divines. It reads:

'that for settling the church in unity and peace, some learned, godly and moderate divines of both persuasions, indifferently chosen, may be employed to compile such a form as is before described, as much as may be in Scripture words; or at least to revise and effectually reform the old, together with an addition or insertion of some other varying forms in Scripture phrase, to be used at the minister's choice; of which variety and liberty there be instances in the Book of Common Prayer.'

The Ministers, whilst prepared to accept a liturgy, are uncompromising in their rejection of ceremonies in worship for which they can find no Scriptural warrant. This repudiation is phrased in characteristically Puritan phraseology:[2]

'That the Lord hath declared himself in the matters that concern his worship to be a "jealous God"; and this worship of his is certainly then most pure, and most agreeable to the simplicity of the gospel, and to his holy and jealous eyes, when it hath least of human admixtures in things of themselves confessedly unnecessary adjoined and appropriated thereunto; upon which account many faithful servants of the Lord, knowing his Word to be the perfect rule of faith and worship, by which they must judge of his acceptance of their services, and must be themselves judged, have been exceeding fearful of varying from his will, and of the danger of displeasing him by additions or detractions in such duties wherein they must daily expect the communications of his grace and comfort . . .'

The Presbyterians clearly laboured under the Great Taskmaster's eye. They also urged that these ceremonies had been abolished by the other Reformed Churches, that they had been bones of contention since the Reformation and had therefore been productive of schisms from the Church. These offensive

[1] *id.* p. 17 [2] *id.* p. 18

ceremonies are enumerated in the conclusion of the 'Proposals' as: kneeling at the Lord's Supper, the crossing of the child at Baptism, bowing at the name of Jesus, the use of the surplice, 'such holy days as are but of human institution', and the erection of altars. There is only one exception: the use of the ring in marriage. The Puritans had strenuously opposed this, but the Presbyterians, in their later detailed critique of the Prayer Book, wished to leave it optional.

The first 'Proposals' were then answered by the Bishops. They maintained that many short prayers were more suited 'for relieving the infirmities of the meaner sort of people' than the longer prayers desired by the Ministers. Repetitions and responsals were defended on the same grounds. The imposition of the liturgy was insisted upon in the interests of uniformity, whilst it was claimed that ministers are not 'denied the use and exercise of their gifts in praying before and after sermon'. Obviously the Bishops held a poor opinion of extemporary prayer, since they continue:[1]

'such praying be but the continuance of a custom of great antiquity, and grown into common use by sufferance only, without any other foundation in the laws or canons, and ought therefore to be used by all sober and godly men with the greatest inoffensiveness and moderation possible'.

Clearly the Bishops stood for the old order. They were equally intransigent in upholding the ceremonies. Holy-days and kneeling at the reception of the Lord's Supper were to be retained. The Bishops were not satisfied with the objections to the use of a surplice, crossing at Baptism or bowing at the name of Jesus, but they preferred that the King should judge whether tender consciences were to be allowed liberty to refuse them or not.

Chilled by the response which their proposals had received from the Bishops, the Ministers now produced 'A Defence of our Proposals to His Majesty for Agreement in Religion'. They begin by defending the honour of the Puritans, whose mantles, they felt, had fallen on their shoulders:[2]

'The great controversy between the hypocrite and the true Christian—whether we should be serious in the practice of the religion we com-

[1] *id.* p. 37 [2] *id.* p. 41*f*

monly profess?—hath troubled England more than any other: none being more hated and derided as Puritans, than those that will make religion their business, and make it predominant in their hearts and lives; while others that hate them, take it up in custom, for fashion, or in jest, and use it only in subserviency to the will of man and their worldly ends, and honour it with compliments, and paint the skin while they stab the heart. Reconcile this difference, and most others will be reconciled.'

This was a brave counterblast to the Bishops, but unlikely to produce an eirenical temper in their opponents. The rest of the document complains that true godliness can only be increased by the promotion of family religion in house-meetings, which are at present frowned upon. It demands that Confirmation be made more strict in its requirements; it again urges that long prayers are more edifying than collects; it roundly condemns the imposition of the liturgy, declaring that the only efficacious method of imposition is

'such an efficacy as the Spanish Inquisition and Queen Mary's bonfires had, to send those to God whom the world is not worthy of'.[1]

The King made his expected pronouncement in the autumn of 1660. In this he declared that, as exceptions had been made to the Established Liturgy,

'we will appoint an equal number of learned divines of both persuasions, to review the same, and to make such alterations as shall be thought most necessary, and some additional forms (in the Scripture phrase as near as may be) suited unto the nature of the several parts of worship, and that it be left to the minister's choice to use one or other at his discretion'.[2]

The scrupled ceremonies were not to be compelled and ministers were to be free to use or disuse the surplice, except in the royal chapel, cathedral or collegiate churches, where the surplice must continue to be worn. The King's warrant convening the Conference at Savoy was issued on the 20th of March, 1661.

The Presbyterian Ministers presented their 'Exceptions against the Book of Common Prayer' to the Bishops at a meeting held on the 4th of May in the same year. These

[1] *id.* p. 56 [2] *id.* p. 73

exceptions are divided into two sections. The first part consists of general principles, the second of detailed criticisms. They range over the whole of the Prayer Book. There are eighteen general exceptions tabled:

i. Their first principle is that any liturgy that is to win widespread approval must contain no questionable materials or controversial inclusions.

ii. The aim should be to produce a liturgy both comprehensive and inoffensive enough to include all who agree in the substantials of Protestantism.

iii. Exception is taken to the repetitions, responsals and alternate readings of the psalms and hymns. Instead the minister is to lead the worship, 'the people's part in public prayer to be only with silence and reverence to attend thereunto, and to declare their consent in the close, by saying "Amen".'[1]

iv. It is proposed that the Litany should be remoulded as a single continuous prayer to be made by the minister.

v. Lent must not be regarded as a religious feast, our Saviour's example being no more imitable 'than any other of his miraculous works were, or than Moses his forty days fast was for the Jews'.[2]

vi. Saints' days and their vigils are to be abolished, or, if retained, not to have a special service devoted to them.

vii. The liturgy must not be so imposed as that the exercise of the gift of extemporary prayer is totally excluded in any part of the public worship.

viii. A new Royal translation of the Scriptures is to be uniformly introduced.

ix. Apocryphal lections are to be omitted.

x. 'That the minister be not required to rehearse any part of the liturgy at the Communion-table, save only those parts which properly belong to the Lord's supper.'[3]

xi. The word 'minister' is to be substituted for the words 'priest' or 'curate' and also 'Lord's day' for 'Sunday', whenever these occur.

xii. 'Because singing of psalms is a considerable part of public worship, we desire that the versions set forth and allowed to be sung in churches be amended; or that we may have leave to make use of a purer version.'[4]

[1] *id.* p. 114 [2] *id.* p. 115 [3] *id.* p. 116 [4] *id.* p. 117

xiii. Obsolete words should be disused. Two examples are given: 'arede' in the gospel-lection for the Monday and Wednesday before Easter, and 'then opened he their wits' used in the gospel-lection for Easter Tuesday.

xiv. It is requested that no portions of the Old Testament or Acts of the Apostles should be called 'Epistles', or read as such.

xv. The Offices assume that all persons are 'regenerated, converted and in an actual state of grace' but this is an assumption which even the utmost latitude of charity cannot allow.

xvi. 'That whereas orderly connection of prayers, and of particular petitions, and expressions, together with a competent length of the forms used, are tending much to edification, and to gain the reverence of people to them: there appears to us to be too great a neglect of both, of this order, and of other just laws of method.'[1] An illustration of this want of method is taken from the structure of the collects.

xvii. It is claimed that the liturgy is defective in the following respects: it lacks a preparatory prayer for the assistance of God, whilst many collects placed in the middle of the service consist of nothing else; the Confession does not clearly express original sin, nor particular sins; there are insufficient forms of public praise and thanksgiving; and the entire Book[1] 'consisteth very much of mere generals . . . without any mention of the particulars in which these generals exist'.[2]

xviii. The liturgy contains many ceremonies which were objected to by many godly men in the first days of the Reformation, which are offensive to sensitive consciences, and must be judged as 'a violation of the royalty of Christ, and an impeachment of his laws as insufficient'.[3]

The first section of the 'Exceptions' closes by declaring that in fulfilling the royal request to compare the present liturgy with the primitive liturgies, they

'cannot find any records of known credit, concerning any entire forms of liturgy, within the first three hundred years, which are confessed to be as the most primitive, so the purest ages of the church; nor any impositions of liturgies upon any national church for some hundreds of years after. We find indeed some liturgical forms fathered on St. Basil, St. Chrysostom, and St. Ambrose, but we have not seen any copies of them, but such as give us sufficient evidence to conclude them either

[1] *ibid.* [2] *id.* p. 118 [3] *ibid.*

wholly spurious, or so interpolated, that we cannot make a judgment which in them hath any primitive authority.'[1]

The second part of the 'Exceptions' is concerned only with detailed objections.

'Some, we grant, are of inferior consideration, verbal rather than material . . . others dubious and disputable, as not having a clear foundation in Scripture for their warrant; but some there be that seem to be corrupt, and to carry in them a repugnancy to the rule of the gospel; and therefore have administered just matter of exception and offence to many, truly religious and peaceable,—not of a private station only, but learned and judicious divines, as well of other reformed churches as of the church of England—ever since the reformation.'[2]

What succeeds is probably the most thorough examination of the Prayer Book ever undertaken. It is a survey of every sentence and every rubric.

These detailed criticisms can most conveniently be considered under five headings: first, alterations that aim at a more exact correspondence with the Scriptures; secondly, changes in the interest of edification; thirdly, reforms to promote the moral betterment of the laity; fourthly, variations in structure to avoid repetition and to maintain the continuity of the theme; and, finally, literal amendments.

The Puritan demand for the closest possible adherence to the Scriptures was reiterated by the Presbyterians. They requested that the longer version of the Lord's Prayer, as given by St Luke, should be used in the liturgy. They asked that the Decalogue should be introduced by its Scriptural preface. In the Lord's Supper, they requested that the Dominical words accompanying the delivery of the elements in the Last Supper might be used. They suggested that the Absolution pronounced in the Order for the Visitation of the Sick should be declarative and conditional, since this was in accordance with the Scriptural teaching that repentance is the condition on which forgiveness is granted.

In the interests of the edification of the people, the following changes were proposed. The lessons should be read, rather than sung. A psalm or a Scripture hymn should be substituted for the *Benedicite, omnia opera*. Preaching should accompany

[1] *id.* p. 121 [2] *id.* p. 122

the administration of the Sacraments. Kneeling should not be insisted upon during the saying of the Commandments, lest the ignorant might assume this was a prayer rather than a profession of obedience and faith. In regard to Confirmation, it was claimed that memorizing of the catechism was insufficient. Candidates should be able to explain their beliefs on being questioned. It was suggested that, by making the laying on of the Bishop's hands at the Confirmation an essential part of the service, the liturgy appears to set a higher value upon it than Baptism or Holy Communion. Furthermore, it was wrong to allege the Apostolic warrant for this practice at Confirmation. It was proposed that the Triune formula should be omitted in the Marriage Service, lest it foster the erroneous opinion that marriage is a sacrament. It was felt to be unwise to demand that Holy Communion should be administered after marriage or after visitation of the sick, since this would allow scandalous persons to receive the sacrament indiscriminately. It was, therefore, urged that the minister should decide whether persons were fit to receive the Lord's Supper. It was particularly urged that in the Burial Service the following words of committal be omitted, 'in sure and certain hope of resurrection to eternal life'. These words, it was urged, could not truthfully be said of the notoriously evil.

The third series of alterations was framed with the aim of increasing the godliness of Christian believers. It was felt to be prejudicial to their best interests to allow them to receive Holy Communion without careful preparation. Moreover, lest believers should neglect the Apostolic warning not to eat and drink to their own damnation, it was insisted that the 'fencing of the tables' should be exercised in a more stringent manner. In the sacrament of Baptism, it was urged that the godparents had unwarrantably displaced the parents:

'Here is no mention of the parents, in whose right the child is baptized, and who are fittest both to dedicate it unto God, and to covenant for it.'[1]

Furthermore the custom by which the godparents answered the interrogatories in the name of the child was disliked:

'We know not by what right the sureties do promise and answer in the name of the infant . . . and therefore we desire that the first two inter-

[1] *id.* p. 133

rogatories may be put to the parents to be answered in their own names, and the last propounded to the parents or pro-parents thus, "Will you have this child baptized into this faith?".'[1]

It was also suggested that the Order for the 'churching' of women should include passages of Scripture suitable to induce humiliation, in case the child recently delivered had been born in adultery. Throughout their critique the Ministers insisted that Communion should be given only to the duly qualified. Hitherto it was the necessary accompaniment of almost every office, as that for the visitation of the sick, marriage and 'churching'.

To avoid unnecessary repetition, it was suggested that both the *Gloria Patri* and the Lord's Prayer should be sung or said less frequently. Of the former, they assert that it is

'appointed to be said six times ordinarily in every morning and evening service, frequently eight times in a morning, sometimes ten; which we think carries with it at least an appearance of that vain repetition which Christ forbids'.[2]

The same criticism applied to the Lord's Prayer as used in the liturgy. The collects were objected to, not simply because short prayers were less conducive to edification than longer prayers, but also because so much of their invocations and conclusions was repetitious.

Finally, many literal changes were demanded. Two archaisms were condemned in the Marriage order: 'with my body I thee *worship*' and 'until death us *depart*'. It was suggested that the Prayer of Humble Access in the Communion order appeared to give a greater efficacy to the blood than to the body of Christ. Exception was taken to the wording of the Collect for Christmas Day. The following words, 'Almighty God, which hast given us thy only begotten Son, to take our nature upon him, and *this day* be born of a pure virgin, . . .' implied that Jesus Christ was born on the very day upon which the prayer was offered. Other collects requiring verbal alterations were those for Whit Sunday, the two collects for St. John's day and Innocents', those for the first Sunday in Lent, the fourth Sunday after Easter, Trinity Sunday, the sixth and twelfth Sundays after Trinity, St. Luke's day and

[1] *ibid.* [2] *id.* p. 124

Michaelmas day. The Litany was criticized meticulously, if not pedantically.

The 'Exceptions against the Book of Common Prayer' was thus a most comprehensive survey of the defects of the Prayer Book from the Presbyterian position.[1] As a painstaking critique it deserves the highest respect. As an eirenical document it failed in two respects. In the first place it concentrates exclusively on the supposed defects of the Book of Common Prayer, with apparently no appreciation of the values of the Liturgy. In the second place no attempt is made to arrange the criticisms in any order of importance. It is in effect an interlinear commentary on the Prayer Book. An arrangement of the criticisms commencing with graver charges and descending to minutiæ would probably have been more effective.

As it happened the critique was coldly received by the Bishops. They maintained the *status quo* vigorously, offering only a few unimportant concessions. Responsals and alternate readings are defended, extempore prayers are scathingly described as full of 'idle, impertinent, ridiculous, sometimes seditious, impious and blasphemous expressions', while the plea that the prayer of Confession should particularize sins is summarily discarded:

'This which they call a defect, others think they have reason to account the perfection of the liturgy, the offices of which being intended for common and general services, would cease to be such descending to particulars.'[2]

They claim that the liturgy has no lack of public thanksgivings. They instance the *Te Deum*, *Benedictus*, *Magnificat*, *Benedicite*, *Sanctus* and the Doxology. As to ceremonies, they contend that they have a right to institute signs as long as they signify something decent and comely. The weaker brethren whose tender consciences are offended by such ceremonies are dismissed as merely 'scrupulous'. The surplice is retained as significant of purity and beauty; the posture of kneeling at the reception of the elements is the most convenient symbol of our obedience to God; whilst crossing in Baptism which was always used in the Church 'in immortali lavacro' is a reminder of the Communion of Saints and a token that the child shall not be ashamed of the Cross of Christ. The shorter version of the

[1] It occupies 32 pages octavo of a modern reprint [2] Bayne *op. cit.* p. 155

Lord's Prayer is retained, since there is a suspicion that the longer ending is unhistorical. The suggested verbal changes in the Litany are dismissed:

'The alterations here desired as so nice, as if they that made them were given to change.'[1]

The reserving of Confirmation to the Bishop, they claim, argues the dignity of the Bishop, not the superiority of the service.

Then follows a list of seventeen concessions. The first three agree that the lections shall be selected from the latest translation, that any non-epistolary lection shall be designated 'For the Epistle' and that the psalms shall be collated with the last translation. Fourthly, they agree that the words 'on this day' shall, in both collects and prefaces, be used on the day itself only, and for the rest of the days 'as about this time' shall be substituted. The fifth and sixth concessions allow for a tightening of the regulations for admission to the Lord's Table. It is agreed, seventhly, that the whole Scriptural preface shall precede the Decalogue, and eighthly, that the second exhortation now in the Communion office shall be read on some Sunday or Holy Day before the celebration. Two other concessions are made in the Communion office. The General Confession may be pronounced by one of the ministers, the people to repeat it after him, all kneeling; also the manner of consecration is to be made more explicit by the insertion of a rubric to that effect. Eleventhly, it is agreed that the font shall be placed where the Baptismal service can most conveniently be heard by all. Then a verbal alteration is made in the office of Baptism, which clarifies the point that the promises are made by the sureties in their own name, not in the child's. The thirteenth concession alters the last rubric before the Catechism to read 'that children being baptized have all things necessary to salvation, and dying before they commit actual sins be undoubtedly saved, though they be not confirmed'.[2] The next concession adds that only those who are desirous and ready to be confirmed shall be presented to the Bishop. The three final concessions are verbal. 'With my body I thee honour' is substituted for 'With my body I thee worship'. 'Till death us depart' is altered to 'Till death us do part'. It was finally agreed to omit the words 'sure and certain' in the committal in the Burial office.

[1] *id.* p. 164 [2] *id.* p. 175

These meagre concessions on unimportant points disappointed the Ministers. The latter complain in their 'Rejoinder' to the Bishops:

'. . . we find ourselves exceedingly disappointed . . . as may appear both by the paucity of the concessions and the inconsiderableness of them, they being for the most part verbal and literal, rather than real and substantial.'[1]

They appear to have realized that the intransigence of the Bishops had lost the cause of comprehension for they take their farewell in bitter terms that are a deeper criticism of the Prayer Book than their exhaustive critique of it:

'Prayer and humility are indeed the necessary means of peace; but if you will let us pray for peace in no words but are in the Common Prayer book, their brevity and unaptness, and the customariness, that will take off the edge of fervour with human nature, will not give leave (or help sufficient) to our souls to work towards God, upon this subject, with that enlargedness, copiousness, and freedom as is necessary to true fervour. A brief, transient touch and away, is not enough to warm the heart aright; and cold prayers are like to have a cold return . . .'[2]

Later in the 'Rejoinder' the real gravamen of the Presbyterian objection to liturgical prayer without an admixture of extempore prayer appears. These words are a worthy expression of the Puritan tradition in prayer:

'yet must we, before God and men, protest against this opium which you would here prescribe or wish for, as that which plainly tendeth to cure the disease by the extinguishing of life, and to unite us all in a dead religion'.[3]

The Ministers claim that sincerity rather than 'comeliness of expression' is the test by which prayers must be examined. They refuse to accept a liturgy 'that pretends to help the tongue' while it 'hurts the heart'. They still profess themselves to be moderates:

'We would avoid both the extreme that would have no forms, and the contrary extreme that would have nothing but forms.'[4]

Their final word is a warning:

[1] *id.* p. 201 [2] *id.* p. 213 [3] *id.* p. 230 [4] *id.* p. 247

'And we must say, in the conclusion, that, if these be all the abatements and amendments you will admit, you sell your innocency and the church's peace for nothing.'

Under the influence of this radical re-examination of the bases of liturgical and extemporary worship, Richard Baxter prepared *The Reformation of the Liturgy*.[1] This production is frequently derided as a mere 'fourteen days' liturgy' because it was apparently the work of a fortnight. If this was actually the case, then it should be remembered that Baxter's liturgy was the mature product of years of reflection and experiment. Indeed three considerations can establish this as a certainty. In the first place the Savoy Liturgy has a close structural resemblance to the outline of the Parliamentary Directory, which suggests that Baxter had tried out variations on the Directory during his pastorate at Kidderminster in the Commonwealth years. His biographer, Dr F. J. Powicke, suggests:[2]

'I think we may account for the swiftness and preparedness with which he afterwards wrote out a whole liturgy of his own in a fortnight, by the fact that he was but writing out and supplementing what he had practised at Kidderminster.'

In fact the Savoy Liturgy may not inaptly be described as Baxter's revised version of the Directory. A comparison of the orders for Morning Service in the Appendix will confirm the derivation.

In the second place Baxter had already conceived of a liturgy that should be composed entirely of Scriptural materials. This is clearly shown in his *Five Disputations of Church Government and Worship* which was published in 1659. There he says[3]

'The safest way of composing a stinted Liturgie, is to take it all, or as much as may be, for words as well as matter out of the Holy Scriptures.'

He defends this assertion by three arguments. Such an undertaking is less liable to be scrupled since

'all are satisfied of the infallible truth of Scripture, and the fitness of its expressions, that are not like to be satisfied by man's'.[4]

Moreover, such a liturgy would have œcumenical advantages and, thirdly,

[1] ed. Hall *Reliquiæ Liturgicæ* vol. iv [2] *Life* p. 95 [3] p. 378 [4] *ibid.*

'There is no other words that may be preferred before the words of God, or stand in competition with them.'[1]

He is also clearly aware of the objections that might be raised and he answers them. If it be claimed that Scripture has not forms enough for all the needs of the Church, he replies:[2]

'it hath matter and words for such forms. Without any additions save only terms of connection, the sentences of Holy Scripture may suffice the Church for all its uses, as to forms.'

If it be objected that the misapplication and misplacing of Scripture may cause men to speak untruths, he replies that, as long as they use no expository terms of their own, perversion is less likely. Moreover, however they are placed,

'the people are left at liberty to interpret them according to the sense they have in Scripture and not according to what men's misplacing may seem to put upon them'.[3]

In the third place the lengthy controversies between the Bishops and the Ministers, in which Baxter had been actively engaged, were preparing him for the production of a liturgy which should be both comprehensive and also free from the exceptions which were made against the Book of Common Prayer. In all these ways the Savoy Liturgy was in the making before it was concluded in fourteen days.

In the preface to the Bishops it is quite clear that it was not intended to replace the Book of Common Prayer. Rather it was to provide a series of alternatives which the Puritans would not scruple, because each office had a Scriptural warrant and was framed, apart from necessary connecting links, entirely out of the words of the Word of God. The Preface begs

'that these alterations and additions may find your favourable interpretation and acceptance, and may, by our joint consent, be presented to his Majesty; to the end they may obtain his gracious approbation, and the several particulars thereof may be inserted into the several respective places of the Liturgy to which they do belong, and left to the Minister's choice to use the one or the other, according to his Majesty's gracious Declaration concerning Ecclesiastical Affairs'.[4]

The Savoy Liturgy is worthy of serious consideration as a landmark in the history of Puritan worship. Whilst the West-

[1] *id.* p. 379 [2] *ibid.* [3] *ibid.* [4] Hall *op. cit.* iv 7*f*

minster Directory was a compromise between the three parties, the English Presbyterians, the Scottish Presbyterians and the Independents, the Savoy Liturgy is representative of the liturgical convictions of one party, the English Presbyterians, and was drawn up by one man, rather than by a committee. It is for that reason a homogeneous production. It is valuable as an indication of how the Westminster Directory might have been written, had the Independents not pressed their views on the Presbyterians. It is also a clear indication that, even whilst the particular liturgy of the Church of England was severely criticized, the Presbyterians had no objection to a liturgy, provided it was not imposed in utter disregard of tender consciences. Moreover, it presents—with the Presbyterian critique of the Prayer-Book—both the denials and affirmations of the moderate Puritans on the subject of public worship.

Its outstanding characteristic compared with the Book of Common Prayer is flexibility. It was to be used as an alternative to the accepted liturgy of the Church of England. And, to allow the maximum of freedom, it contained shorter alternatives to all the longer prayers. Compared with the Westminster Directory, whose child it was, its distinctive quality is variety. This is most clearly shown by a comparison of the orders for the Sunday Morning Service in the two liturgical compilations. The Westminster Directory has an order consisting of eight items only: a Prayer; Readings from the Old and New Testaments in succession; a Psalm; the Prayer before the Sermon; the Sermon; Intercessory Prayer and Lord's Prayer; a Psalm and the Blessing. In comparison with the parallel order in the Savoy Liturgy this is bald and dull. Baxter's order has sixteen items in all:

1. Prayer of Approach
2. One of the three Creeds read by the Minister, the Decalogue, and Scripture Sentences moving to Penitence and Faith
3. Prayer of Confession and Lord's Prayer
4. Sentences of Absolution, followed by a plea for Sanctification
5. A Psalm
6. The Psalms in order for the day
7. Reading of a chapter from the Old Testament

8. Psalm or the *Te Deum*
9. Reading of a chapter from the New Testament
10. Prayer for the King and Magistrates
11. Psalm or *Benedictus* or *Magnificat*
12. Prayer for needs of the Church and in preparation for the Sermon
13. Sermon
14. Prayer
15. Psalm or "Hymn"
16. Blessing

Clearly Baxter has in mind the needs of the congregation in framing this order. Their part in the service is more than doubled (five psalms being sung compared with the Directory's two) whilst prayer-material which is similar in both is divided into five prayers in the Savoy Order, whilst they are only four in the Directory. Concentration on the reading of the Scriptures must have improved by Baxter's separation of the two chapters by a psalm. Baxter was a psychologist, as well as a theologian.

If variety characterized the Savoy Liturgy, no less remarkable was its completeness. It fittingly commenced with a prayer for the acceptance of the worship by God. It followed by professing obedience to him in both mind and heart, by the Creed and the Decalogue respectively. By a natural transition the worshipper was moved to confess his breaches of the Holy Laws. This was made all the more sincere by the use of sentences inciting to penitence and faith. The worshipper rightly begged forgiveness through the merits of his Saviour and as a token of reliance upon him he recited the Lord's Prayer. The Minister then read sentences declarative of God's absolution and comfort, with a Scriptural exhortation to a godly life. This was fittingly confirmed by the congregation who now joined in a psalm of praise. This preparation had made the people ready to receive the Word of God which was now read and preached to them, and they were dismissed with a blessing after they had said 'Amen' to intercessory prayers and sung a concluding psalm. Thus the service ranged over all the Christian moods of adoration, confession, petition and intercession. It comprehended all the Christian needs of forgiveness, faith and exhortation. It included all the Christian duties of belief and conduct. Its completeness was equalled only by the inevitableness of its transitions from one item to the next.

No new liturgy can hope to emulate an ancient liturgy, whose beauty is in its language hallowed by centuries of faithful usage. It is therefore surprising that Baxter's diction has a sustained dignity. This is due partly to Baxter's upbringing on the Book of Common Prayer, but more to his careful choice of Scriptural phraseology. Scripture sentences from widely separated parts of the Bible are juxtaposed most skilfully, without giving the impression that they have been torn from their contexts. And this is combined with an affecting directness of diction in the appeals of the exhortations. The Exhortation in the Communion Order contains an example of this kind of appeal:[1]

'You were lost, and in the way to be lost for ever, when, by the greatest miracle of condescending love, he sought and saved you. You were dead in sin, condemned by the law, the slaves of Satan; there wanted nothing but the executing stroke of justice to have sent you into endless misery; when our Redeemer pitied you in your blood, and shed his own to heal and wash you. He suffered that was offended, that the offended might not suffer. He cried out on the cross "My God, my God, why hast thou Forsaken me," that we, who had deserved it, might not be everlastingly forsaken. He died that we might live . . . See here Christ dying in his holy representation! Behold the sacrificed Lamb of God, that taketh away the sins of the world! It is his will to be thus frequently crucified before our eyes. O how should we be covered with shame, and loathe ourselves, that have both procured the death of Christ by sin, and sinned against it! And how should we all be filled with joy, that have such mysteries of mercy opened, and so great salvation freely offered to us! O, hate sin! O, love this Saviour!'

No formal wording could have the arrow-like directness of this appeal. Baxter's diction excels in the combination of economy of language, sustained dignity and directness.

This liturgy is in several respects an important development of the Calvinist tradition. The element of adoration, which is overshadowed in the previous Genevan liturgies by a sense of the creatureliness of the worshipper, is restored to its rightful place. A new prayer of approach, and the increase in the number of psalms and Scripture hymns allowed, account for

[1] Hall *op. cit.* iv 60–62

this change in emphasis, as also do the words of pardon and consolation which appear as a declaration, not as a petition. The Calvinist insistence upon a holy life as the worship most acceptable to God was underlined. This was effected by the reading of Scripture sentences exhorting believers to a more sanctified life, by a lengthy exhortation on the same subject following the Communion. It was also safeguarded by the inclusion of an Order for 'Pastoral Discipline, Public Confession, Absolution, and Exclusion from the Holy Communion of the Church'.[1] Two other improvements on previous Puritan compilations were the inclusion of an *epiclesis* in the Consecration prayer in the Communion order and the provision of a 'Thanksgiving for the Deliverance of Women in Child-bearing'.[2] Previous Puritan apologists had merely dismissed the order for the 'churching' of women as a Levitical survival from the Old Dispensation. Baxter's attitude was more constructive. He included a prayer in his Savoy Liturgy for those women who desired to give thanks to God for a safe delivery. It was throughout Baxter's chief quality as a reformer that he discerned the use in the abuse and that he therefore advocated amelioration in preference to abolition.

His finest contribution to the Savoy Liturgy is the Order for Communion. This is no mere memorialism as its title suggests: 'The Sacrament of the Body and Blood of Christ'. It commences with a lengthy explication of the 'nature, use and benefits of this sacrament'. It is followed by an exhortation and a prayer of access. As in the traditional order, the offertory then takes place, the bread and wine being brought to the Minister. Then succeeds a brief but comprehensive prayer of Consecration which includes a commemoration of Creation, the *anamnesis* and an explicit *epiclesis*:[3]

> 'Sanctify these thy creatures of Bread and Wine, which according to thy institution and command we set apart to this holy use, that they may be sacramentally the Body and Blood of thy Son Jesus Christ.'

The words of Institution are then read, and a brief prayer of petition is offered up pleading our Lord's intercession and sacrifice. The Fraction is accompanied by the words:[4]

> 'The body of Christ was broken for us, and offered once for all to sanctify

[1] *id.* iv 117*ff*  [2] *id.* iv 115  [3] *id.* iv 68  [4] *id.* iv 70

us: behold the sacrificed Lamb of God, that taketh away the sins of the world.'

The Libation is accompanied with these words:[1]

'We were redeemed with the precious blood of Christ, as of a Lamb without blemish and without spot.'

This is followed by a prayer for a sanctified life. After the Minister has communicated himself, he delivers the elements in the Scriptural formula of the Parliamentary Directory. A post-Communion prayer succeeds and an exhortation to a godly life. The service concludes with a psalm of praise and the Blessing. This is a comprehensive and devout order.

The Savoy Liturgy was framed in the hope that liturgical differences between the Anglicans and Presbyterians might be settled by the adoption of alternative liturgies. For that reason it accepted as much of the structure of the Book of Common Prayer as was possible. The scrupled ceremonies were not included; longer prayers took the place of collects; but notwithstanding these alterations the new liturgy was a serious attempt to be as comprehensive as the old. It failed in its purpose and apparently was never used. The imposition of the Book of Common Prayer in 1662 with the consequent 'Great Ejection' by which two thousand Nonconformist ministers were deprived of their livings, brought the Book of Common Prayer into great disrepute among Dissenters. Hence the liturgical movement fostered by Baxter was strangled soon after birth. For over two centuries the successors of the Puritans confined themselves to extempore prayers.

[1] *ibid.*

# CHAPTER X

## THE PRAISES OF THE PURITANS

The Puritans were more prone to squander the riches of the Catholic heritage in worship than to augment them. Their contribution to worship is in the main a lopping off of dead branches or a pruning of over-luxuriant blooms which bade fair to run to seed, rather than the cultivation of new varieties. It is to their credit, however, that they succeeded in restoring the right of the common people to join in the praise of God. This, however, was a recovery rather than a discovery. Their originality lay in their turning the psalms into metre, which paraphrasing ultimately led, by a legitimate extension, to hymnody. The three stages are: firstly, the restoration of the people's rights to sing the Davidic Psalms in the vernacular; secondly, the versification of these psalms, that they might the easier be memorized by congregations and set to repetitive melodies; whilst the third stage is exemplified by Isaac Watts, in whom paraphrases of psalms develop into hymns.

The Reformers realized that the Vulgate Psalms of the mediæval Western Church had become remote and unintelligible to the untaught laity. These Psalms, apportioned among the seven daily Offices and the Mass, were sung exclusively by priest and choir, antiphonally; this, combined with intricate tunes too subtle for the congregation to follow and often hurried in the execution, rendered them unsuitable for congregational praise. In Germany, the Reformation brought in its train a virile indigenous hymnody, written in the vernacular. In Switzerland and France, under the influence of John Calvin, there was an outburst of metrical psalmody. In this the followers of Calvin remained true to their criterion of reformation 'according to the Word of God'. The Puritans therefore confined themselves to psalmody until the eighteenth century.

The translation of the Psalms into the vernacular on a large scale for the purposes of praise is not to be attributed to Calvin, but to Clement Marot, the court poet of Francis I. He began by translating the sixth Psalm into French verse in 1533;

three years later he had completed thirteen other Psalms; and by 1540 his Psalms were highly popular throughout the French Court. This is borne out by the following statement of Prothero in his *The Psalms in Human Life:*[1]

'When Marot's Psalms first appeared, they were sung to popular tunes alike by Roman Catholics and Calvinists. No one delighted in the *sanctes chansonettes* more passionately than the Dauphin. He sang them himself . . . To win his favour the gentlemen of the court begged him to choose for each a Psalm. Courtiers adopted their special Psalms, just as they adopted their particular arms, mottoes and liveries.'

To Calvin must be attributed the credit for incorporating these Psalms of Marot's from their secular *milieu* into the worship of the Church, at Strassburg. When they were as yet unpublished, he introduced twelve of them into his first Psalter of 1539 ('Aucun Pseaumes et Cantiques mys en chant'). After Calvin's return to Geneva, several larger editions of Marot's psalms were published, until in 1554, the year of Marot's death, the poet had fifty psalms to his name. Calvin who was anxious that the task of translation and versification should be completed, requested Theodore Beza to conclude the task. In 1562 the entire collection was published as *Les Pseaumes mis en rime francoise par Clement Marot et Theodore du Beze.* This particular version later came to be known as the Genevan Psalter and exercised a profound and far-reaching influence on the Continent. It became the exclusive praise-book of Geneva as well as the distinctive mark of the Huguenots in court and in camp. Furthermore, as a precedent for Reformed worship it had a great indirect influence upon the worship of the Puritans both in England and in Scotland, where metrical psalmody was for long the sole medium of praise.

The chief channel of communication which carried Genevan psalmody to the English Puritans was the Anglo-Genevan Psalter of 1556. Originally it was framed as an adjunct to the interim order of worship framed by Knox and Whittingham as Marian exiles in the Church at Frankfort. The Psalm was directed to be sung after the Scripture Sentences and the exhortation 'in meetre in a plaine tune'. This was succeeded by a prayer, Scripture Lessons, a Sermon, a General Prayer, the Apostles' Creed, whilst immediately preceding the Benediction

[1] (ed. 1903) p. 51

another Psalm was sung. Whilst the interim order was revised when the Frankfort exiles seceded to Geneva under Knox's leadership, the Psalter remained intact. The compositions are mainly the work of Sternhold and Hopkins with additions and revisions by Whittingham. A later edition of 1561 shows further enlargement, including Psalms by Whittingham, Pullain and Kethe. When the English exiles returned to their native land both service-book and psalter published in 1556[1] were readily used by Puritans in Scotland and England. They provided a basis for the people's praise in Scotland until in 1644 they were supplanted by the Westminster Directory.

Meanwhile in England, the Established Church substituted a vernacular prose translation for the Vulgate Psalms. This was authorized in the three Prayer Books and was ordered to be read through in the course of a month during Matins and Evensong. Together with this official usage, there grew up the extra-liturgical custom of singing a metrical psalm before and after the prescribed order. This custom, which may possibly be traced to the influence of the returned exiles, appears to have obtained official sanction: for in her Injunctions to the clergy in 1559, Queen Elizabeth directed:

'For the comforting of such as delight in music, it may be permitted that at the beginning or end of Common Prayer, either at Morning or Evening, there may be sung a hymn or such like song to the praise of Almighty God, in the best melody and music that may be devised, having respect that the sentence of the hymn be understood and perceived.'

The result was the publication of numerous attempts to render the Psalms into metre. Among the more noteworthy were those of Archbishop Parker, Sir Philip Sidney and the Seven Penitential Psalms of Edmund Spenser. The two most significant versions, among ten that obtained official approval, are the versions of Sternhold and Hopkins (the Old Version) and of Tate and Brady (commonly known as the New Version). The former of these versions was so popular that it was bound up with the Book of Common Prayer and the Bible. It did not, however, oust the prose Psalter. The latter continued to be sung antiphonally in the cathedrals, or to be said responsively by clerk and people in the parish churches. It became in effect

[1] *The Forme of Prayers &c.*; ed. Maxwell *John Knox's Genevan Service Book* (London 1931)

almost exclusively the one liturgical form in the worship of those who rejected liturgies. For the regular and enthusiastic use of the psalms by the people in their worship we must turn to the Puritans. On the overthrow of Episcopacy, the Parliamentarians demanded a new version of the Psalter, being dissatisfied with the sorry doggerel of Sternhold and Hopkins. As a result Francis Rous published his Psalter in 1641. The Assembly of Divines meeting at Westminster in 1644 included the following rubric in their *Directory for the Public Worship of God*:[1]

'Of Singing of Psalms. It is the duty of Christians to praise God publickly, by singing of Psalms together in the congregation, and also privately in the family. In singing of Psalms, the voice is to be tuneable and gravely ordered; but the chief care must be, to sing with understanding and with grace in the heart, making melody unto the Lord. That the whole congregation may join herein, every one that can read is to have a Psalmbook; and all others not disabled by age or otherwise, are to be exhorted to learn to read. But for the present, it is convenient that the minister or some other fit person appointed by him and other ruling officers, do read the psalm, line by line, before the singing hereof.'

This rubric, whilst encouraging the participation of all the congregation in the praise of God, indulged the expedient of 'lining-out' and so helped to produce the lamentable condition into which psalmody had fallen in the time of Watts, eliciting his complaint of

'the dull indifference, the negligent and thoughtless air that sits upon the face of the whole company, while the Psalm is upon their lips.'[2]

We have evidence of the still unsatisfactory state of psalmody in Richard Baxter's 'Reformed Liturgy' of 1661. There, voicing the convictions of the Presbyterians, he declares:[3]

'We desire that instead of the imperfect version of the Psalms hitherto now in use, Mr. William Barton's version, and that perused and approved by the Church of Scotland there in use (being the best that we have seen), may be received and corrected by some skilful man, and both allowed (for grateful variety) to be printed together in several columns

[1] Hall *op. cit.* iii 81
[2] *Hymns and Spiritual Songs in Three Books*, preface; *Works* iv 253
[3] Hall *op. cit.* iv 44

of pages, and publicly used; at least until a better than either of them shall be made.'

The Psalms in Baxter's rite were allowed an important place. In the public worship one Psalm (the 98th, the 100th or the 84th) was to be said midway through the service, following the Scripture Sentences of Absolution and Comfort; this was to be followed by Psalms sung in the order for the day. The next Psalm may be sung as an alternative to the *Te Deum*, whilst a final Psalm (the 67th, 98th or some other) is to be sung or said as an alternative to the *Magnificat* or *Benedictus*, immediately preceding the Sermon.

The versions mentioned above were not the only ones which were used by the Puritans. Indeed versions produced both in Holland and in New England by the communities residing there, had a considerable influence upon the praise of the English Puritans. The Church founded by the Separatists, Johnson and Ainsworth, at Amsterdam at first neglected singing, but soon the deficiency was remedied. In 1612 Henry Ainsworth, a great Hebrew scholar, produced *The Booke of Psalms: Englished both in Prose and Meeter*. This is of great technical interest, containing a twofold translation so that the departure from a literal translation necessitated by the exigencies of metre and rhyme might be corrected by the juxtaposition of a literal translation in prose. The book also contains a commentary and a careful exposition of the principles of tune-selection. This version, however inadequate its versification, was a landmark in Puritan psalmody. For it did not confine itself to the ballad metre but attempted several others; moreover it provided an alternative to the Old Version of Sternhold and Hopkins and was used by the Pilgrim Fathers in New England for nearly thirty years. The use of Ainsworth's version by the Independents of New England early after its publication is a clear indication that the colonists did not share the scruples of their English brethren concerning the use of a rhymed psalter in public worship. This is clearly corroborated in John Cotton's *Singing Psalmes a Gospel Ordinance*. He allows that all Scriptural 'spirituall songs' may lawfully be sung in Christian Churches. He admits that some scruple the singing of psalms in metre, but he confidently affirms:[1]

[1] (London 1647) p. 56

'pre-supposing that God would have the *Psalmes of David*, and other Scripture-*Psalmes* to be sung of English men . . . then as a necessary meanes to that end, he would have the Scripture-*Psalmes* (which are Poems and Verses) to be translated into English-*Psalmes* (which are in like sort Poems and Verses) that English People might be able to sing them.'

Cotton had to rebut the charge that 'English words are as much an invention of man as English tunes'. He does so by maintaining that these versions of the Psalms are not contaminated by Popish usage; indeed they have been repudiated by the Papists as 'Genevah Gigs'.[1]

'And they be Cathedrall Priests of an Anti-Christian spirit that have scoffed at Puritan-Ministers, as calling the People to sing one of the Hopkins-giggs, and so hop into the Pulpit.'[2]

The last citation is an interesting contemporary allusion to the popularity of the musical settings to the psalms. Cotton regards lining-out as a regrettable necessity until such time as the entire congregations are literate and provided with copies of the metrical versions of the Psalms.[3] The catholicity of the New England Independents is further shown by the statement:[4]

'Nor doe we forbid the private use of an Instrument of Musick therewithall; (to accompany private Psalm-singing). So that attention to the instrument doe not divert the heart from attention to the matter of the Song.'

The next version to appear in New England was the *Bay Psalm Book* published in 1640, and ten years later *The New England Psalm-Book*. The latter, which was prefaced by a discourse on the lawfulness of singing in public worship, represented a great improvement, both verbally and musically, on Ainsworth's version. In the main it was a revision of Rous's version. It had, however, a lasting influence upon the psalmody not only of North America, but also of England and Scotland. Sufficient proof of its popularity and influence is to be found in the fact that it passed through eighteen English and twenty-two Scottish editions.

Amongst the English Dissenters two attitudes towards psalmody were current. These were exhibited both by con-

[1] *id.* p. 61 [2] *ibid.* [3] *id.* p. 62 [4] *id.* p. 15

forming and non-conforming Puritans. Hence the difference of opinion may be described as lateral rather than vertical. On the one hand there were those who were opposed to singing of any kind. Their radical opposition was due to their aversion to the antiphonal use of the prose-version in the Roman and the Established Churches. They were unable to approve of the metrical alternatives, since they were rendered in such a slovenly fashion. Hence they were opposed to singing of any kind in public wórship. On the other hand, there were other Puritans who delighted in singing the songs of Zion and appealed to Scripture as the warrant for their practice.

It now remains to consider the fragmentary evidence as to the use of the Psalms by the Separatists, Independents nd Baptists of seventeenth-century England. The position of the Presbyterians does not demand further consideration, since that is represented by the official approval given to metrical psalmody by the Westminster Assembly of Divines, in which Presbyterians were an overwhelming majority.

From the earliest days of the Reformation, Puritans appear to have lodged protests against elaborate music in the cathedrals, taking particular exception to the organ. In 1539 they apparently fanned the opposition to singing with 'conjoint voices' which led to the burning of Coverdale's *Goostly Psalmes and Spiritualle Songes*. In 1586 the Puritans brought before Parliament the proposal

> 'That all Cathedral Churches may be put down where the service of God is grievously abused by piping with organs, singing, ringing, and trowling of Psalms from one side of the choir to the other.'[1]

This was clearly a rooted dislike of the antiphonal singing of psalms. The attitude of Browne, the father of the Independents, as well as the attitude of his followers, was contrary to the use of metrical psalms. They were radically opposed to the Old Version which was allowed in 1562. There were two points at issue. Firstly, whether it was Scriptural to sing with conjoined voices in worship, since that necessitated a 'set form' of praise; or whether the Scripture was to be interpreted as allowing only a single person at a time to sing, when moved to do so by the influence of the Holy Spirit. The second question raised was: whether it was proper to sing David's Psalms in

[1] *v. A Parte of a Register*

metre at all, since this involved an alteration of the words and often of the thoughts, divinely inspired in the Scriptures.

Barrowe's views were less extreme. He allowed, in the main, the use of the metrical psalter. But his approval was hedged in by qualifications. In his reply to Giffard, who charged him with 'speaking profanely of singing psalms', he declares that he is not against 'that comfortable and heavenly harmony of singing psalms', but opposed to 'the rhyming and paraphrasing the Psalter as in your Church' and 'the apocryphal, erroneous ballads in rhyme sung commonly in your Church instead of the Psalms and songs of the Canonical Scriptures'.[1]

The climax of the controversy was reached in the mid-seventeenth century. It is of interest to note that there was a considerable body of opinion amongst the Quakers which, in the early days of the movement, favoured the singing of psalms in public worship. George Fox and his friend Hubberthorne maintained in the childhood days of the movement that singing, preaching and prayer were integral parts of Divine worship. In 1658 Fox and Hubberthorne declare:[2]

'Those who are moved to sing with understanding, making melody to the Lord in their hearts, we own; if it be in metre, we own it.'

Indeed there is evidence that singing was practised by Quakers as late as 1670, for in his *Truth cleared of Calumnies* of that year, Barclay writes:[3]

'That singing is a part of God's worship, and is warrantably performed among the saints, is a thing denied by no Quaker so called, and it is not unusual among them; and that at times David's words may be used as the Spirit leads thereunto.'

This, however, is no proof of congregational or 'conjoint' singing, but only for that of a single person at the instigation of the Holy Spirit. Later, when Quietism prevailed, the Quakers as a whole abandoned singing in this country, although the practice continued in Holland.

In the Baptist and Congregationalist denominations there was at first strenuous opposition to singing of psalms. In the main this was due to exception being taken to the abuses and corruptions encouraged by the use of elaborate songs in the

[1] Hanbury *Nonconformist Memorials* i 61

[2] Spencer Curwen *Studies in Music and Worship* p. 85 [3] *ibid.*

Roman Mass and Daily Offices, and to a lesser degree in the services of the Established Church. A more serious scruple objected to the danger which was felt to be incurred by the presence of unbelievers and profane persons who could take upon their lips the sacred words of the Scriptures. This danger was all the more real as church-attendance was compulsory in those days. Thus, at the Bunyan Meeting House in Bedford, a Church Meeting assembled in 1690 decided:

'that public singing of the Psalms be practised by the Church with a caution that none other perform it but such as can sing with grace in their hearts, according to the command of Christ.'

Another scruple demanded, despite the precedents established by Marot and Beza, Sternhold and Hopkins, whether the versification of the Holy Scriptures was permissible, since the exigencies of metre and rhyme made a departure from the literal expression of Scripture a necessity. In the third place, the uncouth rendering of the Old Version appears to have produced a distaste for metrical versions of the Psalms. Moreover, even if the legitimacy of singing were granted, it appeared doubtful that more than one person should sing at a time. Scripture expressly insisted that only one person should pray at once and it seemed likely that this precedent should operate in the case of praise. Furthermore the individual was only to sing when he felt himself obliged to do so under the constraint of the Holy Spirit. These cumulative objections on the part of Baptists and Congregationalists therefore left the regular use of metrical psalms to the Presbyterians. Moreover, the practice became less popular even amongst the latter after the passing of the Conventicle Act, by which Nonconformists were forbidden to hold meetings at which more than five persons were present. The singing of psalms was dangerous in such circumstances, since it gave a clear indication to the authorities of the existence of an unauthorized religious assembly. This is substantiated by the following citation from the records of a Church Meeting in St. Thomas's, Southwark:[1]

'1692. April 1st. We met at Mr. Russell's in Ironmonger Lane, where Mr. Lambert of Deadman's Place, Southwark, administered to us the ordinance of the Lord's Supper, and we sang a psalm in a low voice.'

[1] *id.* p. 84

This view is, however, open to serious doubt, since the Broadmead Records show that a combined Baptist and Presbyterian congregation meeting in 1674–5 used to sing psalms immediately they were warned of the approach of the authorities, thus implying that they had not gathered for hearing the Word read or preached to them, but simply for the exercise of singing. This, apparently, was not regarded as a punishable offence. The records state:[1]

'And when we had notice that the informers or officers were coming, we caused the minister or brother that preached, to forbear and sit down. Then we drew back the curtain, laying the whole room open, that they might see us all. And so all the people begin to sing a psalm, that, at the beginning of the meeting, we did always name what psalm we would sing, if the informers or the Mayor or his officers come in. Thus still when they came in we were singing, that they could not find any one preaching, but all singing. And, at our meeting, we ordered it so, that none read the psalm after the first line, but everyone brought their bibles, and so read for themselves; that they might not lay hold of any one for preaching, or as much as reading the psalm, and so to imprison any more for that, as they had our ministers.'

Thus while the Church at Bristol used to sing psalms as an alarm, the Church Meeting in Southwark refused to sing them lest they should give the alarm. In this it appears that the ingenious device of the Broadmead Church was not generally used. The version of the psalms used does not, however, appear to have been a metrical one.

The Independent opposition to psalmody, as envisaged by the Westminster Assembly, is undeniable. Baillie informs us:[2]

'One of the Committee matters is the Psalter . . . Mr. Nye spoke much against a tie to any Psalter, and somewhat against the singing of paraphrases, as of preaching homilies; we, *understand*, will mightily oppose it: for the Psalter is a great part of our uniformity which we cannot let pass until our church be well advised with it.'

It appears, however, from the records of the churches themselves that psalm-singing increased in popularity. Cockermouth Church Meeting, at its foundation in 1651, passed a resolution that psalm-singing was to be one of the practices of

[1] *Broadmead Records* (ed. Underhill, London 1847) p. 226

[2] Hanbury *op. cit.* ii 225

the Church.[1] Beccles Church was using the New England version of the metrical psalter in 1657. Moreover a certain Cuthbert Sydenham records the hope in 1653 that when 'men's hearts come in tune their voices will likewise'.[2] The same writer pleads for more discrimination in the selection of psalms to be sung by mixed congregations. It seems, therefore, that from the mid-seventeenth century onwards the use of the metrical psalters became more widespread among Independent congregations. Ultimately the earlier scruples were overcome without creating a serious cleavage of opinion in the denomination.

It was far otherwise with the Baptists. The General Baptists, with only a few exceptions, disapproved of psalmody. They objected to singing as a worldly occupation and also to the formalism which they believed it produced in worship. On the other hand, the Particular Baptists were more willing to utilize musical forms.

The views of the General Baptists are fairly represented by Thomas Grantham. In his *Christianismus Primitivus* (1678) he rejects

'musical singing with a multitude of voices in rhyme and metre',

yet approves that

'such persons as God hath gifted to tell forth his mighty acts . . . should have liberty and convenient opportunity to celebrate the high praises of God one by one in the churches of God, and that with such words as the nature of the matter and present occasion requires . . .'[3]

In 1689, when the controversy was still acute, the General Baptist Assembly, after discussion, declared that

'it was not deemed any way safe for the churches to admit such carnal formalities . . . the singing of one was the same as the singing of the whole, as prayers of the one are the prayers of the whole congregation.'[4]

Among the Particular Baptists psalmody was more popular. The chief advocate of the use of the Psalter in public worship was Benjamin Keach, pastor of the church at Horsleydown. His fame rests not only on this but also upon his introduction

[1] Spencer Curwen *op. cit.* p. 83 [2] *ibid.* [3] *id.* p. 95

[4] *Minutes of the General Assembly of the General Baptists: 1654–1728* (ed. Whitley, London 1909) p. 27

of hymnody into the worship of the Dissenters. The hymn was employed, by Scriptural precedent, after the celebration of the Lord's Supper. Later the custom was extended to Days of Thanksgiving and, finally, to the Lord's-day worship. Writing directly to his own congregation in the preface of *The Breach Repair'd in God's Worship* (1691), he declares:[1]

'Tis no small grief to me to see (since the Church in such a solemn manner agreed to sing the praises of God on the Lord's Day) to find some of you so offended; I am perswaded 'tis for want of Consideration, for you have no new thing brought in among you. Hath not the Church sung at breaking of bread, always for 16 or 18 years last past, and could not, nor would it omit it in the time of the late Persecution? . . . And have we not for this 12 or 14 Years sung in *mixt Assemblies on Days of Thanksgiving*, and never any offended at it, as ever I heard?'

Keach cites as his precedents the Puritans, and the contemporary examples of the Presbyterians and Independents.[2]

His major defence of the right of Christians to sing psalms is found in *Spiritual Melody*, published in 1691:[3]

''Tis a hard case that any Christian should object against that duty which Christ and his Apostles and the Saints in all ages in their public assemblies were found in practice of, but 'tis no easy thing to break people off of a mistaken notion, and an old prejudice taken up against a previous truth of Christ. The Lord will, I hope, satisfy all his people about the heavenly ordinance in due time, and they shall not call it a carnal nor formal thing any more, nor cry out "'Tis as bad as Common Prayer".'

Keach's most serious opponent was Isaac Marlow. His thesis is contained in the title of his pamphlet: *Prelimiting Forms of Praising God, Vocally sung by all the Church together, Proved to be no Gospel-Ordinance* (1691). There are five arguments adduced to prove his point of view. The first assumes that, the essence of singing being the praise of God, it is not necessarily 'tunable'; secondly, women are prohibited from speaking in public (I Cor. xiv 34–5); thirdly, singing in the primitive Church is no precedent for contemporary singing, since the former was made possible by the dispensation of an extraordinary gift; fourthly, unison singing demands precomposed forms, which are as unwarrantable in singing as in praying; fifthly and finally, there is no ground for believers to

[1] p. ix [2] *id.* p. 69 [3] preface, p. A7 *recto*

unite with unbelievers to sing the praises of God. In answer to these objections Keach produced his *Breach Repair'd*. He will not accept Marlow's definition of singing; if the silence of women were to be taken seriously that would be to forbid them to give an account of their conversion; he denies that singing in the primitive Church was an extraordinary gift any more than were preaching or prophesying; as for prelimited forms, he asserts[1]

> 'I know no more Rule for a precomposed Sermon to be preached, than for a precomposed Hymn that is to be sung, and I am satisfied I have equally in them both the like assistance of the Spirit.'

Finally, as to allowing unbelievers to sing the praises of God, he cites I Cor. xiv 23 and 26, where St. Paul speaks of unbelievers entering the church. He concludes his defence by asking, why should the unbelievers be admitted by the Church to be instructed by preaching, and not for instruction through praise? This controversy has been reviewed at length because in it the arguments for and against the singing of psalms in public worship are exhaustively treated. It also indicates the acuteness of the controversy, and therefore its far-reaching importance amongst the Dissenting circles of the late seventeenth century. The position at that time can be most conveniently gathered from a record of negotiations entered into by the Independents, Presbyterians and Baptists to consider the advisability of holding united congregations in Bristol in 1675. The Presbyterians urged that 'they were for the singing of psalms with others besides the Church'; the Baptists were substantially in agreement, whilst 'others of them could not sing in metre as they were translated; although all of them did hold with singing of psalms'.[2] It would seem therefore that the Baptists adopted the compromise of singing from a prose-psalter, whilst Independents and Presbyterians used a metrical version.

Before the eighteenth-century developments in praise are considered, two further points require elucidation. The first is the manner in which the Psalms were sung; the second, where they were introduced into the orders of service. It was usual for the whole congregation to sing the metrical psalms, but, as we have seen, a certain section of the General Baptists as

[1] p. 137 [2] Spencer Curwen *op. cit.* p. 95

well as the early Quakers allowed only a single person to sing a psalm and only as that person was moved by the Holy Spirit. The information as to the method used is a little confusing. In the Established Church, it was the custom from Reformation days onwards for the parish clerk to read out the appointed psalms line by line, and for the congregation to sing a stave at a time. This method, since it was so dependent upon the whims of an often illiterate clerk, fell easily into abuse. Nevertheless, it was the only practicable way at a time when organs were in disfavour and choirs were unpopular, to say nothing of the scarcity of books and the illiteracy of the common people. Such a custom almost certainly prevailed in Dissenting congregations, except that the Minister took the place of the parish clerk. The earliest evidence for this practice among Dissenters is found in the Westminster Directory under the rubric 'Of Singing of Psalms'. There it is recommended that

'the minister or some other fit person appointed by him and the other ruling officers do read the Psalm, line by line, before the singing thereof.'

This was clearly, however, only a temporary measure but the practice continued until the time of Watts, by whom it was severely castigated in the Preface to *The Psalms of David imitated into the language of the New Testament.*

It is more difficult to determine the position of the psalms in the orders of worship. It would be reasonable to suppose that where only one psalm was sung in a service, it would be at the commencement; where two were sung, the second as a rule followed the sermon, or the prayer immediately preceding the Benediction. Some light on the position of the Psalm in the service is afforded by John Cotton, pastor of the Boston church in New England. He declares:[1] 'Before prophesying it will be seasonable to sing a Psalm.' Elsewhere he says:[2]

'Before Sermon and many times after we sing a Psalm: and because the former translation of the Psalms doth in many things vary from the original, and many times paraphrases rather than translates . . . we have endeavoured a new translation into English metre as near the original as we could express it in our English tongue; so far as for the present the Lord hath been pleased to help us, and those Psalms we sing both in our public churches, and in private.'

[1] *The True Constitution of a Particular Visible Church* (1642) p. 6

[2] *The Way of the Churches of Christ in New England* (1645) p. 67

Whilst this indicates an orderly worship amongst the Independents of New England, their English brethren appear to have conducted their worship in a less orderly manner. Baillie, writing of them in his *A Dissuasive from the Errours of the Time* in 1646, says:[1]

'Concerning the circumstances of the Worship of God, they will have nothing determined; but all which the Scripture hath not determined, to be left so free that all Directories are against their stomachs.'

The final development of psalmody amongst the Puritans is entirely the work of Isaac Watts. He outtops his predecessors both in the understanding of the nature of Christian praise and in his practice of it. His leading principles are expounded in *A Short Essay towards the Improvement of Psalmody*. There he says if

'we would prepare David's Psalms to be sung by Christian lips, we should observe these two plain rules: *First*, they ought to be translated in such a manner as we have reason to believe David would have composed them if he had lived in our day. And therefore his poems are given us as a pattern to be imitated in our composures, rather than as the precise and invariable matter of our psalmody.'[2]

This, the primary aim of Watts, was a radical departure from the literalism of the older versions of the Psalms. Watts hoped by this 'poetic license' to produce a freer and more inspiring verse. But the plea for paraphrase was more than an appeal for greater liberty in technique: it was a demand for a Christian re-orientation of the Psalms. This is indeed the explicit claim of the second principle: 'the translation of Jewish songs for Christian worship'.[3]

This important difference of approach to the Psalms is expounded at greater length in *The Psalms of David imitated in the language of the New Testament and applied to the Christian State and Worship*. Watts points out the unsuitability of David's expressions to meet our experience. He asks:[4]

'Have not your spirits taken wing and mounted up to God and glory, with the song of David on your tongue? But on a sudden, the clerk has proposed the next line to your lips, with dark sayings and prophecies, with burnt-offerings of hyssop, with new moons and trumpets, and

[1] p. 116 [2] *Works* iv 371 [3] *ibid.* [4] *id.* iv 117

timbrels in it, with confessions of sins you never committed, with complaints of sorrows which you never felt; cursing such enemies as you never had; giving thanks for such victories as you never obtained; or leading you to speak, in your persons, of things, places and actions you never knew. And how have all your souls been discomposed at once, and the strings of harmony all untuned!'

It is, therefore, Watts' avowed aim to accommodate the book of Psalms to Christian worship. Where the Psalmist refers to personal enemies, Watts has in mind spiritual adversaries, Satan, sin and temptation; where the essence of religion is conceived as the fear of God in the original, the 'imitation' joins faith and love to the definition:

'where he talks of sacrificing goats or bullocks, I rather choose to mention the sacrifice of Christ, the Lamb of God. When he attends the ark with shouting into Zion, I sing the ascension of my Saviour into heaven, or his presence in his Church on earth.'[1]

He summarizes his aims in one sentence:[2]

'In all places I have kept my grand design in view; and that is to teach my author to speak like a Christian.'

Watts succeeded in his ambitious design and in so doing re-invigorated the dying devotion of the age. In particular he made two alterations which helped to popularize his work. He reduced the original Psalms

'into hymns of such length as may suit the usual custom of churches, that they may not sing broken fragments of sense, as is too often done, and spoil the beauty of this worship; but may finish a whole song and subject at once'.[3]

His second reform was in the interests of intelligibility:

'I would neither indulge any bold metaphors, nor admit of hard words, nor tempt the ignorant worshipper to sing without his understanding.'[4]

In presenting his Christianized psalmody to the public, he added some practical directions for the better rendering of the Psalms. In particular, he is anxious to avoid as far as possible the abuse of lining-out, which destroyed the continuity of the sense and interrupted the devotions of the congregation. He suggests, therefore:[5]

[1] *id.* iv 118 [2] *id.* iv 119 [3] *id.* iv 121 [4] *id.* iv 122 [5] *id.* iv 124

'First, Let as many as can do it, bring psalm-books with them, and look on the words while they sing, so far as to make the sense complete. Secondly, Let the clerk read the whole Psalm over aloud before he begins to parcel out the lines, that the people may have some notion of what they sing; and not be forced to drag on heavily through eight tedious syllables without any meaning, till the next line comes to give the sense of them.'

It is to the credit of Watts that he restored Christian praise to its rightful place in the Dissenting worship of the early eighteenth century. When he set about his task he complained:[1]

'To see the dull indifference, the negligent and the thoughtless air, that sits upon the faces of a whole assembly, while the psalm is on their lips, might tempt even a charitable observer to suspect the fervency of inward religion.'

His *Psalms of David* not only revived the praises of God amongst his contemporaries, but gave to posterity imperishable paraphrases of the Psalms. The more famous of these are the 72nd ('Jesus shall reign where e'er the sun'); the 90th ('Our God, our help in ages past') which is to-day our second National Anthem; the 92nd ('Sweet is the work my God and King'); the 117th ('From all that dwell below the skies'); the 122nd ('How pleas'd and blest was I'); and the 146th ('I'll praise my Maker with my breath'). They are the measure of the poet's success.

He made, however, an even greater contribution to Puritan praise. By his brave defence of the right to paraphrase the songs of the Old Dispensation in the interests of the New, he was delivering the Puritans from the Bibliolatry of the literalists. This liberation from the exact words of Scripture alone made possible the production of Christian hymns. The transition from paraphrase to hymn is made in his famous *Hymns and Spiritual Songs in Three Books*. The first Book consists of paraphrases of the Messianic portions of the Old Testament, but mainly of New Testament paraphrases. The more noteworthy productions are: 'Awake our souls, away our fears' (Hymn 48); 'Come let us join our cheerful songs' (Hymn 62); 'I'm not ashamed to own my Lord' (Hymn 103); 'Come, dearest Lord, descend and dwell' (Hymn 135); 'Join all the glorious names' (Hymn 149). Of the second Book he says that it 'consists of

[1] *Hymns and Spiritual Songs in Three Books*, preface; *Works* iv 253

hymns whose form is of mere human composure; but I hope the sense and materials will appear truly divine'.[1] These hymns include 'Come we that love the Lord' (Hymn 30); 'There is a land of pure delight' (Hymn 66) and 'Give me the wings of faith to rise' (Hymn 140). The third Book, however, represents the greatest departure from tradition, although, as their author points out, these hymns are written 'that in imitation of our blessed Saviour, we may sing an hymn after we have partaken of bread and wine'.[2] One hymn from this collection is certain of immortality and is regarded by that expert hymnologist, Dr Julian, as one of the four finest hymns in the English language.

The hymns and paraphrases of Isaac Watts, although unequal in style, sometimes tawdry in conceits, occasionally descending to the level of doggerel, established themselves as the criterion by which all subsequent metrical versions and hymns came to be judged. They are the finest flowers of Puritan piety.

It would, however, be a mistake to assume that he was the originator of paraphrases or of hymns among the Dissenters. That honour is reserved for Benjamin Keach. Watts wrote no hymns before 1694, whereas Keach had hymns published thirty years earlier.[3] Keach's importance is merely chronological; the significance of Watts lies in the quality of his productions, the variety and orientation of his subjects, and his far-reaching influence. It would not be an exaggeration to say that he was the greatest exponent of public worship in the Puritan tradition. It is true that he had developed beyond his spiritual forefathers; he freed the Puritan tradition from Bibliolatry. At the same time he stood as eagerly as they did for a Biblical basis for praise and his concern for 'gospel-worship' was as deep as theirs. In fact, his main design in paraphrasing the Psalms was to make them more evangelical. If he appeared to depart from the Puritan tradition in prayer in requiring preparation and less dependence upon 'sudden motions', he yet urged that written prayers were a preparative not a substitute for orderly extempore praying and insisted upon an exhaustive use of Scripture expressions in public devotions. It is therefore legitimate to regard him as the inheritor of the Puritan tradition. In his belief in the didactic value of praise, as in his insistence upon intelligibility, his aim, like that of the

[1] *id.* iv 256 [2] *ibid.* [3] Adam A. Reid, art. in *Baptist Quarterly* x 67*ff*

Puritans, was edification. If the Puritan would not subscribe to the Apostles' or the Nicene Creeds, his praises sounded forth his evangelical beliefs. If he would not say his creed, he sang it.

Our consideration of the praise of the Puritans most fittingly concludes with an estimate of the value of the Psalms to the Puritans. They made an intensely personal application of them to their exigencies. Many instances are given in Prothero's *The Psalms in Human Life*. Most famous of these is the occasion when Cromwell called upon his men at Dunbar to sing the 117th Psalm. The General had beaten the enemy with a loss of under twenty of his own men, compared with the enemy's losses of three thousand slain and ten thousand prisoners. The chase was prolonged, Cromwell made a halt, and, in a pious but practical way, called for the shortest metrical psalm.[1] The real value of the Psalms to the Puritans is best shewn, as Hawkins insists,[2] by the treatise, said to have been composed by St Athanasius, which they prefixed to their earlier impressions of the Psalms. These directions advised the choice of particular psalms to meet emergencies. The original Psalms, which were produced in turbulent times, mirror the mood of the Commonwealth days, and, as the following citations shew, seemed extraordinarily apposite to the circumstances of the God-fearing Roundheads:

'If thou seest that evill men lay snares for thee, and therefore desirest God's eares to heare thy praiers, sing the 5 psalme.'

'If thine enemies cluster against thee, and go about with their bloody hand to destroy thee, go not thou about by man's helpe to revenge it, for al men's judgments are not trustie, but require God to be judge, for he alone is judge, and say the 26, 35, 43 psalmes.'

'If they press more fiercelie on thee, although they be in numbers like an armed hoast, fear them not which thus reject thee, as though thou wert not annointed and elect by God, but sing the 27 psalme.'

'If they yet be so impudent that they lay in wait against thee, so that it is not lawful for thee to have any vocation by them, regard them not, but sing to God the 48 psalme.'

'If thou hast suffered false accusation before the King, and seest the divel to triumph therat, go aside and say the 50 psalme.'

[1] Percy Scholes *The Puritans and Music* (1934) p. 272

[2] *History of Music* (1776) ch. cxvi

These citations are sufficient to shew how the Psalms spoke to the hearts and conditions of the Puritans and how, through them, the Puritans were strengthened in their conviction of election by God to a solemn vocation. The Psalms were, therefore, the creeds and the battle-songs of the Puritans. In them they found a supernatural authority for their conduct and a heavenly comfort in perplexity and danger. Through them *vox Dei* became *vox populi*. If the converse of the adage was the danger of Puritanism, this was its inspiration and strength.

## CHAPTER XI

## PURITAN PREACHING

The pure Word of God was the criterion to which doctrine, worship and church government must conform, according to the Puritans. It goes without saying, therefore, that the 'opening' of the Scriptures occupies the central position in Puritan worship. The importance of preaching consisted in the fact that it was the declaration by the preacher of the revelation of God, confirmed in the hearts of the believers by the interior testimony of the Holy Spirit. The Puritans, like the continental Reformers, insisted that the Word of God was above the Church and thus the Church came under its judgment. Calvin was constrained to oppose to the criterion of an infallible Church, the standard of an infallible Book.[1] The Puritans inherited this tradition. For them the very Sacraments, since they were dramatic representations of the Word, are necessarily subordinate to the Gospel. At the same time it was not intended that a high respect for the declaration of the Gospel should be accompanied by a depreciation of the value of the Sacraments. Indeed the Sacraments were the 'seals' of the Word. Thomas Goodwin makes this abundantly clear in the following similes:

> . . .'the moon, though it be a standing ordinance in heaven, yet appears in several shapes, and so the Word, too. But this [*the Lord's Supper*] as the sun is uniform, for the person of Christ (the "Sun of Righteousness") crucified is wholly and entirely the matter of it; and as He is "the same to-morrow and to-day and yesterday"; so is this ordinance.'[2]

This quotation is typical of the 'high' view of the Sacrament of the Lord's Supper held by the Puritans. It is not to be denied, however, that others seemed to think that the sermon in the Puritan order of worship usurped the position of the prayers and praises, as well as of the Sacraments. Dr Hammond is severe on the Puritans for this. He inveighs against

> 'those who place so great a Pietie in hearing, and think so much the more comfortably of themselves from the number of houres spent in that

[1] It is not suggested that Calvin was a 'fundamentalist' in the present-day sense of the term

[2] *Works* (Edinburgh 1845) xi 403

Exercise, which hath of late been the only businesse of the Church, . . . and the Liturgie at most used but as Musicke to entertaine the Auditors till the Actors be attired, and the Seates be full, and it be time for the Scene to enter.'[1]

For a true appreciation of the centrality of preaching, it is necessary to turn to the leading Puritan authors. One of the earliest, William Bradshaw, claims to speak for the whole body of the Puritans in his work *Englishe Puritanisme, containing the maine opinions of the rigidest sort of those that are called Puritanes in the realm of England*. The primacy of preaching is indicated in this quotation from the work:[2]

'They hould that the highest and supreame office and authoritie of the Pastor, is to preach the gospell solemnly and publickly to the Congregation, by interpreting the written word of God, and applying the same by exhortation and reproof unto them. They hould that this was the greatest worke that Christ & his Apostles did.'

A similar view of the supreme importance of preaching is held by the compilers of the Parliamentary Directory, who write:[3]

'Preaching of the Word, being the power of God unto salvation, and one of the greatest and most excellent works belonging to the ministry of the Gospel, should be so performed that the workman need not be ashamed, but may save himself and those that hear him.'

For the Puritan, who emphasized the great abyss that separated God from man, it was infinitely more important that God should cross it and speak to him through the sermon, than that he should traverse it in prayer or praise. There is perhaps no finer definition of the purpose and solemnity of preaching than that of Richard Baxter:[4]

'It is no small matter to stand up in the face of a congregation, and deliver a message of salvation or damnation, as from the living God, in the name of our Redeemer. It is no easy matter to speak so plain, that the ignorant may understand us; and so seriously that the deadest hearts may feel us; and so convincingly, that contradicting cavillers may be silenced.'

[1] *A View of the New Directory and a Vindication of the Ancient Liturgy of the Church of England* (2nd ed., Oxford 1646) p. 73

[2] (ed. 1605) p. 17 [3] Hall *Reliquiæ Liturgicæ* iii 35

[4] *The Reformed Pastor* (ed. London 1860) p. 128

The same author provided the classical description of the urgency of preaching as 'a dying man to dying men'. Under such a persuasion, small wonder that a Puritan preacher mounted the steps of his pulpit as if he were a Moses ascending the mountain of Sinai. A moderate Nonconformist of the next century, in an Ordination sermon,[1] commends the sermons of the Puritans in a passage which is itself an excellent summary of the aims and comprehensiveness of Puritan preaching. He advises the ordinand to deliver sermons that shall contain

'the same doctrine as was deliver'd by St. Paul to Timothy and Titus, and other first Preachers and Publishers of Christianity'.

He continues:

'With all possible seriousness preach to your people the Christ whom St. Paul ador'd, the Grace which he taught, the Faith, the Life, the Spirit, the Hope, the Love, and the Sacraments and other services which he recommended. Open to those that sit under your ministry, the foundation of all Religion, the Divinity of the Scriptures, and their sufficiency, the Covenant of Grace, and the Terms of acceptance with God, and the suitableness of the Mediator provided for lapsed creatures, the Riches and Fulness of the Divine Promises, the odiousness and malignity of Sin, the Nature, Necessity and Excellence of Holiness, and the certainty and importance of things eternal.'

He concludes:

'Let me recommend it to you, to do your part, that that plain Practical Preaching, that was begun by our Good Old Puritans, and by keeping up which, the Modern Nonconformists as much as they have been despis'd have been so useful, may not be lost among us.'

Isaac Watts is within the Puritan tradition when he maintains:[2]

'But let the warmest zeal for God, and compassion for perishing men, animate your voice and countenance.'

He is no less insistent upon the urgency of preaching than Baxter.

'Let the awful and important thoughts of souls being saved by my preaching, or left to perish and be condemned to hell by my negligency,

[1] *The Principles and Practice of Moderate Nonconformity with respect to Ordination* (London 1717) p. 33

[2] *An Humble Attempt towards the Revival of Practical Religion among Christians; Works* iii 31

I say, let this awful and tremendous thought dwell ever upon your spirit.'

The above quotations sufficiently illustrate the Puritan conception of the importance of the sermon. The preacher was the man of God, the prophet, who declared to the congregation the 'mystery' of the Gospel, unfolding the whole plan of salvation, under compulsion to bring men to the parting of the ways that lead to salvation or to damnation. What might appear as mere enthusiasm in the Puritan preacher, was in reality the expression of his sense of urgency. By his preaching of the Gospel he was actually, under Christ, binding and loosing the souls of men. Puritan preaching is thus, in Goodwin's phrase, 'experimental, saving, applying knowledge'. It was far removed from didacticism and from subjectivism. If the Puritan taught, it was 'saving knowledge' that he imparted; if he referred to his own experience it was only by way of illustrating what God in his mercy had done for him. The preaching of the Word was neither a moral homily nor a philosophical disquisition; it was the authoritative declaration of the will of the Blessed God. Therein lay its supreme significance.

The value which the Puritans attached to sermons appeared excessive in the eyes of the Establishment. Hooker, for instance, complains that the Puritans regard preaching as the only method of declaring God's Word:[1]

'. . . whatsoever is spoken concerning the efficacy or necessity of God's Word, the same they tie and restrain only unto Sermons, howbeit not Sermons read neither (for such a thing they also abhor in the Church), but Sermons without book, Sermons which spend their life in their birth, and may have public audience but once.'

Hooker urges that there are other avenues that lead to a saving knowledge of God: in particular, 'conversation in the bosom of the Church', 'religious education', 'the reading of learned men's books', 'information received by conference', as well as the public and private reading of the Scriptures and of Homilies. He refers scathingly to the Puritan claims

'how Christ is by Sermons lifted up higher, and made more apparent to the eye of Faith; how the savour of the Word is made more sweet, being brayed, and more able to nourish, being divided, by Preaching,

[1] *Eccl. Pol.* V xxi 2

than by only Reading proposed; how Sermons are the keys of the Kingdom of Heaven, and do open the Scriptures, which being but read, remain in comparison still clasped . . .'[1]

Indeed Hooker looks askance upon sermons as the corrupt productions of men, whilst the reading of Scripture preserves the Word of God unadulterated. Homilies are preferable to sermons since they have been carefully prepared.

Thomas Cartwright takes an entirely opposite view. He recognizes that reading may make wise unto salvation, but that it is a poor substitute for preaching. It is by sermons alone that the Word of God penetrates the hearts of the congregation.

'As the fire stirred giveth more heat, so the Word, as it were, blown by preaching, flameth more in the hearers, than when it is read.'[2]

But even Hooker makes the grudging admission that sermons are more popular than homilies or Scripture lections.

'Whereas the cause why Sermons only are observed to prevail so much, while all means else seem to sleep and do nothing, is in truth nothing but that singular affection and attention which the People sheweth every where towards the one, and their cold disposition to the other; the reason hereof being partly the art which our adversaries use for the credit of their Sermons, to bring men out of conceit with all other teaching besides; partly a custom which men have to let those things carelessly pass by their ears, which they have oftentimes heard before, or know they may hear again whensoever it pleaseth themselves; partly the especial advantages which Sermons naturally have to procure attention, both in that they come always new, and because by the hearer it is still presumed, that if they be let slip for the present, what good soever they contain is lost, and that without all hope of recovery.'[3]

This unsolicited testimony to the preaching of the Puritans recognizes that in the minds of the people there was no hesitation as to whether sermons were to be preferred to homilies or not.

Indeed it was Archbishop Grindal who first urged the superiority of the sermon to the homily. For his brave defence of preaching made to the Queen, who proposed to silence the unauthorized preaching conferences known as 'prophesyings', he fell from the Queen's favour and was virtually a prisoner in

[1] *id.* V xxii 12 [2] *Eccl. Pol.* (ed. Hanbury) vol. ii, p. 76*n*
[3] *Eccl. Pol.* V xxii 20

his palace for the rest of his days. This famous letter, dated the 20th of December, 1576,[1] contrasts sermons with homilies:

'The Godly Preacher is termed in the Gospel, a Faithful Servant, who knoweth how to give his Lord's family their apportioned food in season; who can apply his speech according to the diversity of times, places and hearers; which cannot be done in the Homilies: exhortations, reprehensions, and persuasions, are uttered with more affection, to the moving of the Hearers, in Sermons than in Homilies. Besides, Homilies were devised by the Godly Bishops in your Brother's time, only to supply necessity, for want of Preachers; and are by Statute not to be preferred, but to give place to Sermons, whensoever they may be had.'

Grindal was, of course, one of the Frankfort exiles during the Marian persecution and he returned to England with the Puritan conception of the sermon.

When Elizabeth was succeeded by James, the Puritans pleaded with the King for toleration. In their appeal, 'Confession and Protestation of Faith of certain Christians in England' (1616),[2] they explicitly requested that preaching may be preferred to the reading of homilies.

'Wee believe that with us the reading of Homilies in divine service is not lawfull, but very unmeete for the congregation of the faithfull; namely where it is held for competent without the imployment of a preaching Pastor; whereas a Pastors diligent, discreet, and judicious preaching, and applying of Gods Word, is the power of God unto salvation ordinarily. Neither doth every of the allowed Homilies in every point conteyne godly doctrine.'

The Establishment feared that the Puritans wanted to use sermons for the dissemination of their distinctive tenets, and they therefore preferred the reading of homilies as a safeguard against heretical or schismatical opinions. Puritans, on the other hand, claimed that it was by preaching alone that the saving truth could be brought home to the hearts of men.

Richard Baxter, who was prepared to see eye to eye with the Established Church on many points, claims that prescribed lections and preaching upon prescribed subjects or the reading of homilies, fail to meet the conditions of the local congregation, which the minister alone knows.

[1] cited by Strype *Grindal* (Oxford 1821)
[2] p. C3 *recto*

'If I know my hearers to be most addicted to drunkenness, must I be tyed up from preaching or reading against that sin, and tyed to Read and Preach only against Covetousness or the like, because it seemeth meet to Governours to tye me a constant course?'[1]

His answer to the question is an unqualified negative.

A characteristic Puritan defence of preaching, as contrasted with reading the Word, is made by Thomas Goodwin. He gives three reasons for preferring the exposition of the Word. First, because the very 'dullness' of many people requires the illumination of preaching. Secondly, preaching is one of the gifts which the ascended Lord bequeathed to his Church. Thirdly,

'It is not the letter of the Word that ordinarily doth convert, but the spiritual meaning of it, as revealed and expounded . . . There is the letter, the husk; and there is the spirit, the kernel; and when we by expounding the word do open the husk, out drops the kernel. And so it is the spiritual meaning of the Word let into the heart which converts it and turns it unto God.'[2]

He sums up preaching as an 'experimental, applying, saving knowledge'.

The debate between Anglicans and Puritans on the relative merits of homilies and sermons, demonstrates the high value, indeed the indispensable value, which the Puritans attached to preaching. This was God's appointed means of bringing men to salvation; it was also the most effective way of gaining the interest of a congregation and of educating it; and, in the third place, only sermons could adapt themselves to the needs of the particular congregations and to the age in which men lived.

From the very beginning the Puritans had been outstanding in their demand for a more thorough knowledge of the Word of God. This found expression in their services which were often preceded by lengthy Scripture lections and, supremely, in their preaching conferences, or 'prophesyings'. These religious exercises prevailed chiefly in the counties of Essex, Norfolk and Northampton. The ministers of a district met at a central church to exercise themselves in the exposition of

[1] *Five Disputations &c.* p. 440

[2] *On the Constitution, Right, Order and Government of the Churches of Christ &c.; Works* xi 364

Scripture. They claimed as the Scriptural precedent for such gatherings the text of St. Paul (I Cor. xiv 31): 'Ye may all prophesy one by one, that all may learn, and all be comforted'. Fuller provides a detailed description of their meetings.[1] The youngest divine would first enter the pulpit and expound a portion of Scripture previously agreed upon on for about half an hour; after him three, four or five other divines, in order of seniority, explained the meaning of the same passage. Finally, a more experienced divine summed up the findings of those who preceded him, and made his comments upon them. The exercises concluded, as they had begun, with prayer. Too often, as Fuller points out, they were made the platform for preaching Puritanism, even where the text did not lend itself to controversial discussion. But even allowing for this defect, they provided the clergy with a better knowledge of the Scriptures and made them, therefore, more efficient preachers of the Word of God. These exercises were themselves a proof of the inadequacy of the Established system to meet the needs of the community, religiously. If the Queen had not abolished them, they might have provided seminaries for the instruction of the clergy. It is also likely that their continuance would have spread the tenets of Puritanism. It was, therefore, for the latter reason that the Queen suppressed them, even though Archbishop Grindal and some of the Bishops, notably Parkhurst of Norwich, supported them.

The demand for the exposition of the Word of God in the services of the Church was powerfully reinforced by the example of the Elizabethan Dissenters. The Barrowist assemblies apparently spent the whole of their Sundays in prayer and exposition of the Scriptures. One of their number reported:[2]

'In the somer tyme they mett together in the feilds a mile or more about London. there they sitt downe vppon A Banke & diuers of them expound out of the bible so long as they are there assembled. In ye wynter tyme they assemble themselves by 5 of the clocke in ye morning to that howse where they make there Coventicle, for yt Saboth daie men and woemen together there they continewe in there kind of praier & exposicion of Scriptures all that daie.'

The Separatists also insisted upon expounding the lessons which they read. The credit for this innovation is due to John

[1] *Church History* IX iv 2, 3 [2] Burrage *Early English Dissenters* i 26

Smyth.[1] His example was followed by the New England Puritans and by Independents and Baptists in England. The Puritans were noted for their method of 'running exposition' of the Scriptures. Baillie informs us that this was characteristic of the Brownist services.[2] He also states that the Amsterdam Separatists had devised another method for educating the people in the Scriptures, which they named a 'Conference',

> 'whereby by way of Conference, Questioning, and Disputation, every one of the Congregation may propound publikely, and presse their Scruples, Doubts and Objections, against anything which that day they have heard'.[3]

John Robinson, the most famous of the Pilgrim pastors, explains that there are seven reasons why he favours 'the exercise of prophecy'. Among them are the following:

> 'That such as are to be taken into the ministry of the church, may both become and appear apt to teach';
>
> 'that the doctrine of the church may be preserved pure from the infection of error';
>
> 'that things doubtful arising in teaching may be cleared, things obscure opened, things erroneous convinced';
>
> 'for the edification of the church and conversion of them that believe not'; and, finally,
>
> 'lest by the excluding the commonalty and multitude from church affairs, the people of God be divided, and charity lessened, and familiarity and good-will be extinguished between the order of ministers and people.'[4]

It will have become evident that the whole body of Dissenters from the Established Church, Separatist and semi-Separatist alike, made the exposition and discussion of the Scriptures the outstanding feature in their worship. The Puritans, reinforced by their example, demanded sermons to be preached instead of the customary reading of homilies, and proceeded to repair the omission by unauthorized 'prophesyings'. These factors, coupled with the Puritan reverence for the Bible as the only standard for worship, combined to produce the Puritan appreciation of the sermon as the culminating point in the worship of God. For them obedient listening to the exposition

[1] *cf.* his *Works* (ed. Whitley) vol. I, p. lxxxvii [2] *A Dissuasive &c.* p. 29 [3] *id.* p. 30 [4] *Works* (ed. Ashton) iii 55–58

of the sacred oracles of God was the climax of the service. Later their central pulpits were to symbolize the centrality of the Word. In their tradition the pulpit overshadowed the communion-table, and fittingly, for the Sacrament was the 'seal' of the Word—a dramatic representation of the Word which they preached.

The lengthy Puritan sermon had a structure of its own. It had a triple division into Doctrine, Reason and Use. The Westminster Directory gives the following instructions for sermon-composition according to this method:

> 'In raising doctrines from the text, his care ought to be, First, that the matter be the truth of God. Secondly, that it be a truth contained in, or grounded on, that text that the hearers may discern how God teacheth it from thence. Thirdly, that he chiefly insist upon those doctrines which are principally intended, and make most for the edification of his hearers.'[1]

Evangelical teaching was the first aim of the sermon. These doctrines had then to be explained to the congregation and their contraries refuted. The second division of the sermon was a logical defence of the assumptions of the first section. The Directory urges:

> 'The arguments, or reasons are to be solid; and, as much as may be, convincing. The illustrations, of what kind soever, ought to be full of light, and such as may convey the truth into the hearer's heart with spiritual delight.'[2]

It is insisted that apparent contradictions are to be reconciled, and that little time is to be taken up in answering trivial objections or mere cavillings. The third section was intended to drive home the practical advantages of belief in the particular teaching advocated. It usually concluded with admonitions and encouragements. Thus Doctrine, Reason and Use might be rendered as the Declaration, the Explanation and the Application of the Christian faith. The first two sections sought to convince the reason, whilst the last section aimed at warming the affections into acceptance of the doctrine. That the Puritan sermon was characterized by this triple division is proved by the following citation from the Anglican divine, Dr Simon Patrick:[3]

[1] Hall *Reliquiæ Liturgicæ* iii 37 [2] *ibid.*
[3] *A Discourse of Profiting by Sermons* (1683) p. 6

'Some indeed, I have heard, find fault with our Sermons for not keeping the old method (as they call it) of Doctrine, Reason and Use.'

This document, written forty years after the Parliamentary Directory, witnesses to the existence of a tradition. Baxter, according to his biographer Dr F. J. Powicke, was a firm believer in this method.

'He tells us expressly indeed, that the preacher's aim should be first to convince the understanding and then to engage the heart. Light first, then heat. And such was his unvarying method. Beginning with a careful "opening" of the text, he proceeded to the clearance of possible difficulties or objections; next, to a statement of "uses"; and lastly to a fervent appeal for acceptance by conscience and heart.'[1]

It was a combination of the methods of St Thomas Aquinas and of St Francis of Assisi. Isaac Watts had the twofold aim of winning mind and heart in sermons, when he gave the following advice:[2]

'Awaken your spirit, therefore, in your composures, contrive all lively, forcible and penetrating forms of speech, to make your words powerful and impressive on the hearts of your hearers, when light is first let into the mind.'

The same author describes the perfect sermon, according to Puritan standards:

'Practise all the awful and solemn ways of address to the conscience, all the soft and tender influences on the heart. Try all methods to rouse and awaken the cold, the stupid, the sleepy race of sinners; learn all the language of holy jealousy and terror, to affright the presumptuous; all the compassionate and encouraging manners of speaking, to comfort, encourage, and direct the awakened, the penitent, the willing, and the humble; all the winning and engaging modes of discourse and expostulation, to constrain the hearers of every character to attend. Seek this happy skill of reigning and triumphing over the hearts of an assembly; persuade them with power to love and practise all the important duties of godliness, in opposition to the flesh and the world; endeavour to kindle the soul to zeal in the holy warfare, and to make it bravely victorious over all the enemies of its salvation.'[3]

The structure of the Puritan sermon was designed to enable it to fulfil these high ends.

[1] *Life* p. 50 [2] *Works* iii 25 [3] *ibid.*

The Puritan sermon was a lengthy one. It appears to have been the unanimous agreement amongst all Puritans that a sermon should be of an hour's duration. Cartwright suggests that it might have been difficult to restrain zealous preachers within the limit of an hour's discourse.

'Let there be, if it may be every sabbath-day, two sermons, and let them that preach always endeavour to keep themselves within one hour, especially on the week-days.'[1]

The Brownists also kept within the same limits.[2] As late as the early eighteenth century the sermon was expected to last for an hour. Edmund Calamy is the informant. Speaking of the average Dissenting minister, he declares:[3]

'He publishes the Will of God both as to Truth and Duty in two distinct Discourses on the Lord's Day, the one in the Forenoon, the other in the Afternoon. Each Sermon is about an hour's length, and begun and closed with Prayer.'

We are indebted to John Howe, who became one of Cromwell's chaplains, for an indication that the prolixity of a sermon was an index of the preacher's abilities in the Commonwealth. Cromwell was anxious to test Howe's pulpit powers, it appears. So, immediately after the prayer preceding the sermon, he altered the text which he had commanded Howe to expound. The worthy divine preached from this text until the monitory sands of the first and second hour had run out. He was called upon to desist only when he was about to turn the glass again.[4] This, however, was a preaching marathon, and congregations were not expected to endure more than an hour's prolixity.

The delivery of the sermon next falls to be considered. Contrary to the common opinion, Puritans were not unanimously in favour of extempore utterance. Goodwin, a leading Independent, was definitely against this. He declares[5] with some heat:

'Whereas some men are for preaching only *extempore*, and without study, Paul bids Timothy meditate and study, and give his mind wholly to these things.'

[1] Neal *History of the Puritans* vol. V, appendix 4, p. xv
[2] *The Brownists Synagogue* p. 6 [3] *A Letter to a Divine in Germany* p. 9
[4] Calamy *Continuation of the Ejected Ministers* (1727) i 250*f*
[5] *Works* xi 379

Later in the same paragraph, he denies the existence of extempore preaching, strictly so-called:

'Neither can they be said to preach *extempore*, or what is at that present revealed, for they preach those things which their thoughts and speeches have been exercised in before.'

Baxter declares in his *Sheet against the Quakers* (1657) that the charge they brought against him of reading his sermons was justified. He wrote and read them except when he was too busy to do so.[1] Dr Powicke is of the opinion 'that all the great preachers of the century did the same'.[2] This claim cannot be substantiated, however. For the Scottish Presbyterians at least did not approve of the custom. Baillie, for instance, informs us that Nye, when he preached in Edinburgh in 1643, 'did not please because he read much out of his paper-book'.[3] The prolixity and the weighty erudition of the printed sermons of the Puritans would make it unlikely that they were preached extempore; whilst it would be an almost impossible burden to commit them to memory. It cannot, however, be roundly stated that all the Puritan preachers delivered their sermons from notes.

The Puritans used vehement gestures in the delivery of their sermons. This is one ground for Anglican ridicule at their expense. One such critic writes:[4]

'How often have you seen a Preacher heat himself, beyond the need of any vestments? Throwing off his Cloak, nay and his Gloves too, as great impediments to the holy performance, squeeking and roaring beyond the example of any Lunatick? Sometimes speaking in a tolerable tone, and presently again crying out as if under some immediate distraction? While the people with great amazement have gaped upon him, and when he hath finished, given him this honourable Encomium, Well, hee's a rare man, a man mighty zealous for the Lord, a powerful Preacher, and one that hath taken abundance of pains that day . . .'

The same writer ridicules the affectations of voice and diction assumed by Puritan preachers:[5]

[1] Powicke *Life of Baxter* p. 256*n* [2] *id.* p. 256
[3] cited Sprott & Leishman *op. cit.* p. 338
[4] *A Free and Impartial Inquiry into the causes of that very great Esteem and Honour that the Nonconforming Preachers are generally in with their followers* (1673) p. 118*f* [5] *id.* p. 119

'Another pretty practice of these men, and that is, the judging men's sanctity, the truth of their Regeneration, by a certain mode or form of speaking. I do not mean the Dramatist's twang of Nose (though you cannot but have observed how modish that was once among the Saints, and you know the Doctor at Oxford we once counted perfect in it) but a peculiar way of wording things; by which men should be judged of them.'

South, the excellent preacher of the Church of the Restoration days, makes a similar complaint against the gestures of Puritan preachers:[1]

'Can any tolerable Reason be given for those strange new Postures used by some in the Delivery of the Word? Such as shutting the Eyes, distorting the Face, and speaking through the Nose, which I think cannot so properly be called Preaching, as Toning of a Sermon.'

He concludes his tirade with an irreverent witticism:

'None surely will imagine, that these Men's speaking as never Man spoke before, can pass for any Imitation of Him.'

The vehemence of the Puritan preacher's gestures was obviously as much approved by the Puritan congregations, as they were abominated by the Anglicans.

Another characteristic of the Puritan sermon was its diction. This is described by South as 'the whimsical Cant of *Issues*, *Products*, *Tendencies*, *Breathings*, *In-dwellings*, *Rollings*, *Recumbencies*'.[2] Another critic of the Puritans claims that men are not listened to if they lack 'the sanctified language'.[3] The same author declares that

'it is notorious to all men, how mighty civil these persons are to their people, how careful to caress all their followers with the glorious names of God's Saints; the Lord's holy ones; the dear people of God, the little flock, the Lambs of Christ Jesus, the Redeemed ones of Sion, the true Remnant of Jacob, and the precious elect Seed'.[4]

There is a much simpler and more convincing explanation of the use of this nomenclature. These are merely the descriptions of the Church of the New Testament, and the Puritans had Dominical or Apostolic precedents for them. The Puritan preachers, it should also be remembered, loved their flocks

[1] *Sermons* (Oxford 1823) iii 34–37 [2] *id.* iii 34
[3] *A Free and Impartial Inquiry &c.* p. 101 [4] *id.* p. 138

but did not hesitate to admonish or chastise them. So that it is fairer to assume that the distinctive diction of the Puritan sermons was due to a familiarity with the Scriptures, not to affectation.

Since Puritan sermons were most carefully prepared for the edification of the people, it was natural enough that their authors should try to make them as memorable as possible. One method of attaching the sermon to the memory of the congregation was to provide headings for the main divisions or doctrines of the sermon, all beginning with the same letter. Baxter, for instance, claims that if this device is used and also another, the numbering of the directions, the sermon can be easily retained in the memory. As an illustration of the method he suggests

> 'as if I were to direct you to the chiefest helps to your salvation, and should name, 1. Powerful Preaching, 2. Prayer, 3. Prudence, 4. Piety, 5. Painfulness, 6. Patience, 7. Perseverance'.[1]

The very insistence that sermons 'should not die at their birth' was characteristic of the Puritan zeal for edification. Baxter insists that it is part of the duty of a Christian to con the sermons that he has heard.

> 'As soon as you come home, while dinner is preparing, it will be a seasonable time either for secret prayer or meditation to call over what you heard, and urge it on your hearts, and beg God's help for the improvement of it, and pardon for all your public failings.'

He also suggests that after the second service of the day is concluded it is the duty of the head of the family to conduct a family service in which he shall repeat, or cause others to repeat, the afternoon sermon.[2] It is quite probable that the more zealous among the congregation took notes of the sermon while it was being preached. This was certainly the practice of some in the Puritan Church of the exiles at Arnhem,

> 'where the chiefest sit and take notes, not a gentlewoman that thinkes her hand to faire to vse pen and Inke'.[3]

Isaac Watts also commends the practice of dividing sermons so that they shall be more memorable:[4]

[1] *A Christian Directory* pt. II, ch. xviii; vol. iv (ed. Orme) p. 255
[2] *ibid.* [3] Burrage *op. cit.* ii 292 [4] *Works* iii 25

'Whatsoever proper and natural divisions belong to your subject, mark them out by the numbers 1st, 2nd 3rd &c. This will afford you time to breathe in the delivery of your discourse, and give your hearers a short season of recollection of the particulars which have been mentioned before.'

It appears, however, that this practice of dividing and subdividing the parts of the sermon could be pursued to exaggerated lengths. For this reason Watts includes this warning:[1]

'But in this matter take care always to maintain a happy medium, so as never to arise to a number of particulars as may make your sermon look like a tree full of branches in the winter, without the beautiful and profitable appearance of leaves and fruit.'

South satirizes the Puritan faults of over-division, prolixity and over-elaboration of the same points in the following account of a typical sermon:[2]

'First of all they seize upon some Text, from whence they draw something (which they call a Doctrine) . . . In the next place, being thus provided, they branch it into several Heads; perhaps twenty or thirty or upwards. Whereupon, for the Prosecution of these, they repair to some trusty Concordance, which never fails them, and by the help of that, they range six or seven Scriptures under each Head; which Scriptures they prosecute one by one, first amplifying and enlarging upon one, for some considerable time, till they have spoiled it; and then that being done, they pass to another, which in turn suffers accordingly. And these impertinent, and unpremeditated Enlargements they look upon as the Motions and Breathings of the Spirit, and therefore much beyond those carnal Ordinances of Sense and Reason, supported by Industry and Study; and this they call a saving way of Preaching, as it must be confessed to be a way to save much Labour.'

In contrast to the sermons of the Caroline Anglican divines, such as Andrewes and Donne, which were weighted down with classical and patristic quotations, the sermons of the Puritans were restricted almost entirely to Biblical citations. Oliver Ormerod in his *Portrait of a Puritan* (1605)[3] pictures a Puritan saying, in a book,

'My heart . . . waxeth colde, and my flesh trembleth to heare you say, that a Preacher should confirme his matter out of the Fathers and

[1] *ibid.* [2] *Sermons* iii 35*f* [3] p. K3 *verso*

humaine writers: doth preaching consist in quoting of Doctors, and alleadging of Poets and Philosophers? In what part of his commission hath a Minister so to doe?'

All Puritans, however, were not of this opinion, although the majority were. Apparently the longest debate, on the subject of preaching, in the Westminster Assembly of Divines, concerned the propriety of quoting the dead languages. Calamy, who was in favour of erudite allusions in the original tongues being included in sermons, supported his point by the following instance:

'A minister told me he was converted by a Latin sentence, *Mallem esse porcus Herodis quam filius*.'

But, on the other hand, Rutherford said 'The pot may be used in the lithing, but not brought in with the porridge'.[1] Even this information shows that the objection was taken to quoting the dead languages in the original, not to the substance of the classics as such.

This attempt to evaluate the Puritan sermon can best continue by examining in some detail two specimens. The first is a sermon preached in London in the year 1674. It is taken as an instance of the heavy fare which Puritans apparently enjoyed, as an indication of the amount of information which was concentrated in a Puritan sermon, and as evidence of the systematic minds the Puritan divines possessed. The text is Acts xvi 30: 'And they brought them out and said, Sirs, what must I do to be saved?' The text is 'opened' thus:

'The words contain in them a weighty question propounded by the trembling jailor, occasioned by a miracle which the Lord wrought for his eminent servants, Paul and Silas.'

The Doctrine is drawn thus:

'That it is the main concernment, and ought to be the continual care of every child of God, diligently to enquire, How he may be saved.'

Then follow the Reasons. The first is

'Because of the Hardness and difficulty here; for though all expect and look for heaven and promise themselves as good a title as the most exact and circumspect walk, but I Pet.4,13, certainly not before God, Hab.

[1] Sprott & Leishman *op. cit.* p. 338

1.13, not before Christ II Thes.1,7, not even before men Mt.7,13 and 14; 16,24; I Cor.6,9 and 10.'

The second Reason given is

'Because all questions unless they may be reduced hereunto are altogether unprofitable and vaine; Psalm 4 and Psalm 15.1. This is a necessary question: Psalm 24.3. Now if God's holiness be such that the righteous, though their sins be pardoned, can scarcely be saved because of their sins, then certainly the wicked whose sins are not pardoned shall certainly be damned.'

This point is driven home by a consideration of 'the vast difference between the godly and wicked in view of their spiritual condition'. The godly have five advantages over the wicked:

'1. The godly were converted; they were regenerated; now by virtue of this they are exalted to know God, but yet for all this they shall scarcely be saved, and through fire. 2. The godly have the effectual and powerful aid of God's Spirit and are partakers of the divine nature; but the wicked are strangers to the Holy Spirit.'

Thirdly, the godly are able to pray in an acceptable manner. Fourthly, they have the promises of God. Fifthly, they have a lively faith.[1] This sermon is not selected as an instance of the best Puritan sermon. It serves to indicate the quality of a fairly typical and average sermon. While it might be considered pedestrian, it has the merit of being sound, of having great clarity and urgency, and of being systematically arranged.

The second summary of a Puritan sermon offered, displays the weaknesses to which Puritan sermons were prone. It was preached in London in October 1682 at a Morning Exercise of the Nonconformist Ministers in London. The subject is 'Whether it be expedient and how the Congregation may say *Amen* in publick Worship.' The text is Nehemiah viii 6: 'And Ezra blessed the Lord, the great God, and all the People answered, Amen, Amen.' It is virtually a sermon on one word, *Amen*. The Doctrine taught is 'That it is a lawful and laudable practice for people at the conclusion of public prayer or praysing God to pronounce an *Amen*.' Then follows a series of

[1] *The Baptist Quarterly* i (1922–23) 233*ff*; the article is entitled 'London Preaching about 1674' and contains summaries of sermons taken down by a listener.

definitions of *Amen*: 1. '*Amen* Substantive' (God himself); 2. '*Amen* Affirmative' (verily); 3. '*Amen* Optative'; and 4. 'Double *Amen*'. This is succeeded by a statement of the Uses of the Doctrine: first, 'it is connatural to Prayer and Praise'; secondly, it has the authority of both Testaments; thirdly, '*Amens* after Prayer and Praise, is the mans consent, judgment and approbation of what is offered unto God'; fourthly, 'This vocal *Amen* is as it were the epitome and summ of all our petitions and praises to God'; fifthly, it 'involves a strong faith'; sixthly, it is 'an assurance that God will accept our Praises and Answer our Prayers'; lastly, 'this unanimous *Amen* of Faith strikes terror on the enemies of the Church, whether Devils or men'.[1] This is an ingenious sermon, but the author has been hard put to it to discover seven 'uses' for the doctrine. The series of definitions of *Amen* is exceedingly pedantic, and the whole sermon wants a sense of proportion in wasting so much labour on an unimportant point. This is an illustration of Puritan prolixity, prodigality and pedantry at its worst. For the best Puritan sermons one must look to the compositions of John Owen, Thomas Goodwin, Richard Baxter and Matthew Henry. They cannot compare with the sermons of Andrewes or Jeremy Taylor for eloquence and sustained diction, nor with Tillotson for sheer oratory, nor with South for urbanity; but for Biblical scholarship, high seriousness and psychological insight they are unrivalled. These are the qualities which they tried to achieve and for which they would be most anxious to be esteemed.

Perhaps the best indication of the value in which sermons were held by Puritans is the frequency of the demand for preaching. Two famous divines will be cited as examples. Baxter provides us in his pastoral diary with an account of his ministerial labours:[2]

> 'I preached before the Wars twice each Lord's Day; but after the War but once, and once every Thursday, besides occasional sermons.'

This, however, did not exhaust his duties, for he spent two whole days of each week in catechizing families. Further, he met a group of his flock every Thursday night at his house

[1] Sermon xxxi in *A Continuation of Morning Exercise Sermons* (ed. Samuel Annesley, 1683)

[2] *Reliquiæ Baxterianæ* (1695) p. 83

'and there one of them repeated the Sermon, and afterwards they proposed what Doubts any of them had about the Sermon, or any other Case of Conscience.'

He also spent another night each week in teaching his young people to pray. He also met with his fellow-ministers for Discipline and Disputation once a month and he presided once every month at the meeting for Parish Discipline. On days of Humiliation also he preached to his congregation. His ardour was indefatigable.

An even more remarkable series of testimonies to the importance of preaching is given by the Northern divine, Oliver Heywood. Reviewing his labours in the year 1689, when he had reached the age of sixty, he declares:[1]

'I doe find that I had travelled 1358 miles, preacht 131 times in week-days, kept 34 fasts, 8 days of thanksgiving, baptized 21 children &c.'

The following year he records that he has preached 135 times in week-days, including two sermons every Lord's day.[2] This remarkable servant of God makes this entry in his diary in his seventieth year:

'My life is still prolonged notwithstanding my many infirmities, especially my sore affliction of the Asthma or short-breathing which hath so increased upon me that I could not walk to my chappel on foot but my friends haue provided me a chair in which two men carry me.'

He continues:

'. . . yet was enabled when I got into the pulpit to preach audibly—baptized 8 children, kept 8 conferences, preacht on week-days 23 times, writ 7 treatises, 4 short for Warly-people, 104 letters, observed 14 fasts, 3 days of thanksgiving, 2 books printed *viz.* the two worlds and Christs intercession—my dear Lord was with me all along.'[3]

This Puritan pastor preached, on an average, five sermons per week. He was not an itinerant preacher, attached to no church. He was the minister of the church at Northowram, near Halifax. He was also an author of great merit in his day. His many sermons were, therefore, preached in the midst of an unusually busy life. One could hardly hope for a more enthusiastic testimony to the high opinion the Puritans had of preaching.

[1] Horsfall Turner *The Reverend Oliver Heywood, B.A., 1630–1702: His Autobiography, Diaries, Anecdote and Event Books* (Bingley 1883) iii 238
[2] *id.* iii 247 [3] *id.* iii 285

It has been pointed out that the Anglican Church produced many eloquent preachers in the seventeenth century. Despite this fact, they were recognized primarily as orators rather than as preachers. The truth is that the Anglican conception of a sermon differed considerably from the Puritan ideal. Canning, the Independent Minister of Ipswich, claims that Anglican sermons do not declare the 'pure Word of God'. Rather are they orations

'of the excellent Constitution of their Church, or of Passive Obedience, or an Exclamation against Schism, or a Discourse of Morality, or only exclaiming against such vices as the very light of Nature condemns'.[1]

By contrast he claims that the true function of preaching is

'to preach Jesus Christ, and sinners need of an Interest in Him, and of His justifying Righteousness, and to magnify the Riches of Divine Grace in Man's Salvation: it is to preach the Doctrines of Faith, Repentance, Regeneration, and Sanctification, and the Necessity of the Power of the Spirit of God, in order to all these'.[2]

In other words, the Puritan complaint against Anglican sermons is that they are not evangelical in content. Anglican preachers were also criticized on the score of delivery. Dr Simon Patrick repeats the Puritan charges:

'Now here two things are found fault withal: first, That our Preachers are not vehement enough in the Delivery of their Sermons; secondly, That they read them.'

The Puritan charges might be reduced to one; the lack of earnestness in the Establishment. For them a true zeal for conversion was discoverable only in a minister who preached the evangelical doctrines, with evident vigour, and who looked his congregation full in the face. The Puritan's concern was light and heat. The Anglican despised enthusiasm in the pulpit, and in his zeal to be a servant of the State, occasionally forgot that he was the servant of God. But the Puritan preacher, whose dominating desire was to win souls, and who supplemented his preaching with diligent visitation, determined, like St. Paul, 'to know nothing save Jesus Christ and him crucified'. To this single aim all was directed. He could not afford to trick out his

[1] *Plain Reasons for Dissenting from the Church of England* (3rd ed. 1736) p. 6
[2] *ibid.*

discourses with the flowers of rhetoric or scholarship. His aim was not to delight his hearers but to strike for a verdict in their souls. Therefore his preaching was Biblical, simple, prolonged, and its urgency was emphasized by the vehemence of his gestures.

Since the Puritan preachers confined themselves to simple, serious evangelical preaching, we look in vain for certain characteristics in their sermons. The wit of South, the brilliant and quaint imagination of Donne, the sustained metaphors of Jeremy Taylor, or the racy language of Latimer, are not to be found there. Their qualities are less obtrusive. Moreover their style is more uniform. They excel in sustained Biblical exposition, in 'existential' thinking, in their knowledge of their congregations, and in sincerity. If their sermons have a quality of anonymity about them, it is because they hid themselves that God might declare his salvation through them. They had, of course, their defects. Among the chief of these were pedantry and prolixity. But if the test of a sermon is the quality of life that it produces, then the Puritan discourses were superbly successful.

## CHAPTER XII

## PURITAN ADMINISTRATION OF THE SACRAMENTS

### I. *The Sacrament of the Lord's Supper*

The very title, 'The Lord's Supper', which the Puritans adopted for the Sacrament of Communion, in preference to 'Communion', or 'Eucharist', is significant. It is yet another indication of the Puritan loyalty to the Word of God. No other name sufficiently indicated the Dominical authority for this sacrament or its Scriptural foundation. It was the universally accepted designation for this sacrament amongst all the Puritans. Since the Puritans preferred Scripture to tradition as their basis for the order of celebrating the Lord's Supper, two conclusions might be expected to follow from this. It would be assumed that all Puritans would be unanimous in their criticism of tradition by Scripture. This in fact happened. All Puritans rejected the Sacrifice of the Mass, and the posture of kneeling at Communion, which they believed lent colour to that doctrine. It might also be presumed that the Puritans would have a uniform mode of celebrating the Lord's Supper according to the pattern of the New Testament. Their frequent criticism of the Communion service of the Anglican Church was that its variations from the Scriptural precedent implied the insufficiency of the Scriptures as a guide to worship. They, on the contrary, maintained the all-sufficiency and clarity of the Word of God as a liturgical guide. But, if this was the case in theory, it was not substantiated in practice. There is a considerable diversity of modes of celebration of Communion amongst the Puritans, which implies that the guidance of the Scriptures was not as all-sufficient or as definite as the Puritans suggested.

There were three main divisions amongst the Puritans: the Independents, the Baptists, and the Presbyterians. Whilst for practical purposes the Independents and Baptists were united in liturgical practices (with the single exception of their celebration of the Sacrament of Baptism), they differed considerably from the Presbyterians both in the method of celebration of the Sacrament of Communion and in their views of the frequency with which it should be administered.

The Baptists, so the *Broadmead Records* inform us, held the Lord's Supper once every month. This was prepared for by a prayer-meeting held in the preceding week. Such was their custom during the Commonwealth.[1] It is probable that in earlier days the Baptists held a weekly Communion. This was certainly the case at the Anabaptist Churches in London, Lincoln, Sarum, Coventry and Tiverton. In 1626 these Churches wrote a letter to Hans Ries, the representative of the Anabaptist Churches in Holland asking to be united with them in one single religious communion. They gave an account of their liturgical practices in this letter, which contains the following statement:[2]

'Oblata iusta occasione impedimenti, affirmamus caenam dominicam omitti posse donec tollantur impedimenta: aut aliter non audemus omittere quoque die sabbati quum convenimus ad praestandum caetera Dei publici Ministerii.'

It is interesting to note that the Baptists in a number of their congregations insisted upon the celebration of the Lord's Supper in the evening, thus following the original time of the institution by our Lord. The Fenstanton Baptists in 1652 made this declaration in their Church Meeting:[3]

'After consideration of the example of Christ, Luke xxii.19,20, and the words of the Apostle Paul, I.Cor.xi.24,25, it was generally concluded from the rule of Scripture, that we ought always to break bread after Supper.'

This custom continued amongst Baptist congregations as late as 1700. It is explicitly laid down in the Covenant of the Baptist Church Meeting at Horsleydown:[4]

'The Lords Supper, in which Bread is blest, and broken; and Wine blest and pour'd forth, and receiv'd by the Church met, and sitting together in the Evening time, as a sign to all, that in the Evening time of the World, Christs Body was broken and his Blood shed for the Remission of Sins; Sealing only to worthy Receivers their saving interest therein.'

[1] *Broadmead Records* p. 57 [2] Burrage *op. cit.* ii 235

[3] *Fenstanton......Records* p. 35

[4] *The Covenant to be the Lords People and to walk after the Lord, sign'd by the Church of Christ meeting at Horsly-Down in Southwark* (London 1700) p. 9

It is also to be noted that only an ordained minister was permitted to administer the Lord's Supper. The General Assembly of the General Baptists made this ruling at its meeting at Goodman's Fields in 1693. The decision was reaffirmed in 1702.[1] The Baptists thus celebrated the Lord's Supper monthly in the evening, the Sacrament being administered only by an ordained minister of their denomination.

The Congregationalists, or Independents, celebrated the Sacrament each Lord's day. In all probability they inherited this custom from their predecessors, the Brownists. Baillie declares of the Brownists:[2]

> 'They teach, that the Lords Supper should be celebrated every Lords day: So preparation-Sermons before, and Sermons for Thanksgiving after the Lords Table, to them are needlesse.'

The same author states that it is the practice of the Independents to celebrate the Lord's Supper 'not as in New England, once in the month, but as at Amsterdam, once every Lord's day'.[3] Baillie also informs us that the Independents in London 'desire to celebrate at night after all other Ordinances are ended'.[4] It was certainly the practice of the New England Independents to have a monthly Communion. Cotton asserts 'The Lord's Supper we administer for the time, once a moneth at least'.[5] This monthly celebration was still maintained at the end of the seventeenth century in New England.[6]

It is equally certain that the English Independents had a weekly celebration of the Sacrament. John Owen's Catechism reads:[7]

> '*Question* 40: How often is the Ordinance of the Lord's Supper to be Administred?
>
> *Ans.* Every first day of the week, or at least as often as opportunity and conveniency may be obtained.'

The official statement of the Independents, Goodwin, Nye, Simpson, Burroughes and Bridge, accords with Owen's practice. In their *Apologetical Narration*[8] presented to the West-

[1] *Minutes of the General Assembly of the General Baptists* (ed. cit.) pp. 39, 70

[2] *A Dissuasive* p. 29 [3] *id.* p. 121 [4] *ibid.*

[5] *The Way of the Churches of Christ in New England* p. 68

[6] *cf.* the *Diary of Samuel Sewall* (Collections of the Massachusetts Historical Society, 5th Series) iii 32 [7] Orme *Life of John Owen* p. 308 [8] p. 8

minster Assembly of Divines, their public practice is described thus:

'Our public worship was made up of no other parts, than the worship of all other Reformed Churches doth consist of. As public and solemn prayer for kings, and all in authority, &c.; the reading the Scriptures of the Old and New Testament; exposition of them as occasion was, and constant preaching of the word; the administration of the two sacraments, baptism to infants, and the Lord's Supper; singing of psalms; collection for the poor, &c. every Lord's day.'

It is less certain that it was the usual custom of the Independents to observe the Sacrament during the evening. Crosby gives an account of the public worship of the early Independents meeting at Deadman's Place, London, which describes a morning celebration of the Lord's Supper. There is, however, complete unanimity amongst the English Independents in the weekly celebration.

The Independent celebration of the Lord's Supper varied from the accepted Reformed usage not only in point of frequency, but also in the manner of the delivery of the elements. It was the Reformed custom for the receivers to come to the Lord's Table and to partake of the elements whilst sitting around the table. The Independents, however, used to receive the elements sitting in their pews. Either the bread and wine were brought to them by the Deacons, who sat at the table with the Minister, or by the Minister himself. The New England practice was for the Deacons to deliver the elements. Cotton, our informant, says:[1]

'In time of the solemnization of the Supper, the Minister having taken, blessed and broken the bread, and commanded all the people to take and eate it, as the body of Christ broken for them, he taketh it himself, and giveth it to all that sit at table with him, and from the Table it is reached by the Deacons to the people sitting in the next seats about them, the Minister sitting in his place at the table.'

The wine is delivered to the people in the same way.

Baillie complains that the Independents, by this mode of reception, have departed from the tradition of the Reformed Churches:[2]

[1] *The Way of the Churches of Christ in New England* p. 68

[2] *A Dissuasive* p. 121

'That their conformity with the Brownists may be full, the New English doe count sitting at a table not only to be necessary, but to be a part of our imitation of Christ and a Rite significant of divers heavenly Priviledges and Comforts, but as the Brownists at Amsterdam this day have no table at all, as they send the Elements from the Pulpit (the place where the Minister preacheth, and celebrateth the Sacrament) by hand of the Deacon to all the Congregation, where in their meeting house they sit up and down in their several places.'

Baillie has evidently misread Cotton's description of the New England Communion-service. Baillie assumes that all the people sit round the table, whereas in fact Cotton states that only the Deacon and the Minister are seated at the table. He continues:[1]

'So the Independents at London doe vehemently contend for the needlesnesse of any to come to the table, what ever be the practice of all the rest of the Reformed Churches. But they will have the holy seales carried from the place where the Minister preaches to the people in their pews, or where ever else they have their ordinary places for hearing of the Word; although most easily in their small Congregations without any disturbance all might bee brought to the Table.'

A further Independent innovation was the characteristic double consecration at their Communion services. Their reason for its introduction was our Lord's precedent given at the Last Supper, when he blessed both bread and wine. The citation from Cotton above shows that first the bread was broken and blessed. The same account then continues:[2]

'After they have all partaked in the bread, he taketh the cup in like manner; and *giveth thanks anew*, (blesseth it) according to the example of Christ in the Evangelist, who describes the institution. *Mat.*26,27. *Mark.*14.23. *Luk.*22.17. All of them in such a way as setteth forth the Elements, not blessed *together*, but either of them *apart;* the bread first by it selfe, and afterwards the wine by it selfe; for what reason the Lord himselfe best knoweth, and we cannot be ignorant that a received solemne blessing, expresly performed by himselfe, doth apparently call upon the whole assembly to look again for a supernatural and speciall blessing in the same element also as well as in the former; for which the Lord will be againe sought to doe it for us.'

This is an example of the blind devotion of the Puritans to the

[1] *id.* p. 122 [2] Cotton *op. cit.* p. 69

very letter of the Scriptures. It is also a singular proof of their belief in the Real Presence. Baillie asserts that this peculiarity in the Independent ordinance is a custom inherited from the Brownists:[1]

'When they come to the action, there is no more but one little discourse, and one short prayer of the Minister, all the time of the participation, there is nothing in the Congregation but a dumb silence: no reading, no exhortation, no Psalmes, their people need no such means to furnish them in their Sacramentall meditations; they have also learned from the Brownists a double and distinct consecration, one for every element apart.'

To a century which had not learned the value of silence in worship, this account of an Independent Communion service naturally seemed bare in the extreme. It must be remembered, however, that the ordinance had been preceded by the Liturgy of the Word. As this often contained psalm-singing, reading and exposition of the Scriptures, and sometimes two Sermons, there was value in a quiet Communion service. The following account of a typical Independent service, at which some Peers were present for the purpose of examining their worship, indicates that a lengthy Communion service would have been unsuitable after the prolix preliminaries:[2]

'The people went on in their usual method, having two sermons; in both which they treated of those principles for which they had been accused, grounding their discourses on the words of our Saviour, "All power is given unto me in heaven and earth." Matth.xxviii,18. After this they received the Lord's Supper, and then made a collection for the poor . . .'

Information as to the detailed procedure of the Independents in the celebration of the Lord's Supper is difficult to obtain. The complete picture can be obtained only by filling in the canvas from the clues and suggestions offered by Cotton and Baillie. Fortunately, there exists a detailed account of the ordinance as celebrated in Rothwell Independent Church in the last decade of the 17th century:[3]

'Every member is required to receive the Sacrament as often as it is administered. The Table stands in the midst of the Congregation, near the Pulpit. The Pastor sits in his chair, near the Table, and the Receivers

[1] *A Dissuasive* p. 121 [2] Crosby *History of the Baptists* i 163
[3] Glass *The Early History of the Independent Church at Rothwell* p. 84

on Forms round about it; the People as spectators, at some small distance behind them. The Pastor prays (all standing) and craves a blessing on the Bread, then sets it apart in almost the same Words which the Church of England uses; then breaks it into small pieces, and puts them on divers Plates, saying whilst he is breaking, Thus was our Lord's body, torn, mangled, broken, &c. The Bread thus broken is carried in the Plates by the Deacons to the several Receivers. The Pastor sits in his Chair eating with the rest. As soon as the Bread is eaten, the Pastor prays; then pours out the Wine, saying, Behold the Blood of Christ poured out for thee, and for me, and for all of us, &c. Drink ye all of this, drink large draughts of the love of Christ, &c.; as he thinks most proper to express himself. Then he drinks and gives to the Deacons. When all have drunk, the Pastor prays, an Hymn is sung, and the assembly is dismissed. They forbid all private prayer at this Ordinance, saying, the Pastor's prayers are sufficient.'

This account with its naïve reporting of the Pastor's commendation to 'drink large draughts of the love of Christ' presents a faithful account of a service in which simplicity is the dominant characteristic. There is also an account available of a Presbyterian Communion service, in which the extemporaneous commendations to the communicants are more felicitously phrased. This account is also of interest because it demonstrates that, by the end of the seventeenth century, the English Presbyterians had abandoned their distinctive custom of sitting around the Lord's table for the Independent custom. The narrator is the New England Judge, Samuel Sewall. He describes the Lord's Supper as it was celebrated in Dr Annesley's church in Little St Helena's, London:[1]

'The Dr. went all over the meeting first, to see who was there, then spake something of the Sermon, then read the words of Institution, then prayed and eat and drank himself, then gave to every one with his own Hand, dropping pertinent Expressions. In our Pue said—Now our Spikenard should give its smell; and said to me, Remember the Death of Christ . . . The Deacon followed the Dr., and when his Cup was empty filled it again: as at our Pue all had drunk but I, he filled the Cup, and then gave it to me; said, as he gave it—Must be ready in new Obedience, and stick at nothing for Christ.'

A detailed account of the celebration of Communion at Dr Watts' church in the early years of the eighteenth century,

[1] *Diary of Samuel Sewall* i 253*ff*

shews that the tradition of Cotton had been retained in its entirety. The service began with the rehearsal of the Institution narrative, followed by the invocation of a Blessing on the Bread.

'Then the Minister says, "Having blessed this bread, we break it in remembrance of our Saviour's body &c." Then the loaves, which are before cut in squares, almost through, are broken by the Minister into small pieces, as big as walnuts, or thereabout, and taking the bread in his hand, he says. "This is the body of Christ, or the emblem or the figure of the body of Christ which was broken for you: take and eat ye all of it in remembrance of our Saviour who died for us", or such like words . . . it is then distributed by the Pastor to the Deacons, and to one or two more of the members who are appointed to it, and it is carried by them to the various members of the church . . . The Pastor proceeds in like manner to pour out the wine, at least into one of the cups, then he asks a blessing on the cup; and then distributes it, as before, to the members or the deacons, and they to some other members of the church, by whom it is carried round to all the seats . . . After this there is a psalm or hymn sung, suited to the ordinance. Then the plate is sent round to collect for the necessities of the poor. After this, particular cases of the members are represented, who desire the public prayers of the church; and then, with a prayer offered on this occasion, together with thanksgiving and the full benediction, the service is concluded.'[1]

This was a typical Independent Communion service, with its double consecration, characteristic of the fidelity of the Independents, as they believed, to the original institution of the Lord's Supper. In one respect only might it be considered to depart from the normal type of Independent celebration: no extemporary reflections, calculated to awaken the response of the communicants, are made by the Minister. A note in the account shows that the Bury Street church was aware of this:[2]

'In many churches the pastor is frequently speaking proper sentences or texts of Scripture to awaken the faith, hope and joy of Christians, and I cannot but approve of it in the main. But our former pastor, Dr. Chauncey, was so much against it, that it was not practised amongst us.'

Later it was revived.

It is often assumed that the Puritans valued the sermon

[1] *Transactions of the Congregational Historical Society* vi 333*ff*: art. 'The Bury Street Church Book (1723)' [2] *ibid.*

more highly than the Sacrament. Goodwin expressly confutes this misrepresentation in the following passage:[1]

'Many things in a Sermon thou understandest not, and haply not many Sermons; or if thou doest, yet findest not thy portion in them; but here to be sure thou mayest. Of Sermons, some are for comfort, some to inform, some to excite; but here in the Sacrament is all thou canst expect. Christ is here light, and wisdom, and comfort, and all to thee. He is here an eye to the blind, a foot to the lame; yea, everything to everyone.'

The same author also declares that, as the moon is variable, so is the proclamation of Christ in a sermon; but, as the sun is constant, so is Christ revealed in the Lord's Supper. Clearly, if he is asked to state a preference, Goodwin values the Sacrament more highly than the sermon.

The most complete statement of the Puritan doctrine of the Lord's Supper is to be found in Matthew Henry's *The Communicant's Companion* which appeared in 1704. Henry's statement of the meaning of the Lord's Supper is as follows:[2]

'It was appointed to be a *commemorating* Ordinance, and a *confessing* Ordinance; a *communicating* Ordinance, and a *covenanting* Ordinance.'

In explanation of the description 'communicating Ordinance' he writes:[3]

'Here are not only Gospel-Truths represented to us, and confessed by us, but Gospel-Benefits offer'd to us, and accepted by us . . . By the Body and Blood of Christ, which this Ordinance is the *Communion of*, we are to understand all those precious Benefits and Privileges which were purchased for us by the Death of Christ, and are assur'd to us upon Gospel-Terms in the everlasting Covenant . . . so in this Ordinance we are *Partakers of Christ.*'

Lest there should be any doubt that this Ordinance is more than a memorial of the death of Christ, or that it merely exhibits the truths of the Gospel, he continues:[4]

'God in this Ordinance not only assures us of the Truth of the Promise, but, according to our present Case and Capacity, *conveys* to us, by his Spirit, the good Things promis'd; *Receive Christ Jesus the Lord*, Christ and a Pardon, Christ and Peace, Christ and Grace, Christ and Heaven;

[1] *Works* (ed. cit.) xi 408 [2] p. 16 [3] *id.* p. 25*f* [4] *id.* p. 27

'tis all your own, if you come to the Terms on which it is offer'd in the Gospel.'

This doctrine is not memorialism—a *signum nudum;* in the full Calvinist sense the Sacrament is a *sigillum Verbi.* It seals to believers the benefits of the Redeemer's Sacrifice.

This was the official doctrine of the Independents, as the *Savoy Declaration* makes evident:[1]

'Worthy Receivers outwardly partaking of the visible Elements in this Sacrament do then also inwardly by Faith, really and indeed, yet not carnally and corporally, but spiritually, receive and feed upon Christ crucified, and all benefits of his death.'

As the Savoy Declaration of 1658 was based upon the *Westminster Confession* issued only four years previously, and with which it agrees in doctrine, if not in ecclesiastical government, this doctrine of the Lord's Supper may be taken as the official view of all the Puritans. It is clearly expressed in directions for the prayer of Consecration in the Westminster Directory, in these words:[2]

'With humble and hearty acknowledgment . . . for this Sacrament in particular, by which Christ and all his benefits are applied and sealed up unto us.'

Presbyterians held a doctrine of the Communion in common with the Independents, but their administration of the Lord's Supper varied considerably from the Independent practice. Independents had a weekly celebration of the Lord's Supper generally, but the interval between one Communion and the next was never longer than a month. It was, however, the general practice of the Presbyterians to have only four Communions during each year. The Parliamentary Directory laid down no definite rule as to the frequency of celebration, but in the debate it was proposed to require at least a quarterly Communion.[3] The one advantage of infrequent Communion appeared to be that its rarity caused the Sacrament to be more esteemed, an illustration of the converse of the adage that 'familiarity breeds contempt'. A further advantage was that infrequent Communions permitted lengthy preparation services for the Sacrament. The infrequency of Communion

[1] ch. XXX §vii [2] Hall *Reliquiæ Liturgicæ* iii 55
[3] Sprott & Leishman *op. cit.* p. 346

amongst the English Presbyterians was probably due to the example of their Scottish brethren. The *Book of Discipline* requests that the Lord's Supper should be celebrated quarterly in burghs and half-yearly in the county-parishes.[1] Communion in Scotland was often more infrequent than this, for there was a popular feeling that the Lord's Supper, like the Passover, ought to be celebrated once yearly.[2] There were, on the other hand, English Presbyterians who would have preferred a weekly celebration. Baxter takes this view:[3]

> 'This Sacrament in the primitive Church was celebrated every Lord's day; yea, and after, even ordinarily on every other day of the week when the churches assembled for communion. And it might be so now without any hindrance to preaching or prayer, if all things were ordered as they should be.'

Despite individual protests, it was the general Presbyterian custom to have a quarterly Communion.

There appears to have been one important difference between Independents and Presbyterians in the manner of administering the elements. It was, however, chiefly practised by the Scottish Presbyterians and pleaded for at the Westminster Assembly. The Independent communicants received the elements sitting in their pews. The Scottish Presbyterians, however, received them at the Table, which was long enough to admit many communicants. The Scottish Presbyterians held tenaciously to this method of reception because they believed it was an accurate attempt to reproduce the circumstances of the Last Supper, whilst it had symbolical value as a declaration that the Lord's Supper was a Feast, at which the Lord was Host and the communicants the guests, rather than a Sacrifice. The point was debated hotly at the Westminster Assembly, but the Scottish Commissioners could not persuade the Assembly to make this manner of reception obligatory. The rubric allows either the Independent or the Scottish Presbyterian method to be adopted. Communion was to be received 'at or about a table'.

The very infrequency of Presbyterian celebration enabled the Communion to take a more elaborate form for them than

[1] McMillan *The Worship of the Scottish Reformed Church* p. 191
[2] Sprott & Leishman *loc. cit.*
[3] *A Christian Directory* pt. II, ch. xviii; vol. iv (ed. cit.) p. 245

for the Independents. The Parliamentary Directory, for instance, contains the following items: an introductory Exhortation explaining the purpose of the ordinance, with a 'fencing of the Table'; the reading of the Institution narrative; the lengthy Eucharistic Prayer; Fraction and Delivery of the Elements; an Exhortation to a worthy life; a post-Communion Prayer; a metrical Psalm of Praise. These are seven in number. The Independent Communion service, by contrast, contains the following elements (according to the practice of the Rothwell Church): the Blessing of the Bread and its Fraction and Delivery; the Blessing of the Wine, its Libation and Delivery; a post-Communion Hymn and the final Benediction. It is not simply that the Presbyterians have seven items compared with the five of the Independents. The Presbyterian prayers, particularly the Eucharistic Prayer, are more comprehensive. From the Rothwell account of the Independent celebration, this would seem to be deficient in two respects. It lacks both an introductory explication and admonition to the communicants, as also a prayer of Intercession on behalf of the Universal Church.

Neither of these items was always lacking in Independent celebrations. Doddridge, in lectures to the students at his theological academy, gives the following instructions as to how the Lord's Supper should be administered:[1]

> 'Introduce the administration with some extempore meditations on some select texts of Scripture . . . In these addresses avoid critical niceties by all means, and pursue a strain the most pathetic.'

It is thus evident that it was frequently the practice to begin the ordinance with an exhortation. He advises that in the pre-Communion prayer the element of confession predominates. He recommends his students to cultivate 'a social temper' throughout the ordinance:

> '. . . give the soul room to expand and soften itself into the most friendly sentiments, not only towards those present, but the whole Church of Christ.'[2]

This direction implies that Intercession for the whole Church of Christ was an integral part of the post-Communion prayer.

The Lord's Supper, as celebrated by the Puritans, is marked

[1] *Works* (Leeds 1804) v 485 [2] *id.* v 486

by three characteristics: first and foremost its fidelity to the Dominical institution of the Supper. This is the meaning of the Presbyterian request that the communicants should receive the elements at the table, as modern representatives of the first disciples. To the Scripture account also must be traced the double 'Consecration' of the Independents. To this, again, must be attributed the practice, universal among Puritans, of singing a hymn or psalm of praise at the conclusion of the ordinance; as also the Delivery accompanied by the original words of the Lord himself as he gave the bread and wine to his disciples. The second characteristic is the strong ethical emphasis given to the Lord's Supper by the Puritans. Only a true disciple of the Lord is worthy to sit at the Lord's Table. The moral sanctity of the ordinance was preserved both by the introductory 'fencing of the Table' and by the exercise of ecclesiastical censures. The demand that communicants should produce the fruits of the Spirit was made by a concluding exhortation, as in the case of the Parliamentary Directory and of the Savoy Liturgy. Finally, the Lord's Supper as celebrated by the Puritans was, in the words of Matthew Henry, 'a communicating ordinance'. It was not a memorial, a tribute to a crucified leader. It was a feast at which the Risen Lord was Host and in which he delivered to his faithful people the benefits of his most sacred Passion. As to its outward form and order, it exhibited, to use John Owen's definition,[1] 'the purity, simplicity and spirituality of evangelical worship'.

## II. *The Sacrament of Baptism*

The Puritans were united in their condemnation of certain features of the Baptismal rite as practised by the Established Church, whilst there was a serious cleavage between the Baptists, who insisted that Baptism was only for adult believers, and the Independents and Presbyterians who practised infant Baptism. Three features of the Anglican Baptismal service were criticized by the three Puritan denominations. The crossing of the child in Baptism was universally disliked by the Puritans. Baxter expresses their unanimous view in his judgment:[2]

[1] *A Discourse of the Work of the Holy Spirit in Prayer; Works* iv 27
[2] *Five Disputations* p. 417

'But of all our Ceremonies, there is none that I have more suspected to be simply unlawful than the Cross in Baptism.'

Whilst he is prepared to admit the Magistrate's right to institute the circumstances of worship, in this matter he cannot, since his action 'is like that of a judge *in alieno foro*'.[1] He regards it as an invented sacrament, pleading that it falls in with the Book of Common Prayer's definition of a Sacrament as 'an outward and visible sign of an inward and spiritual grace'. To add to the prescribed worship of God is to set up oneself in the place of God. That is the gravamen of the objection, and accounts for the ferocity of Puritan opposition to crossing in Baptism. The second criticism was that of the Anglican custom of requiring godparents, or pro-parents, to answer the interrogatories on the child's behalf, promising that it should be brought up in the nurture and admonition of the Lord. The Puritans maintained that the parents themselves alone should be responsible for the spiritual well-being of the child. As they so frequently pointed out, the Scripture promise is 'to you and to your children', and therefore children were baptized on the understanding that their parents were believers and would train their children to be so. The Parliamentary Directory states explicitly, with the Anglican practice in mind:[2]

'The child to be baptized, after notice given to the minister the day before, is to be presented by the father, (in case of his necessary absence, by some Christian friend in his place) professing his earnest desire that the child may be baptized.'

The third criticism of Anglican practice was levelled against the not infrequent custom of private baptism by a private person. The Puritans maintained that Baptism was a Sacrament of the Church and that it ought therefore to be administered in the church by an ordained minister.

If the Puritans were of one mind in their criticisms of the Book of Common Prayer, they were divided in their method of administering the rite. The most serious division of opinion was concerned with the question: Who are to be the recipients of Baptism? The Baptists maintained that only believers should be baptized. The English Baptists sprang originally from the first Independent Church founded by Henry Jacob in 1616.

[1] *id.* p. 418 [2] Hall *Reliquiæ Liturgicæ* iii 45*f*

Whilst Smyth was the first Baptist, he did not found a Church. The first Baptist Church was a secession from the first Independent Church, then under the leadership of Lathrop, in 1633. The Baptists insisted that only believers should be baptized and that the manner should be immersion:[1]

'being convinced of Baptism, yt also it ought to be by diping ye Body into ye Water, resembling Burial & riseing again.'

Edward Draper, a Baptist apologist, gives his reasons for this custom:[2]

'First, From the signification of the word, Baptize; it comes from the Greeke word, *βαπτιζω α βαπτω, i.e. mergo, immergo*, which properly signifies to dip, dive, duck, or plunge under water.'

The second reason is taken from the nature of the ordinance:[3]

'which truly holds forth the death and resurrection of Christ, and our being dead and risen with him: therefore is it said, Coloss.2.12. *We are buried with him in Baptisme.* Now a man that is buried, is covered or hid in the grave: so that . . . persons are, as it were, to be buried under water, which is the most lively representation of the death of Christ.'

This was, therefore, the Baptist substitute for Confirmation, or for the Independent or Presbyterian admission to the membership of the Church.

Both Independents and Presbyterians retained the traditional rite of the Catholic Church in administering Baptism to the infants of believers. Immersion was not regarded as essential:

'Dipping of the person into the water is not necessary, but Baptism is rightly administered by pouring or sprinkling water upon the person.'[4]

The Independents were more strict than the Presbyterians in administering Baptism to infants only where one or both of their parents were believers.[5]

There was probably little difference between the Presbyterian and Independent orders of administration. Each con-

[1] Burrage *Early English Dissenters* ii 303

[2] *Gospel-Glory proclaimed before the Sonnes of Men* (1649) p. 120

[3] *id.* p. 122 [4] *Savoy Declaration* ch. XXIX §iii

[5] Williston Walker *The Creeds and Platforms of Congregationalism* p. 398, note 8

tained an exhortation on the nature and meaning of Baptism; each baptized in the Triune formula; each contained a demand that the parents should promise to bring up the child as a Christian. The only point of difference appears to be that it was the custom of the Scottish Presbyterians to request the father to recite the Apostles' Creed, as proof that he was a believer. The Independents opposed this and it was not demanded, therefore, in the Parliamentary Directory.[1] The unanimity of doctrine between the Independents and the Presbyterians derives from the common Calvinist tenets they held. For both denominations Baptism, like the Lord's Supper, was a *sigillum Verbi*. For both, the presence of the father, rather than of the godfather, was essential (except in the case of his necessary absence) because the child's right to Baptism was its federal holiness, derived through its descent from those who are by profession under the covenant of grace.

The usual pattern of the Independent Baptismal service is given by John Cotton in *The True Constitution of a Particular Visible Church*. This book served as an immense stimulus to the few adherents of Independency in this country and provided them with a rationale and a description of Independent Church order.

'As for Baptism', it read, 'it is to be dispensed by a Minister of the Word unto a Beleever professing his Repentance, and his Faith being a member of the same Church Body as also unto his seed, presented by the Parent unto the Lord & his Church at which time the Minister in Gods roome calleth upon the parent to renew his Covenant with God for himselfe and his seed and calleth upon God as the nature of the Ordinance requireth, for the pardon of originall sinne, and for the sin of the parents and for a blessing upon the Sacrament and Infant and then calling the childe by the name, which the Parent hath given it for his owne edification, and the Childes, he baptizeth it either by dipping or sprinkling into the name of the Father, the Son, and the Holy Ghost.'[2]

This is but the briefest outline of the Independent order. It was left to the discretion of each minister to fill out as best he could. Doddridge gives, in his lectures to his students, directions for clothing the usual Independent bones with flesh. Doddridge's suggested order contains the following items:

[1] Sprott & Leishman *op. cit.* p. 344

[2] *The True Constitution of a Particular Visible Church* p. 6*f*

1. Short Introductory Prayer
2. Discourse on a suitable text
3. Prayer of Confession and Petition for Grace for the Parents
4. Interrogation of Parents
5. Pronouncement of the Triune Name and Baptism
6. Charge to the Parents
7. Prayer of Thanksgiving (for the family and its branches and for Christ's interest in the present generation)
8. The Blessing

This service must have been a very impressive one in practice, if Doddridge's students obeyed his directions. His advice on the 'charge to the parents' is characteristic of the solemnity and the personal intimacy of the Independent services at their best:[1]

'Then give them some particular directions and cautions . . . Especially plead for those parents who have had a religious education, or for whom God hath done anything remarkable in his Providence. Remind them of the obligations they are under to pray for the child, and to resign it to the Divine Will, that if it be taken from this life, the transactions of the baptismal day may be recollected as an engagement to Christian submission. Conclude your discourse with an address to the spectators. If there are any children belonging to the family old enough to be quietly present, desire that they may be, if possible, and drop a word to them touching the meaning of the service.'

This gives an admirable account of how the Puritan pastor who knew his flock intimately was able to speak to their conditions in his discourses, in a manner both intimate and solemn. This account also indicates that in the mid-eighteenth century it was usual to hold Independent Baptismal services in private houses, rather than in the churches. Whilst it was a departure from the Reformed tradition, it enabled the minister to address his hearers in more familiar terms than would have been possible in a Meeting-house. It cannot be doubted that a household of believers was a fitting background for the family ordinance of Baptism. Its one weakness was that the Church members, as the gathered Church, were not able to undertake their corporate responsibility with the parents for

[1] *Works* (ed. cit.) v 483*ff*

the Christian nurture of the child. It was, however, more valuable as a means of serious instruction of the parents, than the service for Baptism in the Book of Common Prayer, which often degenerated into a social occasion at which godparents were invited to take part, not as the Christian custodians of the child, but only as friends of the family who would be expected to provide financially for the child.

The Presbyterian order for Baptism differs hardly at all from the Independent Baptismal service. The Parliamentary Directory gives the following list of items: declaration of the nature of Baptism; admonition of the congregation; exhortation of the parents; prayer for the Lord's blessing on the Ordinance and on the child to be baptized; Baptism in the Triune Name; and a concluding prayer of thanksgiving and petition for the reception of the child into Christ's kingdom. During the exhortation of the parents the Minister is to require the father's 'solemn promise for the performance of his duty'.[1] It is probable that if the Scots Presbyterians at the Assembly of Divines had had their way, even more would have been required of the parents as a proof of their sincerity in desiring Christian Baptism for their child. The Scottish custom, following the example of the Eastern Church and the precedents of Calvin's *La Forme*, Knox's Liturgy, and the Middleburgh and Waldegrave Service-Books, required the parent to recite the Apostles' Creed. Only the strong opposition of the Independents prevented this proposal from being incorporated in the Directory.[2] A mere ghost of the original request survived in the promise required by the Minister from the parent. It has been seen that in the later history of the Independents it was their regular custom to conduct Baptismal services in the home. The Presbyterians, Scottish and English, held firmly to the ruling of the Directory:

'Nor is it to be administered in private places, or privately, but in the place of public worship, and in the face of the congregation, where the people may most conveniently see and hear.'[3]

Apart from these slight differences, the services of Independents and Presbyterians in administering Baptism were uniformly simple, Scriptural and didactic.

[1] Hall *op. cit.* iii 49 [2] Baillie *Letters* ii 258 [3] Hall *op. cit.* iii 45

## CHAPTER XIII

## PURITAN ORDINATIONS

The Puritans in general, and the Independents in particular, by their democratic form of ecclesiastical government, as opposed to the monarchical government of the Established Church, expressed their belief in the doctrine of election and the priesthood of all believers. The inevitable result was that their ministry was not regarded as a priestly hierarchy. It might have been expected that on this account Ordination would have depreciated in value for the Puritans; or indeed that the ordinance might have been altogether neglected. This was not the case. Even the most thorough iconoclasts, the Separatists, held the ordinance in high esteem. This is the testimony of Ainsworth, the learned Hebraist and Separatist leader in Amsterdam:[1]

'I know not one among us that holdeth men without office may minister the Sacraments.'

It may also be remembered that William Brewster asked John Robinson's permission to administer the Sacrament of the Lord's Supper aboard the *Mayflower*, but he was informed that it was inexpedient.

The Separatists of course differed from the Anglicans in their mode and doctrine of ordination. Ainsworth claims that there is strong support in the Old Testament for the ordination of ministers by the whole congregation. For this purpose he cites Num. viii 9–10 as his proof-text:[2]

'In Israel the whole Congregation was assembled at the Ordination of their Ministers and the children of Israel imposed hands upon them. This rule we follow . . .'

The Separatist manner of ordination is also based upon the same passage of Scripture:[3]

'Thirdly for the order and manner of giving, Moses governed the action, to him it was sayd *Thou shalt sprinkle water, thou shalt bring them before*

[1] *An Animadversion to Mr. Richard Clyftons Advertisement* (Amsterdam 1613) p. 69 [2] *id.* p. 53 [3] *id.* p. 54*f*

*the Lord* & then the *Children of Israel* imposed hands: this I understand not of every particular man, but of some of the cheif for the rest: as the Elders, heads of tribes, cheif fathers of families &c as when al the multitute brought an oblation for their sign, the *Elders* put their hands on the head of the Sacrifice, Lev.4.14.15. Accordingly have wee practised in our ordination of officers . . . some of the cheif of the church, the ancients and fathers of families, imposed hands in the name of the rest.'

The Separatists clearly valued Ordination highly, as a Scriptural ordinance; their Teachers and Elders as well as their Pastors were ordained. Moreover the traditional manner, by the laying on of hands, was retained.

The earliest non-Separatist Puritan Catechism in existence shows that the early Independents also valued Ordination highly. To the Question: 'How many Sacraments are there; or holy Signes?' the answer is made:

'Two; Baptisme, & the Lords Table. One other also may be reckoned as a holy Signe of lesse dignity & inferior nature; yt is, Laying on of hands. But beside these Christs Testament knoweth none.'[1]

The author was the first minister of the first English Independent Church, Henry Jacob. Since the first English Baptist congregations were founded by secession from this Church, on the single issue of Baptism, it may be assumed that the English Baptists practised the rite of Ordination, similarly, from the earliest days. The longevity of the Baptist tradition of ordaining their Ministry may be gathered from the following minute of a meeting of the General Assembly of the General Baptists in 1693:[2]

'The Question being put whether a Gifted Disciple as such may Lawfully Exercise Discipline & Administer the Ordinac̄on of the Lords Supper abroad in the Churches without Ordinacon It was resolved in the negative.'

The underlying assumption is that an innovation was proposed allowing a layman to administer the Lord's Supper, but that it was decided to retain the older custom of requiring ordination before administration of the Sacrament. The picture of a complete Baptist Ordination in the eighteenth century includes the following items: First, an introductory discourse, contain-

[1] Burrage *op. cit.* ii 159 [2] *Minutes* (ed. Whitley) p. 39

ing these words: 'We are now come, at the desire of this church, to separate Mr Abraham Booth to the pastoral office in this community, according to the primitive manner, by prayer and imposition of hands.' Then follows an account by a representative of the local Church 'of the steps taken by this community in order to its obtaining a pastor'. The members of the Church are then required to recognize Mr Booth as their pastor by raising their right hands. The new pastor is then to give an account of the reasons why he accepted the invitation of the Church to be its pastor and publicly to declare his acceptance. He was then required to 'deliver a confession of his faith'.[1]

John Cotton, the leading New England Independent of his day, is the earliest authority for the practice of Ordination amongst Independents. His account shows that fasting and prayer began the day of Ordination. He informs us that the rite proper begins when, at the end of the day, an Elder asks if, after having sought God's guidance in prayer, the members still desire to proceed with the election. Silence on the part of the people signifies consent. He then requires the approbation of the assembly for the judgment and practice of the nominee. The election is certified by the raising of hands. The nominee then accepts his election and declares in what ways God has led him to seek ordination. An Elder then reminds the Church of its duties to the ordinand. Then they proceed to ordain the nominee:

> 'He then with the *Presbytery* of that Church if they have any, if not two or three of the gravest Christians among the Brethren of that Church being deputed by the body, doe in the name of the Lord Jesus ordaine him into that Office, with imposition of hands, calling upon the Lord . . . to accept and owne him . . .'[2]

He is also charged to keep the souls of the flock committed to him safe unto the day of judgment. The rite concludes when the Elders give the ordinand the right hand of fellowship as a sign of his reception into the assembly.

It is interesting to note that an early Independent congregation was considering whether to omit the laying on of hands in

[1] W. T. Whitley, art. 'Abraham Booth's Ordination, 1769' in *Baptist Quarterly* ix (1938–39) 246

[2] Cotton *The Way of the Churches of Christ in New England* p. 41

the ordination service, because this ceremony had been interpreted by some in an *ex opere* manner. The Norwich Independent Church elected in 1647 the Rev. Timothy Armitage to be their minister. The Church wrote to the Independent Church at Great Yarmouth seeking advice

'concerning ye manner of ordination, how they shall proceed in it, whether by imposition of hands, or by other ways.'

The reply was received that

'if laying on of hands was significative as the ceremonies were, and for ye conferring of some immediate gift, it was not to be done. But if meerly demonstrative before ye church, noting ye man set apart for ye worke and office unto wch hee is set apart then it might be well done; onely with this caution yt such as were against it would not be offended with ye thing done.'[1]

Whilst it was the general practice amongst Independents to ordain their ministers by the laying on of hands, an ordination was not held to be invalid if the ceremony was omitted. Thus the laying on of hands was felt to be of the *bene esse* not of the *esse* of ordination. The usual practice and doctrine is described in the official Congregational Confession, the *Savoy Declaration* of 1658, as follows:[2]

'The way appointed by Christ for the calling of any person, fitted and gifted by the Holy Ghost, unto the Office of Pastor, Teacher, or Elder in a Church, is that he be chosen thereunto by the common suffrage of the Church itself, and solemnly set apart by Fasting and Prayer, with Imposition of Hands of the Eldership of that Church, if there be any before constituted therein: And of a Deacon, that he be chosen by the like suffrage, and set apart by Prayer and the like Imposition of Hands.'

This was the general method. If exception was taken to the ceremony of laying on of hands, it was permitted to omit this. The next paragraph of the Confession clearly allows for this scruple against the imposition of hands:[3]

'The Essence of this Call of a Pastor, Teacher, or Elder unto Office, consists in the Election of the Church together with his acceptation of it and separation *by Fasting and Prayer:* And those who are so chosen, though not set apart by Imposition of Hands, are rightly constituted

[1] C. B. Jewson, art. 'St. Mary's, Norwich' in *Baptist Quarterly* x 172
[2] cited Williston Walker *op. cit.* p. 404 [3] cited *id.* p. 405

Ministers of Jesus Christ, in whose Name and Authority they exercise the Ministry to them so committed. The Calling of Deacons consisteth in the like Election and acceptation, with separation *by Prayer*.'

The Independent Church at Rothwell ordained as its Minister Richard Davis on March 22nd, 1690:[1]

'. . . the said Mr. Davis by fasting and prayer of the church, and imposition of hands of the eldership, in the name of the said church, was set apart to and installed in the office of Pastor and Bishop of the said Church of Christ at Rothwell.'

At this service only the Elders of the local Church laid hands upon the ordinand, to the grave displeasure of the neighbouring ministers who were present. Several of them abruptly withdrew, saying that 'there was no business for them'.[2] Further confirmation that it was usual and almost universal for Independents to ordain by the laying on of hands is given by Judge Sewall, who witnessed an Independent ordination at Dedham in 1693. He writes:[3]

'. . . saw Mr. Joseph Belchar Ordained. He preached very well from Exod.4.12. Mr. Neh. Hobart asked the Objections; Mr. Sam Torrey solemnly prayed and gave the Charge, Mr. N. Hobart and Mr. Jno. Danforth joining in laying on of Hands. Mr. Moses Fisk gave the right Hand of Fellowship. 118. Psalm sung from the 25th v. to the end; St. David's Tune.'

Apparently even in Watts' day, imposition of hands was not considered to be an essential in the rite of ordination. In a letter to his brother Enoch Watts,[4] he declares that the majority hold to the tenets of Dr John Owen on the matter of ordination:

'. . . that it is not absolutely necessary that a minister be ordained by the imposition of hands of other ministers, but only requisite that other ministers should be there present as advisers and assistants when he is ordained by the Church; that is, set apart by fasting and prayer.'

In another letter[5] he declares that whether imposition of hands is to be practised in an ordination service or not should rest upon the decision of the Church ordaining, since it cannot be shown in Scripture to be essential to the rite:

[1] Glass *op. cit.* p. 33*f* [2] *id.* p. 37*f* [3] *Diary of Samuel Sewall* i 387
[4] Milner *Life of Isaac Watts* (1834) p. 196*f* [5] *id.* p. 231

'The laying on of hands can never be proved from the Scriptures to be an essential requisite to ordination that I can find, nor that an office is thereby ordinarily conveyed; but it has been a sign in use in all ages, agreeably to, and derived from, the nature of things, when a superior has prayed for a blessing on an inferior, or when anything has been devoted to sacred use; I could use it on all occasions with great freedom, or omit it, according as it might be most agreeable to the Church where I minister.'

Clearly Watts and Owen both follow the lead of the *Savoy Declaration* which, whilst commending the laying on of hands, refused to make it indispensable in ordination. It appears that Watts did not receive the laying on of hands at his own ordination on March 14th, 1702. The order of service commenced with a prayer by Mr Matthew Clark, the Minister of Miles Lane Church. Then Mr Pickard, a deacon, asked the assembled members if they agreed to choose Mr Watts as their Minister and if they would submit to him. Assent was given by raising their right hands. Then Mr Watts gave his consent publicly. Then Mr Thomas Collins continued with prayer. Mr Thomas Rowe, the Minister of Girdler's Hall Church, preached on the text Jeremiah iii 15. This was in effect a charge to both Minister and congregation. Mr Benoni Rowe, of Fetter Lane, Mr Ridgley, and the new Minister followed in prayer. A hymn was sung and Mr Watts concluded the duties of the day by pronouncing the Blessing.[1] The order given above makes no reference to the laying on of hands and it may be assumed that this was not included.

The usual Independent Ordination service would contain the following elements: an invitation on the part of the Church to the ordinand to become their Minister, publicly attested; and public acceptance of this invitation on the part of the ordinand. These two statements might be elaborated should the representative of the Church or the ordinand, or both, decide to explain the steps that led to giving and accepting the invitation. Then the ordinand is solemnly set apart to his office by prayer, and if the Church desires, by the imposition of hands. Then follows a sermon exhorting the Minister to be faithful in the discharge of his duties and the Church members to be loyal

[1] T. G. Crippen, art. 'Dr Watts' Church Book' in *Transactions of the Congregational Historical Society* i (April 1901) 36*f*

to their Minister. Alternatively, two separate charges may be given. Then it was customary after other prayers and praises for the newly-ordained minister to conclude the service with a Blessing. Such is the usual Independent Ordination order in outline.

A complete and early account of the Presbyterian manner of ordination is provided in the Waldegrave and Middleburgh Liturgies. Whenever there was a vacancy in a Presbyterian congregation, the Ministers and Elders of the Presbytery convened the members of the Church, desiring them to consider suitable nominations. If more than one candidate was suggested, then the Church appointed that they should be examined by the Ministers and Elders on a certain convenient day. The examination aimed at discovering whether their knowledge of the Scriptures was thorough, and whether their conduct had been blameless. The candidate selected, the congregation was then informed of the choice of the Ministers and Elders, and they were allowed eight days in which to make individual enquiries as to the suitability of the candidate selected. The people are charged to humble themselves before God by fasting and prayer that the decision may be agreeable to God's will and beneficial to the Church: and,

'if nothing be alleged, upon some certain day, one of the Ministers, at the morning sermon, presenteth him again to the Church, framing his sermon, or some part thereof, to the setting forth of his duty'.[1]

The preliminaries completed, the Ordination service took place in the afternoon.

Full details of this service are given in the Middleburgh Prayer-Book. This commences by a lengthy introductory discourse by the presiding minister on the nature of Ordination, based upon the 4th Chapter of the Epistle to the Ephesians. This includes a description of pastoral duties. The Minister is required to preach the Word, to offer prayers on behalf of the whole Church, to administer the Sacraments of Baptism and the Lord's Supper and to maintain the Church in good discipline. The ordinand is then required to answer the three following questions:

'First, I ask you, whether you feel in your heart that you are lawfully called by the Church of God, and consequently by God himself, to this

[1] Hall *op. cit.* i (Middleburgh) 125

holy ministry? Secondly, whether you hold the books of the Old and New Testament to be the only word of God, and the perfect doctrine of salvation; and do forsake all doctrines repugnant unto the same? Thirdly, whether you promise to execute your charge, as before it is described, with all fidelity, according to the same doctrine; and to execute and accompany your instructions with a godly life: as also to submit yourself to the Church censures, according to the common order of the Churches, if it should happen that you should miscarry yourself either in doctrine or life?'[1]

The ordinand is to answer each question with the response 'Yea, with all my heart'. Then follows the ordination prayer, which is said while the presiding minister, and any others who may be present, lay their hands upon the ordinand. The new minister and his flock are then admonished as to their respective duties by another minister. This is succeeded by a prayer that God may ratify the act of ordination. It is concluded by the Lord's Prayer, said by all. The service ends with a psalm of praise.[2] The Waldegrave order of 1584–5 follows this procedure with one alteration: the presiding minister pronounces the ordinand lawfully ordained in these words:

'According to this lawful calling, agreeable to the word of God, whereby thou art chosen Pastor in the name of God, stand thou charged with the pastoral charge of this people, over which the Holy Ghost hath made thee overseer, to govern this flock of God, which he hath purchased with his blood.'[3]

The Middleburgh Prayer of Ordination is a development of this earlier and simpler declaration. The Middleburgh form for Ordination may fairly be taken as the pattern of Presbyterian ordination services during the Commonwealth period, since it was reprinted in *The Service, Discipline and Forme of the Common Prayers . . . humbly presented to the most High Court of Parliament, this present yeare*, 1641. Moreover the second edition of 1643, also presented to Parliament, declares that it was 'approved by most Reverend Divines of the Church of Scotland'. The Parliamentary Directory, intended to serve as a manual of liturgical directions acceptable to both Independents and Presbyterians, naturally omitted an order for ordination, since this would necessarily have been unacceptable to

[1] *id.* i 81*f* [2] *id.* i 126 [3] Hall *Fragmenta Liturgica* i (Puritan) 19

the Independents. For this reason there is all the more justification for believing that the Presbyterian ordinations followed the Genevan model as transmitted by the Waldegrave and Middleburgh Liturgies.

After 1645 the earlier models were unnecessary, as the Westminster Assembly in that year examined and approved a new form, which also received the approbation of the General Assembly of the Church of Scotland. This order requires that the congregation, which finds itself without a pastor, shall ordain a fast at which three or four ministers of the Presbytery shall attend. One of the ministers shall expound to them out of the Word of God directions as to the office and duties of Christian ministers and the duties of the congregation towards the minister. The sermon ended, the presiding minister shall demand of the ordinand

'concerning his faith in Christ Jesus, and his persuasion of the truth of the reformed religion according to the Scripture; his sincere intentions and ends in desiring to enter into this calling; his diligence in prayer, reading, meditation, preaching, ministering the sacraments, discipline, and doing all ministerial duties towards his charge; his zeal and faithfulness in maintaining the truth of the gospel, the unity of the church against error and schism; his care that himself and family may be unblamable, and examples to the flock; his willingness and humility, in meekness of spirit, to submit unto the admonitions of his brethren and discipline of the church; and his resolution to continue in his duty against all trouble and persecution.'[1]

The presiding minister is then to admonish the Church

'concerning their willingness to receive and acknowledge him [*the ordinand*] as the minister of Christ; and to obey, and submit unto him, as having the rule over them in the Lord; and to maintain, encourage, and assist him, in all the parts of his office'.[2]

When these promises have been obtained from both the ordinand and the Church, the ministers of the Presbytery

'shall solemnly set him apart to the office and work of the ministry, by laying their hands upon him'.[3]

Then follows a brief charge to the Minister and his flock on their mutual duties. They are then both commended to God

[1] Neal *History of the Puritans* vol. V, appendix 9: 'The Form of Presbyterian Church-government', p. cix [2] *ibid.* [3] *id.* p. cx

in prayer. The service concludes with the psalm and a blessing. This form, it will be seen, is in the direct line of the Genevan order, and bears many resemblances to the Middleburgh order for ordination.

A comparison of an Independent form of ordination with a Presbyterian order shows that both were essentially alike. In both the work of selection was accompanied by fasting and prayer; in both the ordinand and the flock to which he is to be ordained make solemn promises; in both the central act is an invocation; in both there is a charge to the Minister and to the Church. The differences are slight and are the products of the differing types of church government. In an Independent ordination the presence of neighbouring ministers was not required, since the local Church set the ordinand apart for the work of the ministry. In a Presbyterian ordination the Presbytery sent its representatives who conjointly, by the laying on of hands, set apart the Minister to his office. In Presbyterian ordinations the laying on of hands is a necessary accompaniment of the ordination prayer, whilst in the Independent ordinations it is a regular but not a necessary constituent of the service.

## CHAPTER XIV

## PURITAN EXERCISE OF ECCLESIASTICAL DISCIPLINE

The controlling principles of Puritanism, as of Separatism, were two. First and foremost, the demand that God should be worshipped and obeyed according to the 'purity' of his holy Word. Thus Christian doctrine, worship and government were to conform to that authoritative criterion. The second principle was that God must be served with a corresponding 'purity' of life. It is therefore not to be wondered at that the Puritans were scrupulously rigid in the exercise of Church censures. Justification for the exercise of admonishment, and failing that, of excommunication, was to be found both in the New Testament and in their insistence upon ethical purity.

Richard Fitz, the minister of the 'Privye Churche' meeting in Plumbers' Hall in 1567, declared in his pamphlet *The Trewe Markes of Christes Churches, &c.*[1] that a true Church was characterized by the three following signs:

> 'Fyrst and formoste, the Glorious worde and Euangell preached, not in bondage and subiection, but freely, and purelye. Secondly to haue the Sacraments mynistered purely, onely and all together accordinge to the institution and good worde of the Lorde Iesus, without any tradicion or inuention of man. And laste of all to haue, not the fylthye Cannon lawe, but dissiplyne onely and all together agreable to the same heauenlye and allmighty worde of oure good Lorde, Iesus Chryste.'

Clearly this Separatist values discipline highly because he believes it to be an ordinance of Christ.

The ethical value of ecclesiastical discipline is clearly explained in 'The Order of the Ecclesiastical Discipline' contained in the Waldegrave Liturgy. The paragraph headed 'What Discipline is'[2] maintains that

> 'As the word of God is the life and soul of the Church, so this godly order and discipline is, as it were, sinews in the body, which knit and join the members together with decent order and comeliness. It is a

[1] Burrage *Early English Dissenters* ii 13 [2] Hall *Fragmenta Liturgica* i 76*f*

bridle to stay the wicked from their mischiefs: it is a spur to prick forward such as be slow and negligent: yea, and for all men it is the Father's rod, ever in a readiness to chastise gently the faults committed, and to cause them afterwards to live in more godly fear and reverence.'

We have seen that ecclesiastical discipline was exercised by the Separatists; it was also enforced by the semi-Separatists,[1] the Independents,[2] the Presbyterians,[3] and the Baptists.[4] Its importance may be gauged from the fact that all Puritans, whatever their denomination, were agreed on the necessity of Church censures.

The fullest account of the exercise of ecclesiastical discipline is that given by Thomas Goodwin in his book, *On the Constitution, Right, Order, and Government of the Churches of Christ, &c.* It may be taken as an authoritative exposition since Goodwin was an eminent divine who held high office, as President of Magdalen College, in Commonwealth days. He and Owen, then Vice-Chancellor of Oxford and a fellow Independent minister, were regarded as the twin pillars of Puritanism in their day. In the sixth chapter of the first part of his work he deals with excommunication in great detail. The Scriptural sources adduced for the ordinance are: Matt. xviii 17 and 2; I Cor. v 11 and 3; III John 10; and I Cor. v 5. He insists that the act of excommunication is not simply leaving a man to his own devices:

'Excommunication imports a positive punishment, for it is a spiritual revenge.'[5] 'Such a man hath grieved the Holy Ghost the Comforter, and therefore he is suitably given up to Satan as an accuser and tormentor.'[6]

The severity of the exercise is amply manifested in John Owen's request:[7]

'The Rejection of an offending Brother out of the Society of the Church, leaving him as unto all the privileges of the Church in the state of an Heathen, declaring him liable unto the Displeasure of Christ, and Ever-

[1] *cf.* John Robinson *Works* (ed. cit.) ii 241

[2] *cf. Savoy Declaration* pt. II §xviii

[3] *cf.* the Savoy Liturgy (Hall *Reliquiæ Liturgicæ* iv 117)

[4] *Fenstanton, Warboys and Hexham Records* (ed. Underhill, London 1854) *passim* [5] *Works* xi 45 [6] *ibid.*

[7] Owen *The True Nature of a Gospel-Church and its Government* (1689) p. 202

lasting Punishment without Repentance, is the Excommunication we plead for.'

Such a serious penalty is not, Goodwin asserts,[1] to be inflicted unless the offender is convicted of a grave offence:

'It is scandalous sin that is the matter of censure, sin judged so by common light and received principles; sin that goes afore to judgment, that you may read afar off; I Tim. V 24. Doubtful disputations and sins controverted are not to be made the subject of church censures; for if the weak are not to be received to such, then neither are they to be cast out for such.'

Consciences might so easily be terrorized by the threat of excommunication that prudence required its enforcement only in cases of great offence or of outstanding obstinacy and perversity. Even then it was only to be used when, after repeated admonitions, the offender remained unrepentant.

A comprehensive list of the sins deserving ecclesiastical censures is given by Stephen Ford in his *A Gospel-Church: or, God's Holy Temple opened*,[2] published in the year 1675. The following sins, if persisted in and not repented of, are deserving of excommunication:

'1. Strong and violent passions. 2. Apparent Wrath, Envy, Bitterness and Anger shewed, without great provocation. 3. Apparent Frowardness, Peevishness, Clamour and Strife. 4. Jangling, Disputing and Peace breakings, and all things that directly hinder the Edification and Peace of the Church. 5. Backbitings, and speaking evil against, or of one another. 6. Constant or frequent neglects of Family and Church-duties, and the Ordinances of God in them. 7. Needless Associating and holding Communion with profane and scandalous persons. 8. Defrauding any persons of their first dues any way, on any account whatsoever, when it might have been prevented. 9. Disobedience to the Lawful Commands and Rules of Parents, Masters, Magistrates, Elders, or any other that have Authority over them. 10. Publishing false Doctrines against the Fundamentals of the Gospel, Faith, and Worship. 11. False accusing any Persons, especially any of the Church. 12. Railing at, or reviling others to their face, or behind their backs. 13. Idleness, Tatling, and being Busie-bodies in other mens matters that concern them not.'

This catalogue suffices to make plain the intense seriousness

[1] *Works* xi 48 [2] p. 343

with which the Puritans devoted themselves to the duty of exercising ecclesiastical censures. It also indicates the dangers to which the Puritans were liable in the performance of this part of the government of the Church. These were two: scrupulosity in the governors of the Church, and hypocrisy in those governed. These were, in fact, the two abuses for which the Puritans were most frequently criticized. It is not without significance that the Puritans were also dubbed 'precisians', whilst the hypocritical Puritan is a stock character of the Elizabethan playwright.[1] Many of the offences in Ford's catalogue would appear to be too trivial to be deserving of censure.

That even such peccadilloes as gossiping or occasional laziness were actually punishable by excommunication, is confirmed by an account of the discipline administered by a certain Richard Davis, minister of the Independent Church of Rothwell from 1690 to 1715. Davis describes the offenders as being 'excommunicated for the destruction of the proud flesh, that their souls may be saved, if the Lord will'.[2] The following is part of the list of those excommunicated with a description of their offences:[3]

'Richard Hill for unfaithfulness in his master's service.

Eliz. Campion for being an unfaithful and disobedient servant.

Bro. Campion for proferring love to one sister while engaged to another.

Bro. Palmer for admitting card-playing into his house and playing himself.

Bridget Rowlatt for sloth in business.

Robert Hanan for stealing away a maid's affections at Weekley and now leaving of her, falsifying his word, and going to others.

Bro. Cussens for being overtaken in beer.

Sister Hemington for taking a journey on the Lord's Day.

Bro. Clark for riding over unmowen hay.

Mrs. Wood for borrowing a pillion and not returning of it.

Bro. Crozier for spending a day in an Ale-house and going away without paying his reckoning.

Bro. Hoby for jumping for wagers.

Sister Durdin and Sister Lumley for dancing and other vanities.

[1] *e.g.* in Shakespeare's *Twelfth Night* and Ben Jonson's *Bartholomew Fair* the Puritan characters are, respectively, Malvolio and Zeal-of-the-Land Busy.

[2] Glass *op. cit.* p. 73 [3] *id.* p. 75*f*

John Cussens for threatening to knock his brother's brains out.
Bro. Wright for his cudgel-playing.
Bro. Musket for playing at nine pins.
Betty Coates for whispering and tattling.'

A further entry reads:[1]

'The Church was satisfied with Mrs. Charlton as to the weight of her butter.'

The above information warrants two conclusions on the exercise of discipline by the Puritans. The first is the extremely high standard of conduct which was expected of their Church members. For with the whole Church acting as informers for the most trifling offences, concealment was practically impossible. The second is that some Church Meetings must often have consisted of nothing but personal accusations and protestations of innocency. No wonder that one member of the Rothwell Church was excommunicated 'for his passion in the Church Meeting'.[2] Obviously, what had begun as a protest against the moral laxity of the members of the Established Church, had degenerated by the end of the seventeenth century into a Puritan Inquisition into the private lives of Church members. Ethical earnestness had evaporated into legalistic scrupulosity.

How then was the act of excommunication administered? John Owen claims that two Scriptural precedents provide a complete account of the method, the meaning and the purpose of excommunication. These are the excommunication of Simon Magus by Peter (Acts viii 13, 20–23) and St Paul's demand for the ejection of the incestuous person from the Corinthian Church (I Cor. v 1, 2, 5–7). Having cited these passages, he claims:[3]

'The whole of what we plead for, is here exemplified; as 1. The cause of excommunication which is a scandalous sin unrepented of. 2. The preparation for its execution which is the Churches sense of the Sin and Scandal, with Humiliation for it. 3. The warranty of it, which is the Institution of Christ, wherein his authority is engaged. 4. The manner and form of it, by an Act of Authority, with the Consent of the whole Church. 5. The effect of it in a total separation from the Privileges of the Church. 6. The end of it: with respect unto the Church, its purging

[1] *id.* p. 77 [2] *ibid.* [3] *The True Nature of a Gospel-Church &c.* p. 203

and Vindication. With respect unto the Person Excommunicated, his Repentance, Reformation and Salvation.'

This is a most admirable summary of the rationale of Excommunication, but it gives little information as to the actual method of preparation for the Excommunication. Goodwin, however, is more explicit. He informs us that ecclesiastical discipline goes through three stages. First, the sinner is admonished, then excommunicated, and finally rejected. He continues:[1]

'We have order given for the degrees of the proceedings in these, as orderly as any man can make provision for the indemnity of men innocent and just, proceeding in any civil court in order to amend men.'

He proceeds to make good his claim by showing the care with which each accusation is examined:[2]

'1. If the sin be private, so as thou alone knowest it "That thy brother sin against thee", Mat.xvi 11, 15, "Go and tell him his fault, between him and thee alone, if he hear and repent (as it is Luke xvii 3), thou shalt forgive him", and it shall go no further. This provision hath Christ took to preserve the reputation of persons, so to mend them as not to blaze their faults; and this not for one sinning, but if seven times, that is, never so oft, Luke xvii 4.'

The second stage ensues only when the offender is unrepentant, in which case the directions are

'then take two or three and tell him of it afore them, and if he denies not the fact, and yet repents not, then thou hast two or three witnesses of his not denying the fact, and yet of his obstinacy and hardness in not relenting, and of his impenitency; so it follows, "That in the mouth of two or three witnesses, every word may be established," that is, brought into public.'[3]

The matter is now brought to the notice of the Church on the authority of the Dominical imperative 'If he neglect to hear them, tell it to the church'.

'But if it were a sin that is public, that is, though privately committed, yet made known, commonly reproved, and so commonly known, as it is I Cor.5.1, then the church is to take immediate notice of it publicly . . .

[1] *On the Constitution, Right, Order and Government of the Churches of Christ; Works* xi 48 [2] *ibid.* [3] *id.* p. 48*f*

and those that can accuse, should impeach as I.Cor.v. he shews, and also I Tim.v.20.'[1]

If, on the other hand,

'it be a sin that is suspected and cannot be proved (whether commonly reported or private), and that by two or three witnesses, the officers are to cast it out of the Church proceeding, and not to receive it, "Receive not an accusation", so as to proceed in it, unless it appears evident by two or three witnesses. This rule is given about admonishing officers, II Tim.v.19; but it regards also every man else, Matt.xviii.16. Then, when any sin is thus made of public cognisance, 1, they are to admonish; 2, to excommunicate in case of obstinacy and impenitence.'[2]

This careful and exact account of Puritan discipline renders a common criticism against ecclesiastical censures void. A cursory survey of the apparent trivialities for which the penalty of excommunication might be demanded, would suggest that a malicious person could lodge information against a neighbour, and that an innocent person so charged might find it impossible to clear himself. Public sins could be proven by eye-witnesses. But allegations of private defaults were only a matter for the deliberations of the Church, when the defendant refused to deny the offence in the presence of two or three witnesses, or would not express his penitence. Goodwin's claim that the justice of the ecclesiastical 'courts' was equal to that of the civil courts, is thus established.

Hitherto the subject has been considered in its juridical rather than in its spiritual aspects. The end of Excommunication was not simply to lop off dead wood or poisonous fungus from the tree of the Church; its purpose was corrective, not vindictive. As Owen reminds his readers,[3] this spiritual exercise calls for

'Prayer for the person cut off; Admonition as occasion is offered; Compassion in his distressed estate; Forbearance from common converse, with readiness for the Restauration of love, in all the fruits of it . . .'

Thus it was hoped that, by depriving the offender of the privileges of the Church and by segregating him from the fellowship of the members, he might be brought to a state of remorse. The severity of the sentence of excommunication was mitigated to a certain extent by the following factors: In

[1] *id.* p. 49 [2] *ibid.* [3] Owen *op. cit.* p. 216

the first place the excommunicated person was not prohibited from 'hearing the Word'. In the second place, although the Church members were to keep such a person at arm's length, converse was allowed that had been 'made previously necessary, by Mens mutual Engagement in Trade and the like'.[1] This involved no suspension of family relations or of civic rights. Remembering that the offender's immortal soul was in dire punishment, such treatment does not appear unduly rigorous. This was certainly John Milton's view when he wrote:[2]

'so doth excommunication as dearly and as freely, without money, use her wholesome and saving terrors; she is instant, she beseeches, by all the dear and sweet promises of salvation she entices and woos; by all the threatenings and thunders of the law, and rejected gospel, she charges and adjures: this is all her armoury, her munition, her artillery; then she awaits with long sufferance, and yet ardent zeal. In brief, there is no act in all the errand of God's ministers to mankind wherein passes more loverlike contestation between Christ and the soul of a regenerate man lapsing, than before, and in, and after the sentences of excommunication.'

The exercise of discipline by the Puritans was severely criticized by the clergy of the Establishment. A certain F. Fisher raises the question, whether individual ministers have the right to exclude those whom they judge unworthy receivers from the Sacrament of the Lord's Supper? He asks:[3]

'Whether when the three Evangelists, recording the Institution of the Lord's Supper, do most expresly testifie, that Christ then sate at Table with his 12. Disciples, amongst whom is particularly named Judas Iscariot; and that Christ gave the cup and bread to them all, and that they all did eat of the bread and drink of the cup; Nay when Christ himself saith in the very time and act of celebration, "Behold, the hand of him that betrayeth me is with me at the Table", are they not unworthy to be accounted Christ's Ministers, who shall openly question and deny the truth of Judas his being there and his partaking of the Sacrament?'

Another Anglican, John Humfrey, makes the same point.[4] He

[1] *id.* p. 229 [2] *Reformation in England* (Everyman ed. 1927) p. 99

[3] *Questions Preparatory to the Better, Free and more Christian Administration of the Lord's Supper* (London 1655) p. 3

[4] *A Humble Vindication of a Free Admission unto the Lord's Supper* (London 1652) p. 20

also adduces several other reasons for a free admission to the Lord's Table. He claims that as the Gospel is free for all, so also should the Sacrament be free, as it is the 'Verbum visibile'.

'My third reason I take from the nature of Christian Communion, and Church-fellowship, which ought to be in Charity; in humility; *without judgeing; every one esteeming others better than themselves.*'

His fourth reason arises from 'the vanity, formality, impossibility, of selecting people to this Ordinance'. He also regards this forbidding of unworthy receivers as an entrenchment upon the common liberty of Christians. He concludes by urging that it is a matter of duty; the issue must be left to God. He declares that his motto is: 'Deo gloria, mihi condonatio'.

These criticisms were answered by a Puritan, A. Palmer, in *A Scripture Rale to the Lord's Table*, published in 1654. He denies that the Sacraments are to be received as freely as the Gospel.

'Sir,' he answers Humfrey, 'you know well enough that the Apostles preacht the Gospel to whole Cities, yea Nations, but administered the Sacraments only to such as came and professed repentance and subjection to the Lord Jesus.'[1]

To the objection that Christ allowed Judas to partake of the Last Supper, he replies that Judas had not then committed his crime. He rebuts Humfrey's plea for charity by the rejoinder:[2]

'But what kinde of charity is this to admit ungodly persons, as the members of Jesus Christ, walking indeed as the members of Satan. O merciless flattering pity!'

Palmer admits that it is extremely difficult to assess whether purity is formal or real, but

'We contend, as much as may be for a *reall* purity, and power of godliness; but such as live in open and known profaneness have not so much as a formal purity.'[3]

Finally, he is not prepared to admit that the issue must be left to God, who may be counted on to convert the ungodly. He demands:[4]

'But shew us where he hath *promised* he will, or any *example* of it; 'tis not good arguing from *Gods omnipotency* to his *ordinary* way of dealing.'

[1] *op. cit.* p. 54 [2] *id.* p. 70*f* [3] *id.* p. 79 [4] *id.* p. 84

Because the Puritans regarded unworthy reception of the Lord's Supper as an affront to Christ and his Church, they held discipline in high esteem. This also accounts for the solemn 'fencing' of the Table in their Communion orders. The Waldegrave Exhortation at the Communion expressly forbids unworthy receivers:[1]

'Therefore, if any of you be a blasphemer of God, an hinderer or slanderer of his word, an adulterer, or be in malice or envy, or in any other grievous crime, bewail your sins, and come not to this holy table; lest the devil enter into you, as he entered into Judas, and fill you full of all iniquities, and bring you to destruction, both of body and soul.'

This tradition is maintained in the Communion Offices of the Parliamentary Directory[2] and of the Savoy Liturgy.[3]

It is not to be forgotten that, if the offender repented after his excommunication, he was to be restored to the privileges of the Church. Owen[4] gives a description of the process:

'The outward Manner of the Restauration of such a person consists in 1. His Testification of his Repentance unto the Satisfaction of the Church. 2. The Express Consent of the Church unto his reception. 3. His renewed Ingagement in the Covenant of the Church, whereby he is re-instated or jointed again in the Body, in his own proper place.'

In conclusion it must be emphasized that the Puritan exercise of discipline was not arbitrarily assumed power. They were convinced that Christ had given 'the keys of the Kingdom', the power of binding and loosing, to his Church. The ecclesiastical censures were a partial expression of the Christocracy of the Church. Discipline was, as the Middleburgh Order describes it, 'the sinews of the Body' of Christ. It was required both for the purgation of the Church, that a high standard of Christian profession might be maintained, and also for the good of the offender. It was for the healing of both parties. It was therefore an essential part of church order. This is finely expressed by the anonymous 'T. C.', in his preface to the posthumous publication of Owen's *The True Nature of a Gospel-Church and its Government*.[5] Commenting on τάξις, the word translated 'order' in Col. ii 5, he writes that this is a military word:

[1] Hall *Fragmenta Liturgica* i 60 [2] Hall *Reliquiæ Liturgicæ* iii 52
[3] *id.* iv 60 [4] *op. cit.* p. 230 [5] (ed. 1689) p. 11*f*

'It's the Order of Souldiers in a Band, keeping Rank and File, where every one keeps his place, follows his Leader, observes the Word of Command, and his Right-hand Man. Hence the Apostle joys to see their close Order, and Stedfastness in the Faith, their Firmness, Valour and Resolution in fighting the good Fight of Faith and the Order in so doing; not only in watching as single Professors, but in marching Orderly together as an Army with Banners. There is nothing more comly than a Church walking in Order when everyone keeps his place, knows and practiseth his Duty according to the Rule, each submitting to the other in the performance of Duty, when the Elders know their places, and the People theirs. Christ hath been more faithful than Moses, and therefore hath not left his Churches without sufficient Rules to walk by.'

This almost lyrical tribute to the discipline exercised by the Puritans is proof positive that for them it was a Dominical ordinance of the highest import to the Church.

## CHAPTER XV

## A SURVEY AND CRITIQUE OF PURITAN WORSHIP

Robert Baillie, the Scots Commissioner who was present at the Westminster Assembly of Divines, expressed the opinion that it was difficult to generalize about the tenets of the Independents:

'It is not easie to set down with assurance the *Independents* positions, both because they have to this day declined to declare positively their minds, as also because of their principle of mutability, whereby they professe their readinesse to change any of their present tenets.'[1]

This criticism is born not of understanding but of impatience. The 'principle of mutability' to which he refers, was a profound conviction that 'the Lord hath more truth yet to break forth out of his holy Word'. This advice was contained in the memorable farewell oration made by Pastor John Robinson to the departing Pilgrim Fathers. The Independents held to this counsel because they could not believe that the Holy Spirit, who should lead into all truth, had completed his work of illumination. Luther only partially understood and Calvin too; therefore Robinson advised his hearers to await further guidance as they meditated on the meaning of the Scriptures. The other criticism, that the Independents had not officially declared their mind, is to be understood in the light of their church government. Each local Independent Church was bound to the obedience of Christ and his Gospel but was free from outside State or ecclesiastical interference. It was therefore free, in accordance with the rules of the Word of God, to frame its own policy. In fact, therefore, there could be no official Independent tenets subscribed by every Independent Church, for that would be an overriding of the liberty of the individual Church.

In these circumstances it might be supposed that there would be as many Independent orders of public worship as there were Independent Churches, each one different from the

[1] *A Dissuasive* p. 101

other. Moreover, allowing for the same differences in the Baptist Church services, and a different type of service for the Presbyterians, it would appear impossible to generalize on the subject of Puritan worship, for one would expect the exceptions to outnumber the rule. This, however, is not the case. The predominating impression that emerges after a study of the worship of the Puritans is one of essential agreement and unity. Every Puritan, left-wing or right-wing, was agreed that the Word of God was the standard by which worship was to be judged. All Puritans agreed in their disapproval of the use of the ring in marriage, of crossing in Baptism, of surplices as superstitious garments, and a majority disliked the Prayer Book's insistence that the Communion elements should be received kneeling. On the positive side, the Puritans all insisted that the use of a liturgy, to the exclusion of free prayer, was contrary to the tenor of the Scriptures, disastrous to the exercise of private prayer, and likely to produce an inadequate ministry. Whilst they did not object to a liturgy as such, they refused to subscribe to the Anglican Book of Common Prayer because it was not in all things in accordance with the Word of God. They wished to be able to pray, as did Tertullian, 'de pectore, sine monitore'. Moreover they were united in observing the two Dominical Sacraments, Baptism and the Lord's Supper; in emphasizing the importance of preaching the Word of God, in preference to reading homilies; in reading whole chapters of the Scriptures instead of mere paragraphs; in valuing ecclesiastical discipline highly; in keeping days of thanksgiving and humiliation both public and private; and in the observance of family and private prayer. Their worship was characterized by simplicity, purity and spirituality.

The preceding pages will have shewn that there were differences amongst the Puritans. Over and above these differences of detail, there were certain ordinances peculiar to different denominations at different times during their history. Three in particular are remarkable. The General Baptists practised the ordinance of feet-washing. Whilst the use of it was left to the discretion of each local Church, it was widely observed. A certain Robert Wright introduced it into Lincolnshire in 1653, and the innovation was brought into Kent by William Jeffrey in 1659. It was practised as late as 1771, for in that year Daniel Dobel, the Messenger of the General

Baptists in Kent since 1761, declared:[1] 'I have been in the conscientious practice of it upward of forty years.' The Baptists were also unique in holding love-feasts. The Fenstanton Church agreed to hold this ordinance in 1656 and the neighbouring Church at Warboys passed the following resolution in its Church Meeting held the previous year:[2]

'The order of the love-feast agreed upon, to be before the Lord's Supper; because the ancient churches did practice it, and for unity with other churches near to us.'

This minute would imply that the custom was in general use among the Baptists of that day. Edwards, of *Gangræna* fame, corroborates the use of the custom among London 'sectaries' of Commonwealth days.[3] The third unusual ordinance is that of anointing with oil. It was most certainly practised by the Independents in exile at Arnhem, under the pastoral oversight of John Goodwin. Baillie says, of the Church referred to:[4]

'In that Church also the Doctrine of extreme Unction was so far brought back, That they began to annoint their sick with oyl; taking it as an Ordinance of Christ, and a kind of sacrament for the people, at least a holy ceremony: no lesse of a divine Institution then Ordination and imposition of hands were for Officers.'

Goodwin wished to restore the use of this custom amongst the Independents in England. The Biblical warrants he adduced for it were Mark vi and James v 14 and 15. He admitted that the Roman Church had perverted the use of it and that the Reformed Churches had been right to protest against the Roman abuse:

'only in rejecting it (as in some other things) they went too far, even denying it to have that use of restoring the sick as a seal of the promise, and an indefinite means to convey that blessing, which God in mercy hath appointed it to be.'[5]

Despite Goodwin's plea for the restoration of the use of anointing the sick with oil, there is no evidence to show that this was ever accepted by the Independents. Certainly the custom is not mentioned in the Savoy Declaration. The three ordinances considered: the customs of feet-washing as a pre-

[1] *Transactions of the Baptist Historical Society* i (1908–09) 129*ff* [2] *ibid.*
[3] *Gangræna* pt. i, p. 27 [4] *A Dissuasive* p. 81 [5] *Works* xi 461

paration for the Lord's Supper, love-feasts, and anointing with oil, are no part of the general Puritan tradition. Where they appeared, they were short-lived, and were accepted only by a small minority of the Churches of the denominations concerned.

A stranger entering any Puritan meeting-house would first notice the bareness and simplicity of the architecture and of the furnishings. Probably the only decoration on the walls of the building would be texts from the Scriptures. Apart from the pews, the only other articles of furniture would be the high central pulpit and the Communion-table immediately below it. On a cushion on a ledge of the pulpit would be seen the Bible. Its dominating, central position was no accident: it testified to the authority of the Bible in the worship, doctrine and government of Puritan Churches.

The impression of unadorned simplicity would be maintained at the worship. The minister would ascend to the pulpit, dressed in a grave black gown, its sombreness relieved only by the white of the Genevan bands he wore. The service would commence with a call to worship, consisting of sentences selected from the Scriptures. Then the stranger would kneel or stand, according to the practice of the congregation where he was worshipping, during the prayer of confession. He would then join in a metrical psalm of praise. The minister would then read a chapter from the Old Testament, perhaps pausing here and there to explain some obscure verse. The stranger might then join in another metrical psalm, or he would hear a New Testament lection immediately after the previous reading. If he were in an Independent church he would then hear the minister lead a prayer of intercession. At its conclusion the whole assembly would assent with a vocal 'Amen'. If he were in a Presbyterian church, this item would be postponed until after the sermon, and it would conclude with all saying the Lord's Prayer aloud. He would then notice the shuffling of the congregation as they settled down to listen comfortably to a lengthy sermon, while the minister adjusted the hour-glass. The sermon would be an exposition of a text or a longer passage of Scripture. It would begin with a simple exposition of Scripture, it would continue by controverting any errors which the Scripture condemned, it would conclude with a statement of the advantages of the acceptance of this particular doctrine. The preacher would deliver his conclusion with passionate and perhaps even vehement pleading. The stranger's general impression of the sermon would be that both reason and conscience had been satisfied, and that the preacher had, in the name of God, struck for a decision. The peroration of the sermon would be the climax of the whole service. The service would then end with another metrical psalm and the pronouncing of the Blessing by the minister.

This would have been a typical Puritan service, to be witnessed in almost any Puritan meeting-house on any Sunday morning in the seventeenth century. The stranger would also have found an essential uniformity in the administration of the Sacraments. Had he been present at a Baptism, he would have heard the discourse explaining its nature and purpose, followed by an interrogation of the father, from whom would be extracted the promise that his child should be taught the duties of a Christian. The infant would be baptized in the Triune Name, after which the minister would pray that the child should inherit the promises of God, and in due time make its own Christian profession. Had he been present at the celebration of the Lord's Supper, he would have heard an introductory discourse on the meaning of the Sacrament, the reading of the words of Institution, the blessing of the bread and wine, their delivery to the communicants who received them sitting, in their pews or at the Communion-table, from the hand of the minister or of the deacons. The ordinance would have included a prayer of intercession and would have concluded with a metrical psalm and a blessing.

In each service he would clearly have understood that the way of worship was not simply the manner in which that particular assembly of Christians wished to worship God, but rather that it was the kind of worship that God himself had demanded in his Word. The lengthy readings from the Scriptures, the Baptismal formula taken from the Scriptures, the words of Institution and of Delivery taken from the Scriptures, the Biblical phraseology of the prayers, the careful way in which the sermon elucidated the Scriptures, and the metrical versions of the psalms used in praise, would all have contributed to produce this impression. In fact, it was the Biblical basis of Puritan worship that accounted for the liturgical agreement amongst the Puritans.

This fundamental unity and similarity can easily be shewn in descriptions of Puritan worship, whether in England or New England, whether amongst the Presbyterians or amongst the Independents, whether during the sixteenth century or during the succeeding century. Even the worship of the semi-Separatists did not differ greatly from the usual Puritan order of service. Clyfton, the colleague of Johnson in the pastorship of the Church at Amsterdam, thus catalogues the order of their service:[1]

'1. Prayer and giving of thanks by the pastor or teacher.

2. The Scriptures are read, two or three chapters, as time serves, with a brief explanation of their meaning.

3. The Pastor or teacher then takes some passage of Scripture, and expounds and enforces it.

4. The Sacraments are administered.

5. Some of the Psalms of David are sung by the whole congregation, both before and after the exercise of the Word.

6. Collection is then made as each one is able for the support of the officers and the poor.'

This then was the worship of the left-wing Puritans in exile in Amsterdam during the last decade of the sixteenth century.

The order of service has not greatly altered amongst the Independents of New England fifty years later. John Cotton describes this worship in the year 1645:[2]

'Wee make prayers and intercessions and thanksgivings for our selves and for all men, not in any *prescribed* forme of prayer, or *studied Liturgie*, but in such a manner as the Spirit of grace and of prayer who teacheth all the people of God, what and how to pray, *Rom.* 8. 26,27, helpeth our infirmities, wee having respect therein to the necessities of the people, the estate of the times, and the worke of Christ in our handes. After prayer, either the *Pastor* or *Teacher* readeth a Chapter in the Bible, and *expoundeth* it, giving the *sense*, *to cause the people to understand the reading* according to *Neh.*8.8. And in sundry churches the other (whether *Pastor* or *Teacher*) who expoundeth not, he *preacheth* the Word, and in the afternoone the other who *preacheth* in the morning doth usually (if there be time) *reade* and *preach*, and he that *expoundeth* in the morning *preacheth* after him. Before Sermon, and many times after, wee sing a Psalme . . . The seales of the Covenant (to wit, the Sacrament of Baptisme

[1] John Robinson *Works* (ed. Ashton) iii 485

[2] *The Way of the Churches of Christ in New England* pp. 66*ff*

and the Lords Supper) are administred, either by the *Pastor* or by the *Teacher* . . . Both the Sacraments we dispense, according to the first institution, Baptisme to *Disciples*, and (who are included in them) their *seed*. The Lords Supper to such as neither want *knowledge* nor *grace* to *examine and judge themselves* before the Lord . . . Ceremonies we use none, but are carefull to administer all things according to the primitive institutions. The *Father* presenteth his owne childe to *baptisme*, as being baptized by right of his *Covenant*, and not of the Covenant unto God-fathers & god-mothers . . . and therefore we have no use of them, but omit them in Baptisme; as the Apostle cast out *love-feasts* from the Lords Supper, being both of them alike *superadditions to the Lords institutions*, I *Cor*.11.23,24.'

Cotton's account closes with a description of the way in which the Lord's Supper was celebrated in the Independent Churches of New England, which was quoted in an earlier chapter.[1] This order of service is almost exactly similar to that used by the Church at Amsterdam. The same items are included and in the same order. Cotton's information is doubly valuable on two accounts: he was an English Puritan who had sought religious asylum in New England, and his influence on the English Independents was considerable. Although he is describing the worship of the New England Independents, he is also outlining the pattern to which the English Independents conformed.

Independent worship had not greatly changed a century later. The following account is taken from a record made by the Bury Street Independent Church of London in 1723:[2]

'In the morning we begin with singing a Psalm, then a short prayer follows to desire the Divine Presence in all the following parts of worship; after that, about half an hour is spent in the exposition of some portion of Scripture, which is succeeded by singing a psalm or an hymn. After this the Minister prays more at large, for all the variety of blessings, spiritual and temporal, for the whole congregation, with confession of sins and thanksgiving for mercies; petitions are also offered up for the whole world, for the churches of Christ, for the nation in which we dwell, for all our rulers and governors, together with any particular cases which are represented. Then a sermon is preached, and the morning worship is concluded with a short prayer and the Benediction.'

[1] see above, p. 207*f*

[2] *Transactions of the Congregational Historical Society* vi 333

The one unusual item is the short prayer that follows the sermon and immediately precedes the Blessing. This is, however, explained in a footnote:[1]

'The hymn or psalm which is sung after the exposition should have been sung just after the sermon; but Mr. Watts, our Pastor, being for several years so much indisposed with nervous disorders, desired the hymn to be sung rather before he went into the pulpit, only because his head was unable to bear the sound.'

The one notable alteration from the two earlier service-orders cited, is the introduction of a short prayer of invocation at the beginning of the service, leaving the longer intercessory prayer until later. In Cotton's order the service begins with a comprehensive prayer of intercession. Early Independents appear to have done this solely on the authority of the text, I Tim. ii 1: 'I exhort therefore, first of all, that supplications, prayers, intercessions, thanksgivings, be made for all men; for kings and all that are in high places'. Apart from this single alteration in placing the intercessory prayer later in the order of service, the Independent service remains unchanged.

Further proof of the essential liturgical agreement amongst the Puritans is to be found in two facts. The first is that the Independents and Presbyterians were able to agree on the formulation of a *Directory for the Publicke Worship of God throughout the Three Kingdomes of England, Scotland and Ireland* in 1644. Unless there had already existed a common liturgical tradition, based upon a Biblical foundation, such an undertaking would never have been successfully achieved. The second fact is that in 1717 an English Nonconformist minister was able to write an account of the worship of the English Dissenters at that time, without requiring to enumerate denominational peculiarities and differences. This general account of the worship of the inheritors of the Puritan tradition could not have been given unless there had been a large measure of agreement among the Nonconformists themselves. Edmund Calamy's account is as follows:[2]

'Their stated publick worship on the Lord's days (which they conscientiously devote wholly to religious purposes) is thus managed. The Minister in each Christian Society, offers up to Almighty God the

[1] *ibid.* [2] *A Letter to a Divine in Germany* p. 9*f*

common Requests of the whole Society, in the aptest and most Scriptural expressions he is able. He publishes the Will of God both as to Truth and Duty in two distinct Discourses, the one in the Forenoon, and the other in the Afternoon. Each sermon is about an hour's length and begun and closed with Prayer. The Psalms are sung in Metre by the whole Assembly. In some Congregations there are Evening Lectures, besides the forementioned Forenoon and Afternoon Sermons. In some, the Youth are catechised on the Afternoons of the Lord's Days, in others on the Evenings, and in others on some Week Day. Some ministers use the Lord's Prayer constantly, others frequently, others seldom or never, as reckoning it rather given for a Directory, than to be used as a Form. Some ministers, besides their stated Preaching, do ordinarily expound a chapter, or some lesser portion of Scripture, at the beginning of the Morning Service, while others only read two or three chapters, or a Psalm and a chapter.'

Calamy then describes the usual method of administering the Sacrament of Baptism:[1]

'In the administration of this Ordinance, they give a brief Explication of the Nature and Grounds of it, and offer up a suitable Prayer. An explicit consent to the Apostles Creed, or some other short Summary of the Christian Covenant, is required either of the Parties baptized, or their Parents, if they are Infants: and then water is poured in the *Name of the Father*, *Son and Holy Ghost*, without any signing of the Cross, or any other Addition, saving a Charge to the Parties baptized about an Holy Life, or to their Parents about their Education, &c and a serious Thankfulness to Almighty God, for his rich Mercy and Grace to sinful Man, through Jesus Christ his Son.'

The account of the worship of the English Nonconformists concludes with a description of their way of celebrating the Lord's Supper:[2]

'Their Administration of it consists in breaking of Bread, and pouring out the Wine, and distributing these Elements among the Communicants, after reading the Account of our Blessed Saviour's Institution of that Solemnity, either out of one of the Evangelists, or out of St. *Paul's* first Epistle to the *Corinthians;* and a serious and devout imploring the Blessing of the Great Master of the Feast. During the Time of Receiving the Minister usually endeavours to stir up the Devotions of the Communicants by some suitable suggestions; and after Participation closes

[1] *id.* p. 10 [2] *id.* p. 10*f*

with some serious Admonitions tending to excite to Holiness of Life; and with affectionate Thanksgivings and Praises to God for his rich Mercy and Grace, and singing a Psalm or Hymn. This Sacrament is by some administered in the Evening, but by most at Noon. The Communicants are at liberty to use their own Posture in the Time of Receiving, tho' a Table-Gesture is most commonly us'd in conformity (as is apprehended) to the practice of our Saviour and his Apostles.'

This account makes it clear that there was essential agreement amongst the Puritans in early eighteenth-century England in liturgical matters. At the same time certain differences of detail were prevalent. Not all ministers used the Lord's Prayer; not all congregations received the Lord's Supper sitting; not all ministers insisted that parents of a child about to be baptized should recite the Apostles' Creed; some ministers gave running expositions of Scripture, whilst others read the lessons without comment. In brief, whilst there was a Puritan tradition of worship, there were also minor modifications of it in detail. These depended partly upon the traditions of the denomination's worship, partly upon the preference of the particular minister and the particular congregation concerned. In fundamental matters of principle there was unity, in secondary matters of detail there was diversity.

Differences of detail amongst Presbyterians and Independents in their public worship were noted by Robert Kirk, an episcopalian minister from Aberfoyle, who visited several London churches in the summer of 1689. He records, in his diary, attending a service which was led by Richard Baxter and his clerk. The following is his account of this Presbyterian service:[1]

'His clerk first sung a Psalm, reading the line. Then the reader read 3 Ps., Isaiah 5 and Matthew 22, after he had given an extempore prayer. Then the Minister, reading the papers of the sick and troubled in mind and intending a journey, he prayed and preached a sermon on popery . . . Mr. Baxter prayed in general for the King and Royal Family and Parliament; for Jacobites, Grecians and Armenians enlightening in further knowledge; for Christians distressed with burning, dislodging and oppression of merciless enemies. He repeated the Lord's Prayer at the end of his last prayer. The congregation all kneeled or stood up at

[1] Donald Maclean *London at Worship: 1689–1690* (1928 Lecture to the Presbyterian Historical Society) p. 16

prayer. The most of the men were discovered during the whole time of the sermon, yet some few kept on their hats when the Scriptures were a reading.'

Baxter was evidently a great favourite of Kirk's for a later visit to a service conducted by him and Silvester is described as follows:[1]

'Mr. Baxter, on Jer.17,11. He prayed for the success of King William and Queen Mary in Ireland, a blessed effect of Convocation, that all ministers might have a sound mind and quiet disposition, and for reconciling all differences, that party nor sect be never heard any more among Protestants. As Mr. Silvester, reader and lecturer, with reading of Scriptures repeated the belief (and at the article of hell, said: He descended into the unseen state), and out of Exod. 21. read the ten Commandments, so Mr. Baxter repeated the Lord's Prayer and in blessing at last said, "Blessed of God are all who consider, believe, love and obey this word." When he repeated the Lord's Prayer he said, "Let thy name be hallowed, let thy kingdom come." The people stood all up at time of prayer and belief, and were discovered at time of sermon. The minister and reader both read and spoke (of the charity from house to house that was to be collected for the aged and weak, for the Piedmont people pursued to the Swiss by the French, their young men having returned to recover their land from the French) that this charity was committed by King William to the Lord Mayor and Lord Bishop of London, King's Counsellor.'

Two features of unique importance, in these services conducted by Richard Baxter, are the catholicity of the prayers and the ability to produce freshness in a traditional item of worship. The first is illustrated in the prayer for 'a blessed effect of Convocation', a prayer offered up by one who had suffered from Convocation. The second is shewn in the willingness to adopt a new translation of the petitions of the Lord's Prayer, and in the recital of the Apostles' Creed. The Puritan structure evidently allowed enough flexibility for the expression of a remarkable personality.

Kirk also gives an account of a visit he paid to a service conducted by an Independent minister, Cockain by name:[2]

'This preacher had no Psalms before or after sermon. The people heard sermon with heads covered, and stood at prayer. Few persons of good

[1] *id.* p. 16*f* [2] *id.* p. 21

rank were present, only two coaches or so attended the doors: 200 persons were within and were much straitened for room. Sermon began in the afternoon at half-past one. The preacher prayed not for the Protestant Churches, nor English, nor any Churchmen, only barely for the King and High Council, without naming the Queen. He did plead vehemently with God for a young man at the grave's mouth, the only hope and visible standing of his father's family, saying: "Lord, 'tis rare to find a good man, more a young good man. Thou sparest 10,000ds. of debauched youths, may not this one not dry but tender and fruitful branch escape the blast of thy displeasure. Save his soul. Spare his body. Sanctify all to the parents seeing Thou dost it, not theirs nor ours, but Thy will be done." The preacher was a very low, but a very corpulent man, of good, plain passable parts. He had not the blessing at the end. This was delivered Sunday, June 5, 1690. The minister was vested in a black coat.'

The Independent service, it will be seen, omitted the recitation of the Creed, but the prayers, as at Baxter's service, were comprehensive and personal in intercession. The predominating impression is of simplicity and sincerity. The citations from Kirk's diary reinforce the conclusion that such variety as existed within the Puritan framework of worship, with its psalms, readings, prayers and sermon, was produced by the various personalities who conducted the services. The Puritan service was well-ordered but flexible.

Having surveyed the unity and the incidental variety of Puritan worship, it now remains to sum up the conclusions reached as to its defects and merits. Some hint as to its defects may be obtained from the following adverse criticism offered by Benjamin Calamy D.D., Prebendary of St Paul's and the second son of Edmund Calamy the elder, the famous Presbyterian divine. He writes in 1683:[1]

'I shall only say here, that irreverent sitting at the receiving the Sacrament of the Lords Supper, Mens unmannerly wearing their Hats in time of Divine Worship, and oftentimes putting them off but half way at their Prayers, their indecent postures and antick gestures at their devotions, the extravagancies and follies (not to say worse) some of them are guilty of in their extemporary effusions, the strange uncouth Metaphors and Phrases they use in their Preaching; in a word, the slovenly

[1] *Some Considerations about the Case of Scandal or giving offence to Weak Brethren* (1683) p. 56

performance of Divine Worship amongst the Dissenters is much more *Scandalous* then all the Ceremonies of our Church can ever be.'

It is doubtful if the Puritans can be criticized on the score of irreverence simply because in their reverence for the Word of God they refused to accept what the Anglicans called 'decent' ceremonies. Dr Calamy does, however, rightly point to one defect in Puritan worship that was not uncommon, namely the extravagance to which their extemporary prayers lent themselves. The same charge is made by Samuel Pepys in an entry in his Diary for the 23rd of September, 1660. There he writes:

'Before Sermon I laughed at the reader, who in his prayer desires of God that He would imprint His word on the thumbs of our right hands and on the right great toes of our right feet.'

Puritan diction was often homely and not infrequently marked by bathos, as in this case. The Anglicans were not slow to point out that the use of a liturgy prevented such infelicities of phraseology. It is to be remembered, however, that the Dissenters themselves were aware of this defect and Isaac Watts attempted in his *Guide to Prayer*[1] to remedy this weakness. He counsels ministers to

'avoid these two extremes: I. A confining ourselves entirely to precomposed forms of prayer. II. An entire dependence on sudden motions and suggestions of thought.'

Infelicity of speech was one of the risks that had to be run if the ideal of extemporary prayer was to be realized. This was offset, of course, by the directness and aptness and warmth of extemporary prayer.

The second criticism that can be levelled at Puritan worship is that it made too great demands upon the intellectual and spiritual capacities of both its ministers and its congregations. Hooker defends the use of collects and responses on the ground that these are more suited to retain the interest of the congregation than long prayers, and he urges the need to consider the capacities of the congregation

'. . . forasmuch as in public Prayer we are not only to consider what is needful in respect of God, but there is also in men that which we must regard.'[2]

[1] (ed. London 1864) p. 27 [2] *Eccl. Pol.* V xxxii 2

The Puritans could have benefited greatly from this advice; had it been taken, they would not have overtaxed the attention of their congregations with their long sermons and prolix prayers. Moreover the preparation of lengthy sermons and the need for extemporary prayers taxed the spiritual resources of the ministers. The judgment of a contemporary liturgist[1] is supported by the facts:

'In general, Independent worship has tended to place too great a burden on the minister, and to leave the congregation too much to the minister's direction, with the result that a ministry and worship designed to be prophetic have not infrequently developed features reminiscent of the "sacerdotalism" against which the Independents made their earnest protest.'

The same criticism is applicable to the worship of the Presbyterians also. The worship of the English Puritans strained both the congregations and their ministers. It is not surprising, therefore, to find Increase Mather, the famous New England divine, complaining in the course of a sermon:[2]

'We may here take notice that the nature of man is wofully corrupted and depraved, else they would not be so apt to sleep when the precious Truths of God are dispensed in his Name, Yea, and men are more apt to sleep then, than at another time. Some woful Creatures have been so wicked as to profess they have gone to hear Sermons on purpose, that so they might sleep, finding themselves at such times much disposed that way.'

The fault, we may surmise, was as much in the sermon as in the audience.

The third criticism of Puritans in liturgical matters is that, in their fear and detestation of the Roman Church, they did not give sufficient heed to the customs of the primitive Church, or to the conclusions of the Reformed Church on the Continent. In fact, in their eager haste to run away from the corruptions of Rome, they far outdistanced their leader, Calvin. Calvin desired a weekly celebration of the Sacrament of the Lord's Supper; the Puritans celebrated at monthly intervals. Calvin approved of the use of a liturgy; the earliest Puritans produced their own prayer-books; but, gradually, objections

[1] E. C. Ratcliff in *The Study of Theology* (ed. Kirk) p. 474

[2] Miller & Johnson *The Puritans* p. 374

to a particular liturgy, the Book of Common Prayer, became objections to any liturgy, as extemporary prayers ousted pre-composed forms. Calvin included the Apostles' Creed in his service; the Puritans, probably under pressure from the Independents, left it out of their services, with the exception of a few Presbyterians. Calvin included a Scriptural form of Absolution in his order of service, but the Puritans omitted it from theirs. Calvin approved of Confirmation and of Confession; the Puritans jettisoned both. In their enthusiasm to root out the errors of antiquity, they ignored the wisdom of antiquity. They would have been less iconoclastic if they had heeded Luther's principle, that 'abusus non tollit usum'. Their apparent æsthetic deficiency must also be attributed to their fear of compromising with Rome. According to Bunyan,[1] himself a Puritan,

> 'the famous town of Mansoul had five gates . . . the names of the gates were these—Ear-gate, Eye-gate, Mouth-gate, Nose-gate, and Feel-gate'.

The Puritan made full use of Ear-gate, but he ignored Eye-gate in his worship.

The final criticism of Puritan worship incorporates the previous three. It is that its Biblical criterion was too rigidly applied. The dominant principle in Puritan worship is that only the worship prescribed by God in his Word is acceptable to the Divine Majesty. It is expressed in characteristic fashion by John Owen:[2]

> 'The *end* wherefore God granted his word unto the church was, that thereby it might be instructed in his mind and will as to what concerns the worship and obedience that he requireth of us, and which is accepted with him. This the whole Scripture itself everywhere declares and speaks out unto all that do receive it; as 2 Tim.iii.15–17; . . . it supposeth, it declareth, that of ourselves we are ignorant how God is, how he might be worshipped, Isa.viii.20. Moreover, it manifests him to be a "jealous God", exercising that holy property of his nature in an especial manner about his worship, rejecting and despising every thing that is not according to his Will, that is not of his institution, Exod.xx.4–6.'

The characteristic Puritan reverence for the Scriptures, as

[1] *The Holy War* (1682) §9

[2] *A Brief Instruction in the Worship of God; Works* (ed. Goold, Edinburgh 1862) xv 450

Dr F. J. Powicke remarks,[1] was 'carried to the point of Bibliolatry'. This meant that for every detail of worship Biblical sanction or silence was required. Moreover it also meant that the Pauline Epistles, originally produced as occasional writings, dealing primarily with the exigencies and controversies of the moment, were carefully scanned for liturgical directions. Such occasional hints were erected into principles. This is the only explanation for the Independent insistence that public worship should begin, not with a prayer of invocation, but with an intercessory prayer, on the authority of I Tim. ii 1. This Bibliolatry also accounts for the Independent double consecration at the Lord's Supper. This is also the reason why the Puritans came to despise all liturgies. They had so extolled the principle of reverence for the Scripture as to ignore the accumulated liturgical wisdom of the centuries, and to deny, in theory, the continued guidance of the Holy Spirit in the Church.

If there were defects, there were also outstanding merits in their way of worship. Their reverence for Scripture, which when pursued to the point of Bibliolatry was a defect, was also a great merit in their worship. Puritan worshippers were always conscious of authority in their worship. They were offering to God the worship that he desired, in the purity that he desired. They listened to the exposition of the Word of God from the minister, as if they were hearing one of the prophets. He was not delivering his own opinions, but the sacred oracles of God. The Biblical stamp of the prayers, the praises and the ordinances, deepened the impression that the worship was an act of obedience to God.

The second quality of Puritan worship was that it was never an escape from life as a formal and beautiful liturgical service might be. Worship was never a substitute for Christian service; indeed it was the Puritan's incentive to perform his Christian duties. For that reason Puritan worship was characterized by a sound ethical emphasis. Moreover the family devotions of the Puritans integrated their worship with their life. The exercise of discipline which guarded against the unworthy receiving of the Lord's Supper, the days of thanksgiving and humiliation, the frequent topical sermons preached by Puritan ministers, and the whole conception of a Church 'gathered' out of the unbelieving world, rooted morality in religion.

[2] *Essays Congregational and Catholic* p. 299

The third merit of Puritan worship was its spontaneity and its relevance to the conditions of its worshippers. A formal liturgy might easily dull the affections of a congregation, but the extemporaneous form of the prayers prevented familiarity breeding apathy or contempt. Moreover the prayers and the sermons met the particular needs of the particular congregation in a way that a prescribed liturgy and prescribed homilies could not. Kirk's instance of the moving prayer of Cockain is a case in point.[1] A prayer offered up for a particular person, or a sermon directed against a local abuse, is inevitably more relevant than a general discourse or general prayers. The Puritans would have described this feature of their worship by the New Testament term 'edification'. Prayers and sermons had two aims in view: first and foremost, to glorify God by an obedient worship of him; secondly, to build up the faith of the Church. To the second purpose Puritan worship with its flexibility was admirably adapted.

The evangelical worship of the Puritans was characterized by purity, simplicity and spirituality. It attempted to recreate the Pentecostal fervour and expectation of the Apostolic Church. Where it failed, it was only because spiritual earnestness could not be maintained on such a high plane of worship. Where it succeeded, it could afford to disparage set forms, as a lame man healed casts away his crutches.

[1] Maclean *London at Worship* p. 16*f*, quoted above, p. 253*f*

# APPENDIX A

# A COMPARATIVE ANALYSIS OF PURITAN LITURGIES

THE SUNDAY MORNING SERVICE

THE LORD'S SUPPER

THE ORDER OF BAPTISM

THE EUCHARISTIC PRAYER

| Calvin's *La Forme* Geneva 1542, etc. | Knox: *Forme of Prayers* Geneva 1556 | *A Book of the Forme of Common Prayers*, etc. London, Robert Waldegrave, 1584/5 | *A Book of the Forme of Common Prayers*, etc. Middleburgh 1586, 1587, 1602 | *A Directory for the Public Worship of God* London 1644 | Baxter: *The Reformation of the Liturgy* London 1661 |
|---|---|---|---|---|---|
| Scripture Sentences | | (Reader's Service: chapters of Scripture) Scripture Sentences | (Reader's Service: chapters of Scripture) Scripture Sentences | Call to Worship<br>Prayer of Approach: adoration supplication illumination | Prayer of Approach (long or short alternative)<br>One of the three Creeds, Decalogue, Scripture Sentences } read by Minister |
| Confession of Sins | Confession of Sins<br>Prayer for Pardon | Confession of Sins | Confession of Sins | | |
| Metrical Psalm | Metrical Psalm | Metrical Psalm | Metrical Psalm | Metrical Psalm | |
| Prayer for Illumination | Prayer for Illumination | Prayer for Illumination & Lord's Prayer | Prayer for Illumination | O.T. Lection (one chapter)<br>(Metrical Psalm) | Confession and Lord's Prayer<br>Scripture Sentences of Absolution and Exhortation |
| Scripture Reading (N.T.) | Scripture Reading | (Scripture Reading) Text | (Scripture Reading) Text | N.T. Lection (one chapter)<br>Prayer of Confession & Intercession | Psalm of praise<br>Psalms in order for the day |
| SERMON | SERMON | SERMON | SERMON | SERMON | O.T. Lesson (one chapter)<br>Metrical Psalm or *Te Deum* (said)<br>N.T. Lesson (one chapter) |
| Marriages, Baptisms & Publication of Banns | Baptisms & Publication of Banns (? with Offering for Poor) | | | | Prayer for King and Magistrates |
| Long Prayer or Lord's Prayer in long paraphrase | Long Prayer and Lord's Prayer | Prayer of Intercession for whole state of Christ's Church to conclude with: Apostles' Creed, Decalogue and Lord's Prayer | Prayer of Intercession for whole state of Christ's Church | General Prayer and Lord's Prayer (if no Communion is to follow) | Psalm or *Benedictus* or *Magnificat*<br>Prayer of Intercession |
| Apostles' Creed (either said by Minister or on Communion Sundays sung by people in metre) | Apostles' Creed (said by Minister) | | Apostles' Creed, Decalogue, Lord's Prayer } said by Minister | | SERMON<br>Prayers of Intercession |
| Metrical Psalm | Metrical Psalm | Metrical Psalm | Metrical Psalm | Metrical Psalm | Psalm or 'Hymn' |
| Blessing (Aaronic) | Blessing (Aaronic or Apostolic) | Blessing (Aaronic or Apostolic) | Blessing (Aaronic or Apostolic) | Blessing (Aaronic or Apostolic) | Blessing |

## THE LORD'S SUPPER

| Calvin: Geneva 1542, etc. | Knox: Geneva 1556 | Waldegrave 1584/5 | Middleburgh 1586, etc. | Directory 1644 | Savoy Liturgy 1661 |
|---|---|---|---|---|---|
| Apostles' Creed sung during preparation of the elements | | | | Exhortation<br>Fencing of the Table<br>Setting apart of Elements to holy use | Explanation of the nature of the Sacrament<br>Exhortation<br>Prayer of Access<br>Offertory |
| Words of Institution | Words of Institution | Words of Institution | Words of Institution | Words of Institution | |
| Exhortation | Exhortation | Exhortation | Exhortation | Exhortation | Eucharistic Prayer (Consecration)<br>Words of Institution |
| Eucharistic Prayer | Eucharistic Prayer | Eucharistic Prayer | Eucharistic Prayer | Eucharistic Prayer | Brief Intercession |
| Fraction | Fraction | Fraction | Fraction | Fraction | Fraction<br>Libation of Wine<br>Prayer for sanctified life |
| Delivery | Delivery | Delivery | Delivery | Delivery | Delivery |
| Communion (while Psalm or Scripture is read or sung) | Communion (while Scripture is read) | Communion (while Scripture is read) | Communion (while Scripture is read) | Communion (Minister receiving first) | Communion (Minister receiving first) |
| | | | | Exhortation to a worthy life | |
| Post-Communion prayer | Post-Communion prayer of thanksgiving and petition for a worthy life | Post-Communion prayer of thanksgiving and petition for a worthy life | Post-Communion prayer of thanksgiving and petition for a worthy life | Post-Communion prayer | Post-Communion prayer<br>Exhortation to a godly life |
| *(Nunc Dimittis) | Psalm 103 | Psalm 103 | Psalm 103 | Metrical Psalm of praise | Psalm of praise (23, 100, 103 or 116) |
| Blessing (Aaronic) | Blessing (Aaronic or Apostolic) | Blessing (Aaronic or Apostolic) | Blessing (Aaronic or Apostolic) | Blessing | Blessing: 'Now the God of peace . . .' |

*only in Strassburg (1545) edn.

# THE ORDER OF BAPTISM

| Calvin: Geneva 1542, etc. | Knox: Geneva 1556 | Waldegrave: 1584/5 | Middleburgh 1586, etc. | Directory 1644 | Savoy Liturgy 1661 |
|---|---|---|---|---|---|
| (SERMON) | (SERMON) | (SERMON) | (SERMON) | (SERMON) | |
| Scripture Sentences | | | | | |
| *Qn.* Do you present. . . .? | *Qn.* Do you present. . . .? | *Qn.* Do you present. . . .? | *Qn.* Do you present. . . .? | | |
| Long Exhortation & Explanation | Long Exhortation & Explanation | Long Exhortation & Explanation | Long Exhortation & Explanation | Declaration of the nature of Baptism<br>Admonition of the Congregation<br>Exhortation of parents | Declaration of nature of Baptism<br>Questions to parents<br>Promises |
| Prayer for grace and reception of child into Christ's Kingdom | | | | | |
| Lord's Prayer | | | | | |
| **Qn.* Do you wish this child baptized? etc. | | | | | |
| Apostles' Creed | Apostles' Creed (said by father or his surety as ratification of his undertaking) | Declaration of assent to Apostles' Creed (by the father or the surety) | Apostles' Creed (said by father or his surety as ratification of his undertaking) | | |
| Short Exhortation to instruct child | Prayer for grace and reception of child into Christ's Kingdom | Prayer for grace and reception of child into Christ's Kingdom | Prayer for grace and reception of child into Christ's Kingdom | Prayer for the Lord's blessing on the ordinance and on the child | Prayer for reception of child into Christ's Kingdom |
| | Lord's Prayer | Lord's Prayer | Lord's Prayer | | |
| BAPTISM | BAPTISM | BAPTISM | BAPTISM | BAPTISM | BAPTISM |
| Declaration that the child is a member of Christ | Thanksgiving | Thanksgiving | Thanksgiving | Thanksgiving and Prayer for reception of child into Christ's Kingdom | Thanksgiving<br>Exhortation of parents<br>Exhortation of the people |

*1545 edn. only

### 2nd Prayer Book of Edw. VI, 1552

Sursum Corda
Prayer of Humble Access

Almighty God our heavenly father, which of thy tender mercy didst give thine only son Jesus Christ, to suffer death upon the cross for our redemption, who made there (by his one oblation of himself once offered) a full perfect and sufficient sacrifice, oblation and satisfaction for the sins of the whole world, and did institute and in his holy gospel command us to continue a perpetual memory of that his precious death until his coming again: hear us O merciful father, we beseech thee and grant that we, receiving these thy creatures of bread and wine, according to our saviour Jesu Christ's holy institution, in remembrance of his death and passion, may be partakers of his most blessed body and blood: who in the same night that he was betrayed, took bread, *etc.*

### Knox: Geneva 1556, followed by Waldegrave 1584/5 Middleburgh 1586, etc.

O father of mercy and God of all consolation, seeing all creatures do acknowledge and confess thee, as governor and lord, it becometh us the workmanship of thine own hands, at all times to reverence and magnify thy godly majesty, first that thou hast created us to thine own image and similitude: but chiefly that thou hast delivered us from that everlasting death and damnation into which Satan drew mankind by the mean of sin: from the bondage whereof (neither man nor angel was able to make us free) but thou (O Lord) rich in mercy and infinite in goodness, hast provided our redemption to stand in thy only and well-beloved son: whom of very love thou didst give to be made man like unto us in all things (sin except) that in his body he might receive the punishment of our transgression, by his death to make satisfaction to thy justice, and by his resurrection to destroy him that was the author of death and so to produce and bring again life to the world, from which the whole offspring of Adam most justly was exiled.

O Lord, we acknowledge that no creature is able to comprehend the length and breadth, the deepness and the height of thy most excellent love which moved

### Directory 1644

*Let the prayer, thanksgiving or blessing of the bread and wine be to this effect:*

With humble and hearty acknowledgment of the greatness of our misery (from which neither man nor angel was able to deliver us) and of our great unworthiness of the least of all God's mercies: to give thanks to God for all his benefits, and especially for that great benefit of our redemption, the love of God the Father, the sufferings and merits of the Lord Jesus Christ, the Son of God, by which we are delivered: and for all means of grace, the Word and Sacraments, and for this sacrament in particular, by which Christ and all his benefits are applied and sealed up unto us: which, notwithstanding the denial of them unto others, are in great mercy continued unto us after so much and long abuse of them all.

To profess that there is no other name under heaven by which we can be saved, but the name of Jesus Christ by whom we alone receive liberty and life, have access to the throne of grace, are admitted to eat and drink at his own table and are sealed up by his own spirit to an assurance of happiness and everlasting life.

Earnestly to pray to God, the Father

### Savoy Liturgy 1661

(*a*) Almighty God, thou art the creator and lord of all things. Thou art the Sovereign Majesty whom we have offended. Thou art our most loving and merciful Father, who hast given thy Son to reconcile us to thyself: who hath ratified the new Testament and covenant of grace with his most precious blood: and hath instituted this holy sacrament to be celebrated in remembrance of him till his coming. Sanctify these thy creatures of bread and wine which, according to thy institution and command, we set apart to this holy use, that they may be sacramentally the body and blood of thy son Jesus Christ. Amen.

*together with*

(*b*) Most merciful Saviour, as thou hast loved us to the death, and suffered for our sins, the just for the unjust, and hast instituted this holy sacrament to be used in remembrance of thee till thy coming, we beseech thee by thine intercession with the Father, through the sacrifice of thy body and blood, give us pardon of our sins, and thy quickening Spirit, without which the flesh will profit us nothing. Reconcile us to the Father: nourish us as thy members to everlasting life thee to show mercy, where none was deserved: to promise and give life, where death had gotten victory, but to receive us into thy grace, when we could do nothing but rebel against thy justice.

O Lord, the blind dullness of our corrupt nature will not suffer us sufficiently to weigh these thy most ample benefits; yet nevertheless at the commandment of Jesus Christ our Lord, we present ourselves to this his table (which he hath left to be used in remembrance of his death until his coming again) to declare and witness before the world that by him alone we have received liberty and life: that by him alone thou dost acknowledge us thy children and heirs: that by him alone we have entrance to the throne of thy grace: that by him alone we are possessed in our spiritual kingdom to eat and drink at his table: with whom we have our conversation presently in heaven and by whom our bodies shall be raised up again from the dust, and shall be placed with him in that endless joy, which thou (O father of mercy) hast prepared for thine elect, before the foundation of the world was laid.

And these most inestimable benefits, we acknowledge and confess to have received of thy free mercy and grace, by thy only beloved son Jesus Christ, for the which therefore we thy congregation, moved by the Holy Spirit, render thee all thanks, praise and glory for ever and ever.

of all mercies, and God of all consolation, to vouchsafe his gracious presence, and the effectual working of his Spirit in us, and so to sanctify these elements both of bread and wine and to bless his own ordinance, that we may receive by faith the body and blood of Jesus Christ crucified for us, and so (to) feed upon him that he may be one with us, and we with him, that, he may live in us and we in him and to him, who hath loved us and given himself for us.

*and*

(*c*) Most Holy Spirit, proceeding from the Father and the Son: by whom Jesus Christ was conceived: by whom the prophets and the apostles were inspired, and the ministers of Christ are qualified and called: that dwellest and workest in all the members of Christ, whom thou sanctifiest to the image and for the service of their Head, and comfortest them that they may show forth his praise: illuminate us, that by faith we may see him that is here represented to us. Soften our hearts, and humble us for our sins. Sanctify and quicken us that we may relish the spiritual food and feed on it to our nourishment and growth in grace. Shed forth the love of God upon our hearts, and draw them out in love to him. Fill us with thankfulness and holy joy, and with love to one another. Comfort us by witnessing that we are the children of God. Confirm us for new obedience. Be the earnest of our inheritance and seal us up to everlasting life. Amen.

*Note*. Baxter permits three usages:

(i) That set out in the table (*supra*).

(ii) Bread and wine might be consecrated separately and in that case Prayer of consecration (*a*) was used here.

(iii) Prayer of consecration might include (*a*) together with (*b*) and (*c*) the words of institution standing before the prayer.

## APPENDIX B

# ART AND MUSIC IN PURITAN WORSHIP

Macaulay has popularized a grave misrepresentation of the Puritans as fanatical Philistines, apostles of gloom, utterly antagonistic to the arts and music. This classic caricature is contained in the following passage from his *History of England* (1848):[1]

> 'It was a sin to touch the virginals . . . The solemn peal of the organ was superstitious. The light music of Ben Jonson's masques was dissolute. Half the paintings in England were idolatrous, the other half indecent. The extreme Puritan was at once known from other men by his gait, his garb, his lank hair, the sour solemnity of his face, the upturned white of his eyes, the nasal twang with which he spoke, and, above all, by his peculiar dialect.'

This charge would make all Puritans tone-deaf and colour-blind iconoclasts. Its untruth has been fully and finally rebutted by Dr Percy Scholes in *The Puritans and Music* (1934). It would be superfluous therefore to cover the same ground again. But it would not be out of place to estimate the Puritan attitude towards ecclesiastical art and music.

To the æsthetic Churchman the simplicity of Genevan worship appeared bare and rude. John Donne, for instance, describes the Puritan Crantz as one who

> 'loves her onely, who at Geneva is call'd Religion, plaine, simple, sullen, yong, contemptuous, yet unhansome;'[2]

The objection to the ceremonial and furnishings of the Established churches was not due to a failure to appreciate beauty. It can be accounted for mainly on theological grounds.

In the first place, the Puritans aimed at a simplicity in religion which they believed characterized the original primitive Church. This simplicity was the will of God and to worship him in ways other than he had explicitly commanded was the height of pride and disobedience. It seemed to them that the Second Commandment, which forbade 'graven images', necessarily demanded the removal of any representations of the Divine Majesty on glass or wood or stone. Whilst representations of the Virgin Mary or of the Saints were not for-

[1] chapter I [2] *Satyre III* lines 50–52

bidden by the Scriptures they were prohibited by the Puritans as a potential danger to the 'weaker brother'. They were the monuments of an older religion, 'the badges of Anti-Christ'; their very existence might revive the abuses they brought to memory. But, more than this, they were often instrumental in promoting abuses. For they bore testimony to the mediæval prayers offered to the Virgin and the Saints. The Apostle Paul's injunction to 'avoid the appearance of evil' was at the root of Dowsing's iconoclasm.[1] The continued bareness of the chapels when the danger of a resurgence of abuses had passed was mainly the result of economic necessity. The impoverished Dissenters were unable to afford lavish and elaborate ecclesiastical edifices, even if they had desired to build them.

It is also to be remembered that Puritans had never valued their meeting-places in the way that the Anglicans esteemed theirs. If the clergy of the Establishment thought of the Church as an edifice, the Puritans meant by the Church the people of God indwelt by the Holy Spirit. The differing attitudes towards buildings for public worship is seen in a comparison of Hooker, the leading Anglican apologist, with Gillespie, a Scottish Presbyterian of distinction. For Hooker the church is a sacred building; for Gillespie the sanctity rests in the 'saints', under the inspiration of God's spirit. Hooker writes:[2]

'... the very Majesty and holiness of the place where God is worshipped, *hath in regard of us* great virtue, force and efficacy, for that it serveth as a sensible help to stir up devotion; and, *in that respect*, no doubt, *bettereth* even our holiest and best actions in this kind.'

Gillespie, on the contrary, writes:[3]

'How much more soundly do we hold with J. Rainolds, That unto us Christians no land is strange, no ground unholy; every coast is Jewry, every house Sion; and every faithful company, yea every faithful body a Temple to serve God in ... whereas the presence of Christ among two or three gathered together in his Name (Matthew xviii.20) maketh any place a Church, even as the presence of a King with his attendants maketh any place a court.'

[1] *v. The Journal of William Dowsing* (ed. Evelyn-White, Ipswich 1885) *passim* [2] *Eccl. Pol.* V xvi 2

[3] *Dispute against the English Popish Ceremonies* (1660) p. 123

This conviction made the construction of religious edifices as utilitarian as possible.

Finally, ceremonial and elaborate furnishing were superfluous to the Puritans. They needed no such stimulants for the imagination; their imagery was vividly Biblical. As Shakespeare relied on few artificial aids as spurs to the imagination, substituting the transcendental imagery of his verse for the fictitious aids of scenery; so the Puritans rejected the ecclesiastical 'scenery' of the mediæval Church for the symbolism and imagery of the Bible. For them the four Gospels and the Book of Revelation provided a more vivid background to faith than human manufactures in glass or wood or stone could do. This is excellently expressed by B. L. Manning:[1]

'To call on the name of God, to claim the presence of the Son of God, if men truly know and mean what they are doing, is in itself an act so tremendous and so full of comfort that any sensuous or artistic heightening of the effect is not so much a painting of the lily as a varnishing of sunlight.'

The attitude of the Puritans to music was not dissimilar. The more extreme Puritans regarded music as a carnal snare; as for instance one John Mulliner, who counted music well lost if religious peace of mind were gained instead:[2]

'I have been so troubled, as I have been playing that I have laid my instrument down, and have reasoned with myself after this manner, and fell a crying to God, it is tru I love this musick, but what good can these sounds do me when my soul wants Peace with God; and this doth but stir up Laughter and Lightness of Spirit, to make me forget my Maker and this will last but a little while, and I had better seek my peace with God, and then, *At his Right Hand are Pleasures for evermore;* and these thoughts I had then so that my Musick began to be a Burden to me.'

This attitude was not, however, representative of the average Puritan. The Puritan did not object to the arts as such: indeed, the Puritans numbered amongst their adherents such poets as Edmund Spenser, Sir Philip Sidney, John Milton and Andrew Marvell. The typical attitude is that of John Cotton, who

[1] *Christian Worship* (ed. N. Micklem, 1936) p. 162

[2] *A Testimony against Periwigs and Periwig-Making* (1667): from a facsimile published at Northampton in 1872

declares that whilst instrumental music is banned in the worship of the Church,

'Nor do we forbid the private use of any instrument of musick therewithal.'[1]

The Puritans objected only to elaborate church music which did not edify the congregations and, indeed, the very complexities of such music made it impossible for the common people to sing the praises of God.

Robert Browne in his *True and Short Declaration* (1583) refers to antiphonal singing of the psalms by the two sides of a cathedral choir, with great distaste. But his objection, be it noted, is theological not musical:

'Their tossing to and fro of psalmes and sentences is like tenisse plaie, whereto God is called to Judg who can do best and be most gallant in his worship; as bie organs, solfaing, pricksong chanting, bussing and mumling verie roundlie, on divers handes. Thus thei have a shewe of religion, but in deed thei turne it to gaming, and plaie mockholidaie with the worship of God.'[2]

A more rhetorical vituperation of contemporary church music would be hard to find than this of Prynne's:[3]

'As for the Divine Service and Common prayer, it is so chaunted and minsed and mangled of our costly hired, curious, and nice Musitiens (not to instruct the audience withall, nor to stirre up mens mindes unto devotion, but with a whorish harmony to tickle their eares:) that it may justly seeme not to be a noyse made of men, but rather a bleating of bruite beasts; whiles the Coristers ney descant as it were a sort of Colts; others bellowe a tenour, as it were a company of oxen: others barke a counter-point, as it were a kennell of Dogs: others rore out a treble like a sort of Bulls: others grunt out a base as it were a number of Hogs; so that a foule evill favoured noyse is made, but as for the wordes and sentences and the very matter it selfe, is nothing understanded at all; but the authority and power of judgment is taken away from the music and from the eares utterly.'

In this criticism there is clearly an inability to appreciate the beauty of the music condemned, but the main ground of the objection is that such music does not tend to edification.

[1] Cotton *Singing Psalmes a Gospel Ordinance;* cited by Percy Scholes *The Puritans and Music* p. 58 [2] Scholes *op. cit.* p. 217 [3] *id.* p. 218

In conclusion, the Puritans must bear their share of the blame for the wholesale destruction of many beautiful monuments at the hands of such iconoclasts as William Dowsing. But their aim was not Philistinism. It might have been misguided, but it was nevertheless sincere. They thus hoped to uproot all idolatrous practices which God had not required in his worship. Their motto, to which they held inflexibly, was: 'Quod non jubet, vetat'. But if beauty was forced to abdicate from the churches, she was accorded a coronation in their homes. The Puritans objected to Sunday dancing, to the use of instrumental music in the worship of the Church, and to ecclesiastical representations of the Trinity and the Saints. But it is utterly untrue to affirm that therefore music, dancing and art were banished from the Commonwealth. Dancing was encouraged by Cromwell, celebrated by Milton in *L'Allegro;* it was an essential part of the education of Colonel Hutchinson's family, and it was at the height of the Puritan regime that Playford published his *English Dancing Master* (1651). As to the private encouragement of music, it will suffice to remember that 'Opera, so far as Britain is concerned, was actually an importation of Puritan times'.[2] A group of people who produced Milton, and who popularized the Psalms, are unfairly described as Philistines. Privately they encouraged the arts and, if they objected to the use of the arts in the service of the Church, their conviction was not æsthetic but religious in basis. It was not that they disliked art, but that they loved religion more.

[2] *id.* p. 195

## APPENDIX C

## THE PURITAN ATTITUDE TO THE CREEDS

It is surprising that the Puritans who trace their theological descent from John Calvin, whose famous *Institutio* is a commentary on the framework of the Apostles' Creed, should have discarded the Creed in public worship. It was in universal use among the Reformed Churches and was included in the first Puritan Prayer-Books. Baillie, a Scottish Commissioner at the Westminster Assembly, lays the blame for the disuse of the Creed at the feet of the Brownists:[1]

> 'The Apostles' Creed they detest, as an old Patchery of evil stuff; Christ's descent into hell, they count a blasphemous Article.'

This attitude came to be shared by the Independents. They desired to rid their public worship of any association with the corruptions of Rome and, as the Creed was an integral part of Roman Catholic worship, they discarded it. Milton expresses the Independent viewpoint admirably:[2]

> 'They object that if we must forsake all that is Rome's, we must bid adieu to our creed; and I had thought our creed had been of the apostles, for so it bears title. But if it be hers, let her take it. We can want no creed so long as we want not the scriptures.'

The Creed was a convenient summary of the articles of faith, it was agreed, but if Roman usage had polluted it, the Puritan would not use it. Indeed so long as he knew his Bible he did not need it.

The Presbyterians were anxious to retain the Creeds. They had originally intended, in the first draft of the Baptismal Order of the Directory, that the father should recite the Apostles' Creed as evidence that he was a believer. Moreover when the Westminster Divines were revising the Thirty-Nine Articles before a separate Confession was thought of, they proposed to re-translate the Creeds, explaining the harsher clauses of the Athanasian Creed. There was no intention of disowning them. They went as far as to send up to Parliament the following revision of the VIIIth Article:[3] 'The Creeds that go under the name of the Nice Creed, Athanasian Creed and

[1] *A Dissuasive &c.* p. 30

[2] *Apology for Smectymnuus* (Everyman ed. 1927) p. 155

[3] Sprott & Leishman *op. cit.* p. 355

that which is commonly called the Apostles' Creed are thoroughly to be received and believed, for that the matter of them can be proved by most certain warrants.'

The left-wing Puritans had two substitutes for the Creeds. The Independents or Congregationalists had their own Confession of Faith, the *Savoy Declaration*. The Presbyterians used as their doctrinal basis, for the purposes of catechizing, the *Westminster Confession*.[1] The second substitute was the use of a covenant as the basis of church-membership, which all new members of the local Church subscribed on being admitted into its fellowship. This was used mainly by the Independents and by the Baptists, but it did not win favour among the Presbyterians, although its principle was accepted in the 'Solemn League and Covenant' of 1643, by which Parliament had given Presbyterianism the status of the official Church in England.

The sole difference between the *Savoy Declaration* and the *Westminster Confession*, which were verbally similar, was that the former declared a consensus of opinion amongst the Independents, whilst the latter was accepted as morally binding amongst the Presbyterians. The character of the Independent Declaration is made plain in the preface:

> '. . . such a transaction is to be looked upon but as meet or fit *medium* or *means* whereby to express *that* their *common faith and salvation*, and no way to be made use of as an *imposition* upon any: whatever is of force or constraint in matters of this nature causeth them to degenerate from being *Confessions of Faith*, into *exactions* and *impositions of faith*.'[2]

The memory of other 'impositions', which had brought fire and faggot in their train, was too vividly present in the minds of the Independents to allow them to repeat the mistake. The Presbyterians, however, made their Confession the basis of their Sunday afternoon catechizing.

The second substitute for a Creed was the Covenant. This was an important part of Independent church-order and worship. The first Independent Church in England, founded in 1616 under the leadership of Henry Jacob, was constituted on the basis of a covenant entered into by all the members. A day was appointed

[1] This was, of course, the Westminster Shorter Catechism of 1647.

[2] Williston Walker *op. cit.* p. 354*f*

'to seek ye Face of ye Lord in fasting and Prayers, wherein that particular of their Union togeather as a Church was mainly comended to ye Lord: in ye ending of ye Day they ware United, Thus, Those who minded this present Union & so joyning togeather joyned both hand each wth other Brother and stood in a Ringwise: their intent being declared, H. Jacob and each of the Rest made some Confession or Profession of their Faith & Repentance, some ware longer some ware briefer, Then they Covenanted togeather to walk in all Gods Ways as he had revealed or should make known to them.'[1]

Later Independent Churches, founded in the days of the Commonwealth, on a covenant basis, were: Yarmouth in 1643, Norwich a year later, Walpole in 1647, Bury St Edmunds a year later, Wrentham in 1649, Woodbridge in 1651, Beccles, Guestwick and Wymondham in 1652, Bradfield probably in the same year, Wattesfield in 1654 and Denton and probably Bassingtown in 1655.[2] Jacob's church-covenant was simple and comprehensive in form and served as the basis and model of all subsequent Independent covenants. Later examples are more elaborate. Occasionally, as in the case of the Bassingtown covenant, they are more impressive. Indeed the solemnity of the latter covenant could hardly be equalled. As a prelude to the Lord's Supper it was an equivalent to the *Sanctus* of venerable use. It was read by all the members standing. It proceeds:[3]

'We do in the presence of the Lord Jesus the awful crowned King of Sion and in the presence of his holy angels and people, and all beside here present Solemnly give up ourselves to the Lord and to one another by the will of God, solemnly promising & engaging in the aforesaid presence to walk with the Lord, and with one another in the observation of all Gospel Ordinances and the discharge of all relative duties in this Church of God, & Elsewhere as the Lord shall enlighten and enable us.'

This solemn admission into the fellowship of Christ's Church was the Independent substitute for Confirmation.

Covenants were not acceptable to all the Puritans. The Presbyterians never appear to have used a church-covenant. At first the Baptists protested against it. Hanserd Knollys,

[1] cited Burrage *op. cit.* ii 294

[2] Burrage *The Church Covenant Idea* (Philadelphia 1904) p. 126

[3] *id.* p. 137

their accepted leader in the days of the Commonwealth, led the attack by challenging the Independents to show that the Scriptures demanded any conditions for admission to the Church other than faith in the Lordship of Christ, repentance and willingness to be baptized.[1] There was even a difference of opinion among the Independents themselves. John Goodwin, the Independent Minister of Colman Street Church, London, was engaged in controversy on this point with Thomas Goodwin, later to be President of Magdalen College, Oxford.[2] Gradually, however, Baptists and Independents adopted church-covenants. The first Baptist covenant is that of the Broadmead Baptist Church, Bristol, which was produced in 1640. They declared

'That they would, in the strength and assistance of the Lord, come forth out of the world, and worship the Lord more purely, persevering therein to their end.'[3]

The same Church reformulated its covenant five years later. It is also known that in 1656 the Longsworth Baptist Church was organized on the covenant-basis. There are, however, few Baptist covenants available before the end of the seventeenth century. This is an indication of the truth of Burrage's contention:

'even as late as 1660, probably as late as 1696, the English Baptists as a body had in reality come to no settled agreement in regard to the method of organising their churches.'[4]

By this time, however, most Baptist Churches had their covenants.

Annexed to the taking of the covenant in the Baptist and Congregational Churches, is a ceremony peculiar to these two denominations. It is termed the 'right hand of fellowship'. This was given by the Pastor of the Church to new members as a sign of their entry into the fellowship of the Church. An account of the manner of receiving new members into the fellowship of the Independent Church at Burwell describes the ceremony thus:[5]

'Then he gave them the right hand of fellowship: he took them by the right hand and said, Sister, you having given yourself to the Lord and

[1] *id.* p. 151*f* [2] *id.* p. 125 [3] *id.* p. 151*f* [4] *id.* p. 125
[5] *Transactions of the Congregational Historical Society* vi 419

to us by the will of God; in the name of Christ and with the consent of this church I Admit you a member of this church of the living God, and give you the right hand of fellowship, and the lord bless you in Zion.'

The same custom was in general use amongst Baptists.[1]

Thus, while the Presbyterians retained their veneration for the Apostles' Creed longer than the other two Puritan denominations, they and the Independents produced a modern statement of belief. Independents and Baptists used a kind of Creed as the basis for church-membership. It was not primarily a statement of belief; it was rather a promise by members of their fidelity to Christ and to his Church. Hence it was named a covenant rather than a Creed.

[1] Burrage *The Church Covenant Idea* p. 149

## APPENDIX D

## PURITAN FAMILY WORSHIP

In his *Autobiography*, Baxter tells of how the villagers of his district used to spend their Sunday evenings dancing under the maypole to the strains of a tabor and a pipe,

> 'so that we could not read the Scripture in our family without the great disturbance of the tabor and pipe and noise in the street.'

He admits that, in those early years, his inclination was all for joining the villagers, but

> 'when I heard them call my father Puritan it did much to cure me and alienate me from them; for I considered that my father's exercise of reading the Scripture was better than theirs, and would surely be better thought on by all men at the last; and I considered what it was for that he and others were thus derided.'[1]

The Puritan was thus characterized by the seriousness of his practice of the duties of private religion.

Two factors contributed to the high esteem in which Family Worship was held by the Puritans. In the first place, religion was not associated with a sacred building for them, as it was for the Church members of the Establishment. Their religious buildings were called 'meeting-houses', not churches. For them the word 'church' referred exclusively to a company of God's faithful people gathered to hear the Word expounded to them. So that, by an easy transference, they could conceive of 'the church in the house' on the analogy of the gatherings of the persecuted Christians of the primitive Church, or on the even earlier precedent of the Apostolic gatherings for worship. The second factor tending to promote the observance of Family Worship was the new significance given to family life by the Reformers. God's covenant, which was invariably read at Baptismal services, was 'to you and to your children' and this welded family life into a solidarity in Christ. The head of the family, who had promised at the baptism of his children to supervise their Christian nurture, was in duty bound to teach his children the Scriptures, to lead them and instruct them in prayer and praise. If he were conscientious in the discharge of his duty, he would conduct family prayers twice each day. At

[1] *Autobiography* (ed. J. M. Lloyd-Thomas, 1931) p. 6

the very least, he was expected to expound the catechism to his family every Lord's day.

Baxter gives a large place to the duties of Family Worship in his *Christian Directory*. There he maintains that every Christian household should meet for family prayers twice each day. He argues that if the worshippers of the Old Dispensation made their morning and evening sacrifices, Gospel-worshippers are all the more obliged to offer their two daily sacrifices of praise. Not only Scripture, but reason and experience point to the necessity for family worship.

'Experience proveth that family sins are daily committed, and family mercies daily received, and family necessities daily do occur.'[1]

He then shows that it is most suitable to the spiritual rhythm of the Christian's life to engage in daily prayer.

'And reason tells us, 1. That it is seasonable every morning to give God thanks for the rest of the night past. 2. And to beg direction protection and provisions and blessing for the following day. 3. And that the evening is a fit season to give God thanks for the mercies of the day, and to confess the sins of the day, and ask forgiveness, and to pray for rest and protection in the night.'[2]

Baxter's arguments all presuppose a great earnestness and sincerity in the profession and practice of religion. He not only assumes that there will be a morning and evening session for family devotions, he also recommends that the Christian individual should begin and end each day with private prayers. He gives detailed instructions to the head of the family as to how he is to perform his duties on the Lord's day. This is to commence with family prayers, which are to serve as a solemn preparation for the public services of the day. He continues:[3]

'After dinner call your families together, and sing a Psalm of Praise, and by examination or repetition or both, cause them to remember what was publickly taught them.'

The family are to be convened again after the afternoon church service:[4]

'When you come home, call your families together and first crave Gods assistance and acceptance: and then sing a Psalm of Praise: and then

[1] *A Christian Directory* (ed. 1673) II iii 507 [2] *ibid.*
[3] *id.* p. 572 [4] *id.* p. 573

repeat the Sermon which you heard; or if there was none, read out of some lively profitable book; and then pray and praise God: and with all the holy seriousness and joy which is suitable to the work and the day.'

Then, after supper, the head of the family is requested to examine the children and the servants on what they have been taught during the day. Then the religious duties of the day conclude with family prayers and praises. He concludes his directions with the plea:[1]

'And now I appeal to Reason, Conscience, and Experience whether this employment be not more suitable to the principles, ends and hopes of a Christian, than idleness, or vain talk, or cards, or dice, or dancing, or ale-house haunting, or worldly business or discourse?'

It is unlikely that even Baxter's own members of the Kidderminster Church kept these exacting directions. Puritanism made few concessions to the inclinations of the natural man, and hence it may be supposed that, even amongst Puritans, the ideal was rarely achieved. Family 'duties', as they were called, must have been extremely irksome to the younger members who were present. The lengthy prayers, with their extended confessions of actual and original sin, can have meant little to the children of the household. Indeed there is evidence that the children of the celebrated Northern Divine, Oliver Heywood, were actually caught playing during family prayers. He had to give them 'seasonable correction which brought them into an exact complyance in the outward man'.[2] It may be doubted, however, if the inward man complied.

A most intimate picture of Puritan family worship in the household of Sir Thomas Abney is given by the Rev. Jeremiah Smith, the knight's minister. Abney was a leading Nonconformist who became Lord Mayor of London. But his chief claim to the gratitude of posterity lies in the fact that he was the patron of Isaac Watts for 36 years. The famous hymn-writer spent many years in his home and acted as his private chaplain. Smith describes the family gathering for worship as follows:[3]

[1] *ibid.*

[2] cited by A. G. Matthews in *Christian Worship* (ed. cit.) p. 185

[3] Orme *Memoirs of the Life, Writings and Religious Connexions of John Owen, D.D.* (1820) p. 369*f*

'Here were every day the morning and evening sacrifices of prayer and praise, and reading the Holy Scriptures. The Lord's day he strictly observed and sanctified. God was solemnly sought and worshipped, both before and after the family's attendance on public ordinances. The repetition of Sermons, the reading of good books, the instruction of the household, and the singing of the Divine praises together were much of the sacred employment of the holy day; variety and brevity making the whole not burdensome but pleasant; leaving at the same time room for the devotions of the closet, as well as for intervening works of necessity and mercy. Persons coming into such a family, with a serious tincture of mind, might well cry out, "This is none other than the house of God, this is the gate of Heaven." Besides the ordinary and stated services of religion, occasional calls and seasons for worship were also much regarded. In signal family mercies and afflictions, in going journeys, in undertaking and accomplishing any matters of great moment, God was especially owned by prayer and thanksgiving; the assistance of ministers being often called in on such occasions. Through the whole course of his life he was priest in his own family, except when a minister happened to be present.'

The concluding sentence of this encomium is a striking illustration of the Puritan belief in the priesthood of all believers.

Another illustration of the ardour of private Puritan devotions occurs in Samuel Clarke's *A Collection of the Lives of Ten Eminent Divines, &c.*[1] The author is describing the spiritual life of John Cotton, the New England Independent divine:

'He began the Sabbath on the Saturday evening: and therefore then performed Family duties after Supper, being larger than ordinary in Exposition, after which he catechized his children and Servants, and then returned into his Study. The morning following, Family Worship being ended, he retired into his Study untill the Bell called him away. Upon his return from the Congregation, he returned again into his Study (the place of his Labour and Prayer) unto his private devotion; where (having a small repast carried him up for his dinner) he continued till the toling of the Bell. The publick service being ended, he withdrew for a space into his aforementioned Oratory, for his sacred addresses unto God, as in the forenoon: Then came down, repeated the Sermon in his Family, prayed, and after Supper sang a Psalm, and, towards bed time betaking himself again to his Study, he closed the day with Prayer. Thus he spent the Sabbath continuously.'

[1] (ed. 1662) p. 69

Nothing could emphasize the high seriousness of the Puritan more thoroughly than the indefatigable way in which he conducted the devotions of the family, and catechized the children and servants of the household. The motto of the Puritans was: Every house a household of faith; every father a priest in his own family.

It is not to be supposed that the morning and evening family prayers, and the Lord's-day catechizing, exhausted Puritan family devotions. Over and above these, Puritan families used to keep private days of thanksgiving or humiliation. Moreover such days are not to be confused with national days of thanksgiving and humiliation. Any occasion in the life of a family that called for gratitude to God was celebrated as a day of thanksgiving.

If, for instance, the mistress of the house was safely delivered of a child, or if the master of the house returned safely after a long and hazardous journey, the family celebrated the occasion with a day of thanksgiving. On these occasions the minister was expected to conduct the family's devotions. Oliver Heywood writes in his diary for October 7th, 1679:[1]

'My wife and I rode to little Horton, we kept a solemn day of thanksgiving at Mr. Sharps for his wife delivered of a daughter a month before.'

The same divine writes on March 5th, 1680:[2]

'we had a solemne day of thanksgiving at my house for my wives and sons recovery, my son Eliezer begun, Mr. Dawson, John proceeded, I concluded with preaching, prayer, we feasted 50 persons and upwards, blessed be God.'

Such days of thanksgiving appear to have been a family festival to which neighbours were invited. There were also days of fasting and humiliation kept by Puritan families. Heywood notes in his diary for December 2nd, 1679:[3]

'I rode to Wyke, kept a solemne fast at Joshua Kersheys, he being in a consumption, god helped me in discoursing extempore on Jer. 17. 13. 14 and praying, it was a good day blessed be god.'

Such private fasts were also held in preparation for receiving the Sacrament of the Lord's Supper. Moreover, Heywood informs us that he and others frequently met for private fasts

[1] *Diary* ii 107 [2] *id.* ii 110 [3] *ibid.*

when persecution of Nonconformists was severe. Some idea of the number of these days of fasting and thanksgiving may be obtained from Oliver Heywood's diary. In the year 1690 he was present at 40 fasts and 17 days of thanksgiving; the next year he officiated at 37 fasts and 11 days of thanksgiving; in 1692 he was at 50 fasts and 14 days of thanksgiving; and in 1693 he presided at 35 fasts and 12 days of thanksgiving.[1] Innumerable others would also be held to which the minister was not invited.

Further evidence as to the importance Puritans attached to the culture of the spiritual life is to be found in the considerable number of devotional books which they produced. Foremost among these were *The Practice of Christianity*, by Richard Rogers; *The Saints' Everlasting Rest*, by Richard Baxter; *The Communicant's Companion* and *The Method of Prayer*, by Matthew Henry; and Isaac Watts' *Guide to Prayer*. Matthew Henry spoke for all Puritans when he declared:[2]

'A golden thread of Heart-Prayer must run thro' the Web of the whole Christian life: we must be frequently addressing ourselves to God in short and sudden Ejaculations, by which we must keep up our Communion with God in Providences and common Actions, as well as in Ordinances and religious Services. Thus prayer must be *sparsim* (a sprinkling of it in every Duty) and our Eyes must be ever towards the Lord.'

The relevance of prayer in the Puritan's life is shewn convincingly in the life of Cromwell who, in the midst of his military and political duties, insisted upon finding time to recommend himself to God. His letters abound in advice to others to seek the will of God in prayer.[3] On one occasion, when he and other generals of the Parliamentary army were convinced that, by their temporizing with the King and their consequent lack of popular support, God was displeased with them, Cromwell called a special meeting of the Army Leaders at Windsor in 1648. The purpose of this meeting was, in the words of Adjutant Allan:[4]

'To go solemnly to search out our own iniquities, and humble our souls before the Lord in the sense of the same; which, we were persuaded,

[1] *Diary* iii 247, 254, 262, 264 [2] *The Method of Prayer* (1710) p. A3 *recto*
[3] *Oliver Cromwell's Letters and Speeches* (ed. Thomas Carlyle) i 121, 167
[4] *id.* i 264

had provoked the Lord against us, to bring such sad perplexities upon us that day.'

Accordingly they spent a whole day in prayer and cross-examination of their consciences, and on the second day, after the exposition of Scripture and further prayers, Cromwell addressed them urging upon them

'a thorough consideration of our actions as an Army, and of our ways particularly as private Christians: to see if any iniquity could be found in them; and what it was, that if possible we might find it out, and so remove the cause of such sad rebukes as were upon us (by *reason* of our iniquities, as we judged) at that time.'[1]

This high estimate of the importance of prayer was not peculiar to Cromwell but it was shared by his commanding officers, as this extract from a letter written to him by Major-General Harrison shews:[2]

'My Lord, lett waiting upon Jehovah bee the greatest and most considerable busines you have every daie; reckon it so, more than to eate, sleep, or councell together. Run aside sometimes from your companie, and gett a word with the Lord. Why should not yow have three or four pretious soules allwaies standing at your elbow, with whom you might now and then turne into a corner? I have found refreshment and mercie in such a waie.'

We may be sure that such advice was accepted by Cromwell.

Because the Puritan lived ever under the eye of the Great Taskmaster, and because he was convinced that without God he could do nothing, he was frequently on his knees in confession or thanksgiving or petition. The sheer relevance of prayer to his every concern is demonstrated in the list of suitable occasions for prayer which Matthew Henry supplies in his *Method of Prayer*. The sixth chapter of this work is entitled: 'Of Addresses to God upon particular Occasions, whether Domestick or Publick'. It is intended for the use of 'Ministers, Masters of Families and private Christians'. The prayers provided are suitable for morning and evening devotions and for blessings before and after meat. Besides these regular occasions for prayer, Henry includes prayers for going on and returning

[1] *id.* i 265

[2] *Original Letters* (ed. J. Nicholls) p. 10; cited A. G. Matthews in *Christian Worship* p. 186

from a journey, for preparation for the Lord's Supper and the services of public worship on the Lord's day. Others are included suitable for other occasions, as, the Baptism of a child, a Funeral, a Marriage, and Ordination, 'upon occasion of the want of rain', 'upon occasion of excessive rain', 'upon occasion of infectious diseases', 'upon occasion of fire', 'upon occasion of great storms'. Having provided prayers for almost all possible calamities, he provides prayers suitable 'for the cares and burdens and afflictions of particular persons'. These are so comprehensive that they include all human moods, such as melancholy, or doubt or distress; others are adapted to the conditions of an illness and vary according to the health of the person who is prayed for. Another meets the need of an insane person, another of a child in sickness, yet another is for a woman in travail. Even parents 'whose children are a grief to them' are provided with a suitable prayer. There are prayers on behalf of prisoners and for condemned malefactors that have but little time to live, whilst those who are braving the dangers of the sea are not forgotten. This extensive catalogue is ample evidence that the Puritan's life was penetrated with prayer, and that only a small proportion of the prayers that he heard were the public prayers in the meeting-house. By far the majority of his prayers were his own, offered up either in the solitude of his own room or in the company of his family. Milton declared:[1] 'We can want no creed, so long as we want not the Scriptures'. The Puritans could have said with equal truth: 'We want no liturgy to teach us how to pray, so long as we have the Scriptures'. They required little help from manuals or directories, since from their knowledge of God, revealed in the Word, and in the Word made flesh, they could cry 'Abba, Father' with all the seriousness and simplicity and confidence of children.

[1] *Apology for Smectymnuus* p. 155

# BIBLIOGRAPHY

(This list of the books consulted is not to be regarded as exhaustive. It is a catalogue of the most important authorities, the majority of which are cited in the text of this thesis. Where the place of publication is not named, it is to be assumed that the volume was published in London.)


## A

Anonymous:

*A Free and Impartial Inquiry into the Causes of that very great Esteem and Honour that the Nonconforming Preachers are generally in with their followers* (1673).

*A Godly Treatise . . . written by some Doctor of Divinity* (1589). (Author reputed to be Robert Some.)

*Anatomy of the Service Book* (1651).

*A Parte of a Register*, MS. in the Doctor Williams' Library, London (*circa* 1590).

*Plain Reasons for Dissenting from the Church of England* (1736).

*The Brownists Synagogue* (1641).

*The Principles and Practice of Moderate Nonconformity with respect to Ordination* (1717).

H.D.M.A. *A Sober and Temperate Discourse concerning the Interest of Words in Prayer* (1661).

Ainsworth, Henry. *A Booke of Psalms . . .* (1612).

Ainsworth, Henry. *An Animadversion to Mr. Richard Clyftons Advertisement*, Amsterdam (1613).

Annesley, Samuel, edited by. *A Continuation of Morning Exercise Sermons* (1683).

*Apologeticall Narration.* By the Independents (1664).

Arber, Edward, edited by. *A Brief Discourse of the Troubles at Frankfort: 1554–1558* (1908).

## B

Baillie, Robert. *A Dissuasive from the Errours of the Time . . .* (1646).

Baillie, Robert. Letters, Vol. II, edited for the Bannatyne Club, Edinburgh.

Baird, C. W. *Eutaxia, or a Chapter on Liturgies* (1856).

Bancroft, Richard. *Dangerous Positions . . .* (1595).

Baptists, The. *Transactions of the Baptist Historical Society*, Vols. I, IX & X. *The Baptist Quarterly*, Vols. I & X.

Barclay, A. *The Protestant Doctrine of the Lord's Supper*, Glasgow (1927).

Bartlet, J. V. Articles in *The Contemporary Review* for July 1897 and April 1902.

Baxter, Richard. *A Christian Directory* (1673).

Baxter, Richard. *Autobiography*, edited J. M. Lloyd-Thomas (1931).

Baxter, Richard. *Five Disputations of Church Government and Worship* (1659).

Baxter, Richard. *The Reformed Pastor* (edition of 1860).

Baxter, Richard. *Reliquiæ Baxterianæ* (1695).

Bayne, Peter, edited, with Introduction by. *Puritan Documents* . . . (1862).

Bishop, Edmund. *Liturgica Historica*, Oxford (1918).

Bradshaw, William. *English Puritanisme* . . . (1605).

Brightman, F. E. *The English Rite*, 2 vols. (1915).

*Broadmead Records*, edited by E. B. Underhill (1854).

Brook. *The Lives of the Puritans*, 3 vols. (1813).

Browne, Robert. *A True and Short Declaration* . . . (1582).

Browne, Robert. *A Booke which sheweth* . . . (1582).

Burn, J. S. *The History of the French, Walloon, Dutch and other foreign Protestant Churches in England* (1846).

Burrage, Champlin. *The Early English Dissenters in the light of recent Research*, Cambridge (1912), 2 vols.

Burrage, Champlin. *The Church Covenant Idea*, Philadelphia (1904).

C

Calamy, Benjamin, D.D. *Some Considerations about the Case of Scandal or giving offence to Weak Brethren* (1683).

Calamy, Edmund. *A Letter to a Divine in Germany giving a Brief but True Account of the Protestant Dissenters in England* (1717).

Calderwood, David. *Altare Damascenum* (1623).

Calendar of Letters and State Papers relating to English Affairs, preserved principally in the Archives of Simancos (1894).

Calvin, John. *The Institutes of the Christian Religion*, trans. Allen (1838).

Calvin, John. *J. Calvini opera quae supersunt omnia*, edited by Baum, *Corpus Reformatorum*, Vol. XXIX, Brunsvigæ (1834).

Cambridge Modern History. Volume II (1903); Volume IV (1906).

Carlyle, Thomas, edited by. *Oliver Cromwell's Letters and Speeches* (1845).

Clapham, Henoch. *A Chronological Discourse* (1609).

Clarke, Samuel. *A Collection of the Lives of Ten Eminent Divines* (1661).

Clemen, Carl. *Quellenbuch zur praktischen Theologie*, Giessen (1910).

Coleman, T. *Independent Churches in Northamptonshire* (1853).

Congregationalists, The. *The Transactions of the Congregational Historical Society*, Vol. VI.

Cotton, John. *A Practical Commentary . . . upon the First Epistle Generall of John* (1656).

Cotton, John. *Singing Psalmes a Gospel Ordinance* (1647).

Cotton, John. *The True Constitution of a Particular Visible Church* (1642).

Cotton, John. *The Way of the Churches of Christ in New England* (1645).

Cranmer, Archbishop. *On the True and Catholic Doctrine and Use of the Lord's Supper*, edited by C. H. H. Wright (1907).

Crippen, T. G. *Transactions of the Congregational Historical Society*, Vol. I, Article: *Dr. Watts' Church Book.*

Crosby, Thomas. *History of the Baptists*, Vols. I and II (1738–1740).

Curwen, Spencer. *Studies in Music and Worship*, 5 vols (1880–1885).

D

Dexter, H. M. *Congregationalism of the Last Three Hundred Years as seen in its Literature* (1880).

Doddridge, Philip. *Opera*, Vol. IV, Leeds (1804).

Donne, John. *Poems*, edited Sir H. J. C. Grierson, 2 vols., Oxford (1912).

Doumergue, E. *Jean Calvin*, Vol. II, Lausanne (1902).

Dowsing, William. *The Journal of William Dowsing*, edited by C. H. Evelyn White, Ipswich (1885).

Draper, Edward. *Gospel-Glory proclaimed before the Sonnes of Men* (1649).

Durel, John. *A View of the Government and Publick Worship of God in the Reformed Churches beyond the Seas* (1662).

E

Edwards, Thomas. *Gangræna*, Parts I and II (1646).

Evans, H. J. *John à Lasco: his earlier life and labours* (1886).

F

*Fenstanton, Warboys and Hexham Records*, edited by E. B. Underhill (1854).

Fisher, F. *Questions Preparatory to the Better, Free and more Christian Administration of the Lord's Supper* (1655).

Ford, Stephen. *A Gospel-Church: or God's Holy Temple opened* (1675).

Foxe, John. *Acts and Monuments*, edited J. Pratt (1877).

Frere and Douglas, edited by. *Puritan Manifestoes* (1907).

Fuller, Thomas. *Church History of Britain* (1655).

G

Gillespie, George. *Dispute against the English Popish Ceremonies* (1637). Edition of 1660 consulted.

Glass, Norman. *The Early History of the Independent Church at Rothwell* (1871).

Goodwin, Thomas. *Opera*, Vol. XI, Edinburgh (1845), for *On the Constitution, Right, Order and Government of Churches of Christ.*

H

Hall, Peter. *Reliquiæ Liturgicæ*, Vol. I, Middleburgh; Vol. III, Directory; Vol. IV, Savoy (1847), Bath.

Hall, Peter. *Fragmenta Liturgica*, Vol. I, Puritan (1848), Bath.

Halley, Richard. *Lancashire, its Puritanism and Nonconformity* (1869).

Hammond, Henry. *View of the New Directory*, Oxford (1646).

Hanbury, Benjamin. *Nonconformist Memorials*, 3 vols. (1839–1844).

Hawkins, John. *History of Music* (1776).

Heiler, F. *The Spirit of Worship* (1926).

Henry, Matthew. *A Method of Prayer . . .* (1710).

Henry, Matthew. *The Communicant's Companion* (1704).

Herbert, George. *Poems.*

Heywood, Oliver. *Diaries*, Vols. I and II, Brighouse (1882); Vol. III, Bingley (1883), edited by J. Horsfall Turner.

Hislop, D. H. *Our Heritage in Public Worship*, Edinburgh (1935).

Hooker, Richard. *Of the Laws of Ecclesiastical Politie*, Book II (1594), Book V (1597).

Horsley Down Church. *The Covenant to be the Lord's People and to walk after the Lord sign'd by the Church of Christ meeting at Horsly-down in Southwark* (1700).

Humfrey, John. *A Humble Vindication of a Free Admission unto the Lord's Supper* (1652).

J

Jewson, C. B. *St. Mary's Norwich*, article in Vol. X of *The Baptist Quarterly*.

Johnson, Francis. *An Inquirie and Answer of Thomas White . . .* (1606).

K

Keach, Benjamin. *Spiritual Melody* (1691).

Keach, Benjamin. *The Breach Repair'd in God's Worship* (1691).

Kidd, B. J. *The Later Mediæval Doctrine of the Eucharistic Sacrifice* (1898).

Kennedy, W. M. *The Interpretations of the Bishops* (1908), Alcuin Club Tracts, VIII.

L

Laing, David. *The Works of John Knox*, 6 vols., Edinburgh (1855).

Luther, Martin. *Luther's Primary Works*, edited Wace and Buchheim (1896).

M

Maclean, Donald. *London at Worship: 1689–1690*, 1928 Lecture for the Presbyterian Historical Society, Manchester.

Marlow, Isaac. *Prelimiting Forms of Praising God* (1691).

Masson, David. *The Life of Milton*, 6 vols. (1859–1880).

Mather, Cotton. *Magnalia Christi Americana . . .* (1702).

Matthews, A. G. *Christian Worship* (1936), Chapter XI.

Maxwell, W. D. *An Outline of Christian Worship* (1936).

Maxwell, W. D. *Church Service Society Annual* (1929–1930). An Article.

Maxwell, W. D. *The Liturgical Portions of the Genevan Service Book* (1931).

McMillan, William. *The Worship of the Scottish Reformed Church: 1550–1638* (1931).

Micklem, Nathaniel, edited by. *Christian Worship* (1936).

Miller and Johnson. *The Puritans*, New York (1938).

Milner. *Life of Isaac Watts* (1843).

Milton, John. *Apology for Smectymnuus* and *Of Reformation in England*, in the Everyman edition of the *Prose Works* (1927).

Moffatt, James. *Christian Worship* (1936), Chapter VIII.

Mulliner, John. *A Testimony against Periwigs and Periwig-making* (1667).

N

Neal, Daniel. *The History of the Puritans*, 5 vols. (1822).

O

Orme, William. *Life and Times of Richard Baxter*, 2 vols. (1830).

Orme, William. *Memoirs of the Life, Writings and Religious Connexions of John Owen, D.D.* (1820).

Ormerod, Oliver. *The Picture of a Puritan* (1605).

Owen, John. *A Brief Instruction in the Worship of God*, in *Opera*, edited Goold, Edinburgh (1862), Vol. XV.

Owen, John. *A Discourse concerning Liturgies and their Imposition* (1662), in *Opera*, edited Goold, Edinburgh (1862), Vol. XV.

Owen, John. *A Discourse of the Work of the Holy Spirit in Prayer* (1662), in *Opera*, edited Russell, London (1826).

P

Palmer, A. *A Scripture-Rale to the Lords-Table* (1654).

Parker, I. *Dissenting Academies in England*, Cambridge (1914).

Patrick, Simon. *A Discourse of Profiting by Sermons* (1683).

Peel, Albert, edited by. *Essays Congregational and Catholic* (1931).

Peel, Albert. *The First Congregational Churches*, Cambridge (1920).

Pepys, Samuel. *Diary*, edited by Lord Braybrooke (1825).

Picart, Bernard, illustrated by. *Cérémonies et Coutumes Religieuses de tous les Peuples du Monde*, Tome IV, Amsterdam (1736).

Pike, G. H. *Ancient Meeting-Houses in London* (1870).

Powell, Vavasor. *Common Prayer-Book No Divine Service* (1661).

Powicke, F. J. *A Life of the Reverend Richard Baxter* (1924).

Powicke, F. J. *Essays Congregational and Catholic*, Chapter XIII (1931).

Prothero, R. E. *The Psalms in Human Life* (1907).

R

Ratcliff, E. C. *Christian Worship and Liturgy*, being Chapter XI of *The Study of Theology*, edited by K. E. Kirk (1939).

Reed, F. O. *Public Worship in Sixteenth Century Calvinism* (1933), an unpublished thesis in Mansfield College, Oxford.

Reid, Adam A. *Baptist Quarterly*, Vol. X. Article.

Robinson, John. *A Treatise of the Lawfulnes of Hearing the Ministers* (1634).
Robinson, John. *Opera*, edited by Robert Ashton, 3 vols. (1852).

S

Schaff, Philip. *The Creeds of Christendom*, Vol. III, New York (1882).
Scholes, Percy A. *The Puritans and Music* (1934).
Sewall, Samuel. *The Diary of Samuel Sewall*, 5th Series, Collections of the Massachusetts Historical Society.
Skeats and Miall. *A History of the Free Churches in England* (1891).
Smyth, C. H. *Cranmer and the Reformation* (1925).
Smyth, John. *The Differences of the Churches of the Separation* (1608).
Smyth, John. *Opera*, edited W. T. Whitley, Cambridge (1915).
South, Robert. *Sermons*, Oxford, Vol. III (1823).
Sprott, G. W., edited by, *The Liturgy of Compromise*, published by the Church Service Society (1905).
Sprott and Leishman. *The Book of Common Order* . . . (1868).
Strype, John. *Annals*, Oxford (1824).
Strype, John. *The History of the Life and Death of Edmund Grindal, Archbishop of Canterbury* (1710).
Strype, John. *The Life and Acts of John Whitgift, Archbishop of Canterbury* (1718).

T

Taylor, Jeremy. *Two Discourses* . . . (1652).
Terry, R. R. *Calvin's First Psalter: 1539* (1932).

U

Underhill, E. B., edited by. *Broadmead Records* (1847).
Underhill, E. B., edited by. *Fenstanton, Warboys and Hexham Records* (1854).

W

Walker, Williston. *The Creeds and Platforms of Congregationalism*, New York (1893).
Watts, Isaac. *Guide to Prayer* (1716), Vol. III of the *Opera* (1810).
Watts, Isaac. *The Psalms of David Imitated in the Language of the New Testament, and applied to the Christian State and Worship* (1718), in Burder's 1810 edition of the *Opera*.
Watts, Isaac. *Hymns and Spiritual Songs* (1707).

Watts, Isaac. *An Humble Attempt towards the Revival of Practical Religion among Christians* (1731).

Whale, J. S. Chapter X of *Christian Worship* (1936).

Whiting, C. E. *Studies in English Puritanism* (1940).

Whitley, W. T. *The Minutes of the general Assembly of the General Baptists: 1654–1728* (1909).

Whitley, W. T. *The Works of John Smyth*, Cambridge (1915).

Whitley, W. T. *A History of British Baptists* (1923).

Whitley, W. T. Article, *Baptist Quarterly*, Vol. IX.

Will, Robert. *Le Culte*, Strassburg and Paris (1925).

Wood, Anthony. *Athenae Oxonienses* (1691).

## Z

*Zurich Letters*. Edited by Hastings Robinson for the Parker Society, 2 vols. (1845).

# INDEX

# INDEX

*(Page references appear in arabic numerals and chapters in roman numerals)*